VOID

Library of
Davidson College

THE HUMAN DIMENSION OF TECHNICAL ASSISTANCE
The German Experience at Rourkela, India

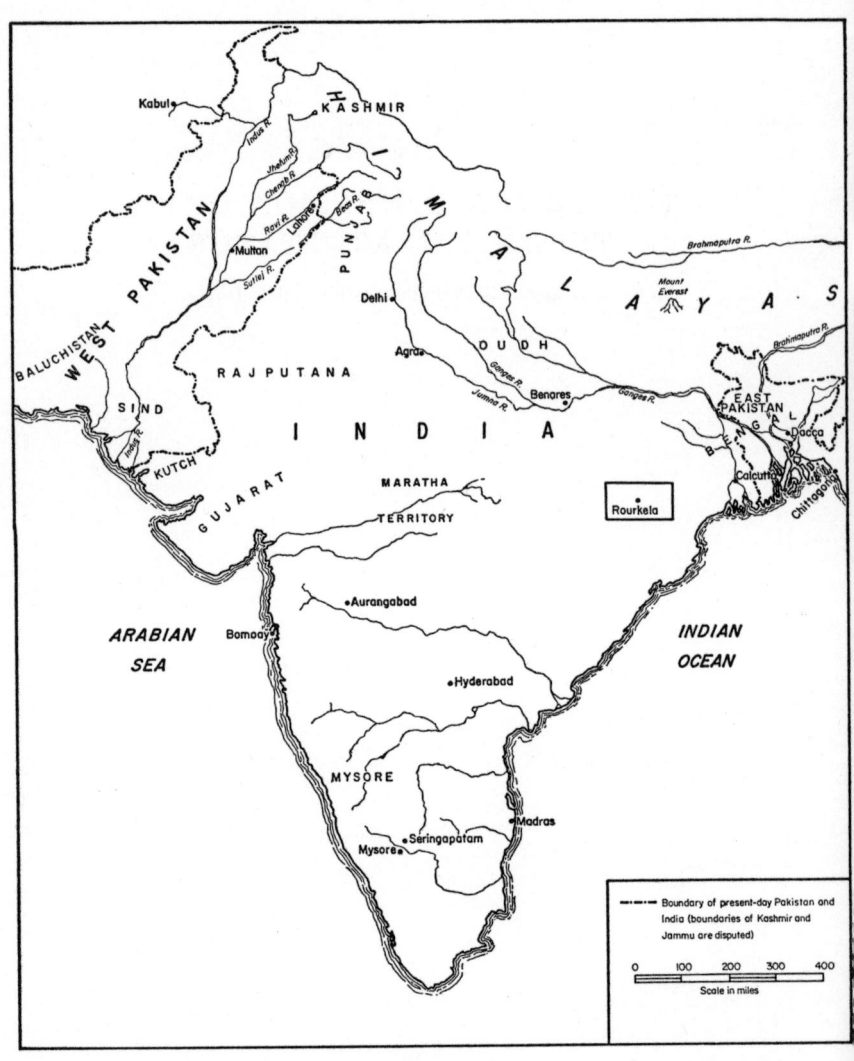

The Indo-Pakistan subcontinent, showing the location of Rourkela

THE HUMAN DIMENSION OF TECHNICAL ASSISTANCE
The German Experience at Rourkela, India

By Jan Bodo Sperling
Foreword by Klaus Mehnert
Translated from the German by Gerald Onn

Cornell University Press
ITHACA AND LONDON

English translation copyright © 1969 by Cornell University

All rights reserved. Except for brief quotations in a review, this book, or parts thereof, must not be reproduced in any form without permission in writing from the publisher. For information address Cornell University Press, 124 Roberts Place, Ithaca, New York 14850.

Originally published in the Federal Republic of Germany under the title *Die Rourkela-Deutschen* by Deutsche Verlags-Anstalt GmbH., Stuttgart, 1965.

Standard Book Number 8014-0528-9
Library of Congress Catalog Card Number 78-87024

PRINTED IN THE UNITED STATES OF AMERICA
BY VAIL-BALLOU PRESS, INC.

CONTENTS

Preface to the English Edition ix
Foreword, by Klaus Mehnert xiii

1 / Germans for Rourkela 1

Origins and Composition 1
   Construction personnel 1
   Operation and maintenance personnel 3
Motivations 4
   Construction personnel 4
   Operation and maintenance personnel 8
Some Personal Characteristics 9
   Gift for organization, sense of order, and pedantry 10
   Intolerance, lack of consideration, and coarseness 13
   The pleasures of drink 16
Knowledge of Languages 18
Prejudices and Stereotypes 20
Off to India Unprepared 24
Suitability and Selection 27

2 / The Indians in Rourkela 33

Origins and Composition 33
   Original inhabitants: The Adivasis 33
   Principal inhabitants: The Oriyas 34
   Immigrant workers 35
   Regional differences 35
The Indians' Attitude toward the Germans 36
   Indian attitudes toward Western economic aid 37

How does the Indian see the German? 46
What attitude had the Germans to expect from the Indians upon arrival? 53

3 / *The Germans in Rourkela* 55

The Climate and Its Effects 55
   Acclimatization 55
   Fitness for life in the tropics 59
   Medical welfare 61
   Errors of diet 66
   Consumption of alcohol and general license 67

The Germans' Way of Life 71
   Living accommodations 71
   Servants 81
   The woman problem 86
   Social life 95
   Structuring of leisure 101
   The German Social Center 105
   Club life in Rourkela 108
   School children and the German school 114
   The churches 117

Special Problems of Adaptation 118
   Homesickness 120
   Exotic environment 122
   Interest in the environment 124
   The German yardstick 127
   The wives 130
   New arrivals 132
   Press and politics 134

Collaboration in the Plant 139
   The Germans' initial position 142
   German power of authority 145
   Behavior patterns of the Indians 145
   Behavior patterns of the Germans 149

Social Structure: The Group 150
   In-group and we-feelings 153
   Out-group and they-feelings 162
   Ethnocentrism 163

	CONTENTS
Isolation in the ghetto	165
Frustration and Aggression	173
4 / *Implications of Rourkela*	179
Preliminary Discussions in Germany	180
Suitability and Selection	183
Preparation	185
Welfare	190
Public Relations	193
Appendix	195
Notes	201
Bibliography	213
Index	223

PREFACE TO THE ENGLISH EDITION

This book is a case study and a critical report on the human problems of one of the largest industrial aid projects ever carried out by a Western nation in a developing country. It deals with the adaptational problems faced by more than a thousand German engineers and technicians while living and working together with national counterparts in India during the construction of a steel mill near the small village of Rourkela in the jungles of the state of Orissa.

The Rourkela project was one of the three most ambitious industrial undertakings in the framework of the Second Five-Year Plan (1957–1962) of the government of India. Three huge steel mills with a yearly capacity of one million tons each were constructed with the help of three countries: Durgapur with British, Bhilai with Soviet, and Rourkela with German, partners. About forty well-known German companies participated actively in the Rourkela project, coordinating a total of more than 3,000 suppliers from the Federal Republic of Germany.

In its first stage the Rourkela plant required an investment the equivalent of almost 500 million United States dollars and can be considered the largest German aid project undertaken so far. At this writing Indian and German engineers are about to complete the second stage of the project, stepping up its capacity to 1.8 million tons. A third stage of expansion is in the process of final planning and preparation.

The field study upon which this book is based was conducted during four years the author spent in Rourkela. While living with the German personnel as the director of their social, cultural, and medical services, he had ample opportunity to study their performance, the difficulties they experienced within their own group, and the manifold problems of their relations with their Indian partners.

This book *demonstrates* how German attitudes toward work and performance, commitments to a sense of order and punctuality, and a certain lack of pedagogical skill, patience, and tolerance, as well as feelings of superiority and social habits, clashed with Indian behavioral patterns and values. This clash affected all aspects of the human relationship between the German personnel and their Indian counterparts in a manner which continuously threatened the success of the project.

This report also *analyzes* the reasons for this clash. It deals with the motivations, the attitudes, the specific experience, and the national character of the Germans, all of which had a bearing on this particular technical-assistance project. The analysis attempts to trace the background of the manifold reactions of the Indians, taking into consideration their cultural and political past.

The performance of both Germans and Indians in this vast project is also *evaluated*. The findings suggest that both parties were not at all well prepared for an undertaking of this kind. The Germans, in particular, did not know enough about the country they had come to work in or anything about the complexity of Eastern society. They had come overconfident in the superiority of their Western technique and with an exaggerated attachment to the Western craftsman's ethic. It was exactly this attitude that turned out to be their Achilles' heel. Nobody had bothered to tell them otherwise.

This evaluation is a challenge to the American reader, since both Americans and Germans face similar problems in their activities in developing countries. They are exposed to strange environments and to people from entirely different cultural backgrounds. Neither Americans nor Germans had much experience of this sort when, some ten to twenty years ago, the challenge of development aid took them into these countries by the thousands. In particular,

PREFACE TO THE ENGLISH EDITION

Americans and Germans tend to base their judgments of people mainly on the question of work and efficiency. They tend to ask, "What do you *do?*" rather than "Who *are* you?" as do many people of the East. To Americans and Germans, work performance has become more important than principles of social standing and heritage. This trait poses similar problems to both in dealing with the difficult task of living and working among people with an alien culture.

And so this book deals with the human dimension in international relations. It is directly concerned with one of the key practical requirements of today's political world: coexistence. The practicability of coexistence is constantly endangered by people's being entangled in different value-systems. This case study of the Germans, in a situation which repeats itself again and again in varying magnitudes for Germans and Americans alike, attempts to illuminate the problems that people in the Western world must set out to overcome.

JAN BODO SPERLING

December 1968

FOREWORD TO THE GERMAN EDITION

When I visited the German steel plant in Rourkela, accommodations in the guest house were all taken. Jan Bodo Sperling, the head of the "German Social Center," offered me a room in his house. And so I became acquainted with him and his work. The "Sheriff of Rourkela," as the Germans jokingly called him, was there to ensure that the German personnel—some 1,500 at that time—got along with one another as smoothly as possible. There was always something happening somewhere. At night, when the telephone in the next room roused me from sleep, I would hear Sperling jump up and drive off within a matter of minutes. The following morning he would tell me what had hauled him out of bed: a group of new workers had arrived from Germany and couldn't find their accommodations, or there had been a dispute in the bachelors' hostel that had called for arbitration, or a drunk had gone to sleep in the wrong bed, or some misunderstanding had arisen between Indians and Germans that had required the services of an interpreter. . . .

In the following pages the reader will be introduced to the many and varied tasks with which the head of the German Social Center in Rourkela was confronted. He had to deal with everything concerning the daily lives of the German personnel, who had come from every social class and from every part of Germany to work in the furnace of Rourkela: with their adaptation to their entirely novel living and working conditions, with the problems of communal living, with their collaboration with the Indians (who were also a mixed bunch, coming from different castes and different re-

FOREWORD TO THE GERMAN EDITION

gions), with their language difficulties, with the frictions that arose both within and among the different national and racial groups.

Only a man who had been caught up in this bustling life for a considerable period of time (1958–1962) could have written a book about the Rourkela Germans—and this is a book that had to be written. For decades to come economic cooperation between the industrialized nations and the developing countries is going to carry enormous influence on the international economy and on international politics. Many a new Rourkela will rise up as a result of the fanatical urge for industrialization that now grips the nations of the "Third World"; each will pose the same human problems as did Rourkela, the greatest of German construction sites in a developing country.

If working conditions on future projects are to be improved, then we must be prepared to learn from the experience gained in Rourkela. And the best way to do this is to read an honest report, one that does not set out to fool the reader and that calls a spade a spade. In his book Sperling not only describes the problems with which the Rourkela Germans had to contend; he also describes the Rourkela Germans themselves, who constitute a segment of the German nation, a German microcosm. This is not a very pleasant picture to look at. The storms that have descended on the German people in recent decades have left their imprint on the nation and on every individual German. But there is no point in harboring illusions about ourselves, especially if we are planning new Rourkelas.

After proving himself in Rourkela, Jan Bodo Sperling received tempting offers from the business world, which he refused. Instead he went to Aachen, to the intellectual atmosphere of a German university, to think about his experiences in India and to set them down on paper. Considering the tempo of modern life, which is always confronting us with new tasks before we have had time to learn from the old, this choice deserves special commendation.

This book does not deal with the technical aspects of the construction work in Rourkela. It is, after all, well known that the Germans are able to build steel plants. But experience has shown that

FOREWORD TO THE GERMAN EDITION

the human side of foreign aid is far more complex than any technical aspect. Those firms that are engaged on the Rourkela project and on many other construction projects around the world will find valuable suggestions in this book and cannot help but appreciate and admire the frank but responsible way in which the author has proceeded.

The billions of marks that Germany is providing for the industrialization of the "Third World" will only produce the desired results if the human beings involved in this process also play their part. And so the human factor has to be taken into account, which means that we must get to know it. Sperling's book helps us to do just this. It shows us the human problems that arise—even in such a magnificent technical operation as that conducted in Rourkela—and it indicates various ways of combating them in the future.

KLAUS MEHNERT

THE HUMAN DIMENSION OF
TECHNICAL ASSISTANCE
The German Experience at Rourkela, India

1/ GERMANS FOR ROURKELA

Origins and Composition

The installation of the Rourkela steel plant took place in two main phases. First came the period of actual construction, in which the building works were carried out and the machinery was assembled; this was followed by a second period in which the steel plant was commissioned and then operated as a going concern. Accordingly, the Rourkela Germans may be divided into construction personnel on the one hand and operation and maintenance personnel on the other—the form of classification normally adopted by the German firms. In this study of the Rourkela Germans, which investigates both the attitudes that they held before their departure for India and their behavior patterns after their arrival in Rourkela, the difference between these two groups will be dealt with in detail.

Construction personnel

The construction personnel consisted for the most part of fitters, engineers, and a small number of administrative officers. In certain instances various other specialist trades may also be considered under this heading, such as transport specialists. Most of the German fitters sent to Rourkela between 1957 and 1961 were members of the permanent staff of German construction firms and had therefore already been engaged on previous projects for their parent firms either within the German Federal Republic or abroad.

But apart from these members of their permanent staff the German firms also sent to India "itinerant" fitters who were employed on particular tasks or specific aspects of construction in Rourkela. This meant, of course, that the firms in question had no previous knowledge of these workers, who were to be found on the payroll of virtually every one of the companies engaged on the Rourkela project, especially during the early months of the construction period. Later the balance between permanent and itinerant workers was redressed in favor of the former. In fact, as work progressed, the technical and general standard of the construction personnel was seen to rise.

The first of the German workers—who came in 1957—were the bridge builders and those engaged on civil engineering work. They were a much tougher lot than, for example, the large group of electrical fitters, the majority of whom did not arrive on the site until the rough work had been finished and the steel plant was nearing completion. The more the work progressed, the more complex were the technical demands made on the workers.

Every large construction project overseas must inevitably attract a certain percentage of itinerant workers. In the case of Rourkela—a particularly important undertaking—it is also true to say that the conditions of full employment obtaining within the Federal Republic created a special situation in which the German firms engaged on the project appeared to find some difficulty in supplying a sufficient number of reliable tradesmen from their own permanent staffs. The following rather extreme case gives an idea of this situation and of the way in which some itinerant fitters were recruited. In January, 1959, a German working in Rourkela was involved in an unpleasant incident, as a result of which he was sent back to Germany and instantly dismissed. A few days later this same man was signed on by another firm, which was also engaged on the Rourkela project but which was evidently quite ignorant of his previous record, and was sent out to Rourkela again.

Among the construction personnel there were a number of non-

Germans—for example, a group of Dutchmen and a group of Austrians who worked on a particular project in the steel melting shop throughout the whole of the construction period and later, when the plant was actually in operation, and whose total complement was some sixty-five men.

Some of the German fitters had foreign wives: in the majority of cases they had met and married these women in the women's own countries, where they had been engaged on previous projects. Consequently Rourkela was able to boast German wives from England, Canada, Egypt, Latin America, Korea, and several other countries.

Our statistical knowledge of the family status of the construction personnel in Rourkela is far from complete, but from innumerable conversations with these workers the author was able to establish that the number of single men was greater than the number of married men and was also greater than the number of single men among the maintenance and operation personnel, who followed them.

Operation and maintenance personnel

When the construction work was completed in 1961–1962, German personnel were needed for the operation and maintenance of the plant. The men sent out to India for this purpose came almost without exception from steel plants within the Federal Republic. But since very few of the firms which had supplied the construction materials and undertaken the building of the steel plant were themselves producers of iron and steel, they were obliged to "borrow" their operation and maintenance personnel from other German firms.

Most of these men—engineers, setters-up, skilled and semiskilled operators—came from steel plants in which they had worked for some considerable time. This meant that they were able to bring with them specialized knowledge of the particular processes of production for which they had been engaged; but what they were not able to offer, save in a few isolated cases, was previous experience of work overseas.

Compared with the construction personnel, far more of the operation and maintenance personnel were married men and far more of those who were married brought their wives and families with them to Rourkela. As with the construction personnel, there was a relatively large group of non-Indian foreign workers, namely Americans. These men had been especially engaged to work the wide strip mill after it had proved impossible to find a German team for this particular task.

Motivations

In view of the origins and composition of the German work force it should not surprise us to find that the reasons which prompted the construction personnel to sign on for Rourkela differed from those which motivated the operation and maintenance personnel. We propose, therefore, to proceed as before and consider the possible motivations of these two groups under separate headings.

Construction personnel

It is probable that the construction personnel, especially those who had had previous experience abroad (a type, incidentally, by no means uncommon in Rourkela), were moved by a kind of wanderlust, which in its turn was prompted by a pretty strong desire on the part of these men for freedom, both in their work and in the conduct of their private lives. The Rourkela fitter who could look back to long experience on construction sites in various lands often gave the impression in private conversation that the Rourkela site was "far too big for his liking" and that he was anxious "to be on the move again." One had the feeling that this particular type of fitter, accustomed to a nomadic sort of existence, was bored with the life in Rourkela and felt that he had been "tied down," a condition which appears to have been aggravated by the isolation resulting from the lack of adequate transport facilities. In the case of such men, whose whole attitude to life was informed by a sense of restlessness, wanderlust would certainly seem to have been one source of motivation.

In a speech which he gave in Rourkela on November 11, 1960, Theodor Heuss (then President of the German Federal Republic) described wanderlust as one of the positive characteristics of the German race: "It is a fine thing that we Germans still have some of this 'wanderlust' in us, that we still feel the urge to 'go abroad for a while.' " But apart from a few isolated cases it is unlikely that the German fitters who signed on for Rourkela were prompted to do so for any *one* reason. The majority were influenced by a variety of reasons, which, although isolated here for purposes of this inquiry, in actual fact frequently appeared only in combination.

The motivation most closely linked to wanderlust is, of course, the spirit of adventure. Although it was restricted to a surprisingly small percentage of the construction personnel, this spirit of adventure was in fact manifested in a great variety of ways: some bought horses in order to reconnoiter the surrounding countryside; others acquired automobiles and set off in small groups on similar explorations. These people were extremely mobile; they wanted to see as much as they possibly could of Rourkela and its surroundings; above all they wanted to see "something new." And then there were the hunting expeditions (tiger hunts with sawed-off shotguns, in which the tigers fortunately did not come within shotgun range), whose appeal quite evidently lay less in the sporting aspect of the occasion than in the prickling sense of adventure.

Exceptional cases apart, it is difficult to assess the extent to which any of the construction personnel may have gone to Rourkela in order to escape from personal problems, for these were matters which the men were usually reluctant to discuss. Nonetheless, the author did get to know a number of Rourkela Germans who were running away from such personal problems as the payment of maintenance allowances, the approaching birth of an illegitimate child, difficulties with parents or with wives and families, pressing debts, and so on. One fitter, whose former wife was suing him for an increase in the maintenance contribution for the child of their dissolved marriage, wrote to the local court at which the action was being brought to the following effect: If you don't stop hounding me, I'll give in my notice to my firm (parent firm in the Federal Republic) and remain abroad for good. Then I'll have no German salary and my ex-wife can whistle for the maintenance. Others, who had married while working on previous construction projects overseas and discovered meanwhile that their foreign and in many cases "exotic" wives were not accepted by their friends and relations at home, had also sought refuge in Rourkela. They hoped that, by escaping abroad, they would find a solution to these social difficulties.

Escape from and compensation for apparently insuperable personal problems or personal failures are two forms of motivation which are also closely related. The German political scientist Oberndörfer is no doubt quite right when he says that "the stigma of failure, which closed every door in the old class society, quickly fades in the highly mobile society of our day. Nor is it necessary for the black sheep of the family to emigrate to America or Australia, for the innumerable financial and professional opportunities afforded by our industrial society offer a refuge." [1] And yet it would seem as if men with personal problems still do seek refuge in overseas service. The author encountered such cases in Rourkela. A number of the fitters openly admitted that they had come to Roukela for reasons of this order: there were those who wanted to get away from the frictions of married life, others who were trying to forget everything following a divorce case or some professional setback, and a few who had made an abortive attempt to set up in business on their own account.

The German fitter also feels that his status is higher abroad than it is at home. This impression is of course greatly strengthened in a land where, because of his technical knowledge, the color of his skin, and many other alleged virtues, he automatically considers himself superior to the local inhabitants. And then there is also the fact that when he is working abroad he is able to associate with the more senior members of his own firm and with his social superiors in both German and indigenous circles, a thing which he could never do at home. This gratifies his need for personal recognition and so constitutes an additional motivating factor. In this respect the German wives deserve a special mention; what tempts them is the social life, the fact that they can keep servants and "be somebody." But this kind of attitude is by no means peculiar to German workers. It is constantly referred to in the literature dealing with the behavior patterns of Americans abroad, where it is defined as the "V.I.P. feeling": what keeps the workers abroad is the sense of their own importance.

Service overseas nearly always carries higher rates of pay. According to the records of the Deutsche Bundesanstalt für Arbeitsvermittlung und Arbeitslosenversicherung (German Federal Office of Labor and National Insurance), the most common motive given by those accepting work overseas was their desire to receive further professional training, the financial appeal of such employment being relegated to second place.[2] But as far as the construction personnel were concerned, it is unlikely that the desire for further training was the chief factor, save perhaps in the case of the engineers and the superintendents, many of whom hoped to gain promotion within their firms by proving themselves in Rourkela.

For the fitters the question of pay was doubtless more important. A general overseas allowance of upwards of 20 per cent of their basic wage, expenses that were paid out in Indian rupees to the value of six to eight dollars a day (with correspondingly higher rates for foremen and engineers), and various other allowances were reason enough for many of those who signed on for Rourkela. The Austrian workers made no secret of the fact that they had come to Rourkela primarily for the money, and certainly they lived extremely frugal lives. Not many of the German workers tried to save, although there were exceptions, namely those who had come in order to finance some special project, perhaps to build a house, to pay off a mortgage, to pay for their children's education, or to provide a dowry for a daughter. A few of the younger men also dreamed and talked of more immediate ambitions, such as the acquisition of an expensive sports car. One worker who was always talking about a Mercedes 190 SL left Rourkela upon completion of his tour with the triumphant remark, "Now I'm off to buy that Mercedes—you won't be seeing me again." A few months later he was back in Rourkela with a new contract. His Mercedes was a total wreck and the insurance company had disallowed his claim. Now he had to earn a new one, and that would take a few more years.

Work abroad, especially in a developing country, usually brings greater opportunities for professional advancement, greater and more far-reaching responsibilities—especially for the younger men. At home they had been accustomed to working conditions in which they were frequently prevented from exercising their professional initiative by the guidance, supervision, criticism, and faultfinding of older colleagues and superiors. Abroad everything is different. Their sphere of responsibility is far greater, they are expected to act upon their own initiative and to perform tasks and solve problems that are rendered more complex by difficult working conditions. As a result they find a quite different and a far greater sense of satisfaction in their work, which younger people particularly appreciate.

Operation and maintenance personnel

The motives of the construction workers did not apply to the operation and maintenance personnel; their motivation was of quite a different order. The financial incentive was more important; high wages and salaries were the greatest single factor in persuading the operation personnel to leave their positions in the Federal Republic and go to Rourkela for an average term of eighteen months. The wages and salaries bill went up considerably upon their arrival, for they earned much more than the fitters, in some cases several times as much. When asked why they had come to Rourkela, many members of the operation staff stated quite openly that their only reason had been the prospect of high renumeration.

To some extent, however, the wishes of their firms will also have contributed to their decision. German industry had responded to the needs of the Rourkela plant by placing operation and maintenance personnel at its disposal and so, quite apart from the firms directly engaged on the construction of the plant, many other German concerns were also trying to spare staff for Rourkela. They selected a number of their men and suggested that they should sign contracts for India.

In many cases the firms in question coupled persuasion with promises: they undertook to keep their workers' old positions open for them and also spoke of chances of promotion in the future. In fact, unlike the construction personnel, for whom such a practice is neither customary nor indeed possible, the operation personnel who went out to India had to be guaranteed their old positions. And those who held higher posts, especially the senior engineers, were also given the prospect of promotion upon their return and some even received contractual guarantees to this effect.

But there is a further motive which may conceivably have influenced some of the men, namely the desire to learn something from their stay in Rourkela, the desire to widen their horizons, in other words, the quest for knowledge. There really were Germans in Rourkela who were clearly intent on just such a quest, which means that it must be considered as a factor within the over-all framework of motivation. However, the number of such men was small; they were to be found among the operation personnel rather than among the fitters, whose spirit of adventure, although closely linked with a healthy curiosity, could scarcely be called a quest for knowledge. This kind of curiosity has been aptly described in a recent inquiry carried out by the Study Group for Tourism in the Federal Republic: "The unique quality of a foreign land, its indigenous culture, is often regarded simply as a backcloth and not as a means of widening one's horizons." [3]

Some Personal Characteristics

The Rourkela Germans revealed a number of personal characteristics that often had unfortunate consequences for their work, for their adaptation to their new environment, and for the reputation and good name of the German community as a whole.

Gift for organization, sense of order, and pedantry

Not all of these characteristics would normally be considered negative; to possess a talent for organization or a well-developed capacity for orderly and solid work is by no means bad in itself. An apprentice carpenter in Germany is taught that when he drives home a set of screws the grooves in the heads must be parallel. This and similar principles are impressed on him over the long years of his apprenticeship until they become second nature to him and constitute an essential part of his working technique. It was with this kind of technique that German carpenters came to Rourkela to work alongside unskilled Indian workers. It was not easy for the German fitters to explain to the Indians why the grooves in the screws had to be parallel. But they did their best—and created bad feeling on both sides. Could it be that the explanation for this lies in a tendency, which has been traditionally attributed to the Germans (and often quite rightly so), to adopt a perfectionist attitude, to insist on "all or nothing"?

We encounter a similar problem with regard to the use of modern working methods and machines. The German fitters, especially the younger ones, showed little understanding for the traditional methods employed by the Indian laborers, who shifted enormous weights with just jute ropes and bamboo poles.[4] Instead of letting the Indians work in their own way, the Germans, with the exception of a few experienced hands, insisted on using cranes, overhead tackle, or pulleys. The Americans involved in technical assistance had already come up against this difficulty in many other places and drawn their own conclusions. They advised against the use of modern methods unless absolutely essential. It is quite clear that to attribute undue importance to the niceties of professional or craft ethics is likely to prove the Achilles' heel of all development aid.[5]

From the point of view of the Rourkela Indians it would doubtless have been far better if, instead of demonstrating their undoubted genius for organization, the German fitters had tried to restrain their innate desire for ordered conditions and concentrated more on adapting themselves to Indian conditions: instead of rejecting the native methods out of hand and replacing them by their own, they could have considered them on their merits and retained what was serviceable. The fact of the matter is that construction work in the developing countries is a highly complex problem, which will doubtless have to be approached more in terms of its social, cultural, and even religious implications than from a purely economic point of view. It will not be solved by traditional methods of orthodox development aid alone. Development presupposes profound changes in the indigenous social structure, but it also demands a corresponding readjustment on the part of the development workers.[6]

This process of readjustment was not always easy for the German construction personnel in Rourkela. They found difficulty in coming to terms with their Indian colleagues and accepting their working methods. Their passion for accuracy and the pleasure they took in their own proficiency prevented them from doing so. German pedantry and dogmatism were very much in attendance and were resented by the Indians, especially the engineers, who felt offended and consequently adopted a hostile attitude. Kurt Hesse's dictum provides an apt description of the situation which existed in Rourkela: "People who know everything better at home and are fond of playing the 'schoolmaster' are generally useless on construction sites abroad." [7]

German staunchness, precision, and thoroughness provoked similar reactions; although the Indians admired such industry, they did not find it congenial. Not only do the Germans work hard, but they keep on telling everyone that they work hard. This "gently gets on the Indians' nerves and they come to see it for what it is, namely boastful and in bad taste." [8] Hofstätter, the social psychologist, referred to an inquiry that was designed to establish the autostereotypes of Germans, Englishmen, Americans, Frenchmen, Italians, and Norwegians (based on 1,000 samples in each case).[9] Its findings showed that of these six nationalities only the Germans

(90 per cent) regarded "industriousness" as their most prominent characteristic; the English (77 per cent), the Americans (82 per cent), and the Norwegians (69 per cent) considered themselves to be primarily "amiable," while the French (79 per cent) and the Italians (80 per cent) opted for "intelligence."

In Rourkela there was a noticeable difference in the industry and zeal displayed by the construction personnel on the one hand and the operation personnel on the other, although in this connection some allowance must be made for the fact that the construction work was far more interesting and consequently more satisfying than the operation and maintenance work. In a sense construction was a unique pioneering and technical adventure, which began with the clearing of virgin jungle and reached its gratifying conclusion when the various plant units came into production. Most fitters made no secret of their inner identification with their work; the life of the site and its problems continued to occupy them in their leisure hours and was freely discussed for its own sake and not simply because the men were bored or lacked other subjects of conversation. The fitters appeared to take a personal interest in the objectives of the construction program and were willing to sacrifice a Sunday or to work into the evening to keep to schedule. However much they may have shamed and offended their Indian colleagues and supervisors with their absolute passion for work and their phenomenal output, however much they may have taxed the Indians' understanding and even provoked their scorn, their achievement throughout the years of construction was tacitly acknowledged and created a certain standard. In later years the Indians themselves came to recognize that the operation personnel did not always live up to this standard.

Indians in Rourkela—and elsewhere—said as much quite openly, and often their statements were not without a hint of criticism.[10] For example, the well-known Indian newspaper, *The Hindu,* said of the German worker that

the days when he exemplified all the virtues of the sober, steady and serious employee who toils like a horse for a low wage and never bickers are definitely over. . . . Today he has apparently begun to realise that one can be satisfied without working that much. . . . Moreover it appears that the workers' interest and enthusiasm have substantially declined.[11]

The Indians would have been spared their disappointment if the Germans had not set such a high standard to begin with, only to undergo such a marked transformation in the course of the years. As it is a paradoxical situation arose, and the Rourkela Germans were censured for having relaxed the overzealousness that had originally caused the Indians such annoyance.

Intolerance, lack of consideration, and coarseness

After visiting Rourkela an American observer wrote: "it didn't help that the Germans often appeared unused—and temperamentally unsuited—to handling the Asians, who are extremely touchy." [12] What prompted this observation and what is it about this temperament of theirs that made it so difficult for the Germans to relate to the Indians in Rourkela?

Indians often lodged complaints about the intolerance and coarseness of the Rourkela Germans. The rough way in which the German fitters treated their colleagues on the site—both German and Indian—frequently gave rise to unpleasant situations that, in view of the language difficulties, could not always be resolved. Unlike the Germans themselves, the Indians did not regard the grobianism, the crudity, which the Germans displayed in both their personal and their work relationships as boisterous but friendly horseplay. On the contrary, they felt that such blunt behavior, which in Germany would be positively assessed as indicative of an open and forthright character, was unrefined, if not barbaric. This was something which the German fitters often simply did not understand. It did not occur to them that the Indians might feel offended by their blunt manner of speaking. Occasionally one also gained the impression that the Germans felt they must go on repeating their blunt remarks in more and more forcible terms until they were understood, which meant of course that the Indians were subjected to a virtual barrage of coarseness.

The German philologist Küpper has succeeded to a point in

demonstrating the coarseness and querulous brashness of the modern German by reference to German colloquial usage:

Colloquial usage is incapable of rendering intermediate, let alone subtle, conditions; its methods are those of exaggeration and bombast. In no time at all quite trivial events are at the very least a filthy swindle. . . . Coarse, blasé attitudes and primitive snobbery are expressed in the colloquial jargon of our time with precious little respect. . . . In his colloquial usage the German is revealed as an absolute egoist: he stands at the center of the world and rules over all his fellows. . . . From forcefulness to coarseness is but a step, and this step is one which colloquial usage is only too happy to take. Out of a sense of power it prefers gross and strong language. It is rough and often crude, coarse and robust, blunt and brash.[13]

The Africans seem to have greater understanding for the fact that the German "does not really mean it like that." There is an East African saying to the effect that the German is outwardly hard but inwardly good, the Englishman outwardly good but inwardly hard.[14] Many of the Indians in Rourkela, however, felt repulsed by the rough outer surface. Nor should they be blamed for this. They acknowledged the German's plea that he "had not really meant it like that" with a polite smile that may have appeared forgiving; but in actual fact the forms of social intercourse of the German *Grobian* ("roughneck") were quite beyond them. In a general study of the German character this sort of situation has been described as typically German:

Subsequently the *Grobian* very often . . . regrets his blustering and shouting; it may well be that he will clap the other person on the shoulder and let out a hearty laugh in the belief that he too will now be able to join in the laughter and without the slightest idea that the offended person is quite incapable of performing such an abrupt psychic somersault.[15]

Unfortunately the keen observer is obliged to note that those peoples in the developing countries who are able to look back on an ancient and venerable culture of their own are pretty uniformly agreed that discretion, tact, courtesy, a sympathetic approach to local customs, and understanding for religious rites and taboos are not exactly the strong points of the Europeans and Americans who have appeared in their midst. Moreover, with the constant growth of Western-type education within the developing countries, Europeans and Americans are losing to an ever greater extent the special position which they previously enjoyed, or thought they enjoyed. As a result, the annoyance felt at their failure to adapt adequately is all the more widespread today.[16]

This general criticism also applies to the Germans who came to Rourkela. The qualities which they had to offer were not appreciated by the Indians and made collaboration difficult. Unlike their Indian colleagues, the Germans thought less in terms of contemplation than of manipulation. They were not inclined to accept things, but preferred to change them, acting on the general assumption that what was needed was "a bit of real order." They simply failed to understand that *their* kind of order, which they regarded as order per se, was not universally desired.

Courtesy and discretion were rare qualities among the Rourkela Germans. They were not even polite to one another and there was no generally accepted form of greeting within their circles. The same is true of factory life in Germany. The worker-priest Horst Symanowski, writing on his factory experiences, commented: "It was not customary to say 'good morning.' If you did so the workers looked at you in astonishment."[17] This was the state of affairs in Rourkela among both the construction and the operation personnel, but more especially the latter. In his inquiry into the German character, Hellpach speaks cautiously of the German's "aversion to formal considerations," by which he means his coarseness. Faced with Asiatic courtesy many of the Rourkela Germans responded in the acrid tones beloved of German officialdom and with the well-tried rowdyism of the soccer stadium. They also ensured that their swear words were "internationalized" as quickly as possible by teaching them to the Indians, many of whom repeated them without knowing what they were saying. Swearing and cursing are completely alien to the Indians; in Rourkela they were initiated into this practice by their German colleagues and supervisors. Hellpach is quite right when he says of the Germans: "There can surely be no other race who swear and curse, moan and grumble, shout and bellow quite as much as the Germans in the course of a day's work and who yet accomplish their task with such absolute certainty." [18] A German postgraduate student who worked in Rourkela for several months as a trainee of the Deutscher Akademischer Austausch-Dienst (German Academic Exchange Service) and lived as an Indian among Indian trainees was particularly well placed to gain their confidence and to discover the attitude of the younger Indians to their German colleagues. He commented: "In their working relations the German fitters are accused . . . of being coarse, loudmouthed and violent. . . . It is significant that the majority of the Indians know the meaning of the words 'shit' and 'get out.'" [19]

This impoliteness is accompanied by a certain intolerance. One observer has said that "the Germans are to be feared when they are looking for scapegoats." [20] There is scarcely a country in the world which is so ready to stigmatize those who think differently. This intolerance is even stronger when the point at issue has to do with work, with the accomplishment of a given task. It feeds on the German sense of what constitutes a correct working style, on the idea of perfectionism.

The educated specialist looks with impatience upon the ignorance of most people in matters that are commonplace to him, and allows his irritation to affect his whole attitude towards the common people. The latter reciprocate by regarding him as a strange kind of being, quite unlike themselves, and by way of compensation may dub him a "highbrow" or "snob." [21]

The pleasures of drink

The account furnished by Erasmus of Rotterdam of the kind of life which went on in the inns and alehouses of sixteenth-century Germany needs to be only slightly amended to fit the German Club in Rourkela in 1959.

The shouts and the noise which are raised when the heads grow heated with drink are quite amazing to hear. No man understands his neighbor. Clowns and buffoons often join in this tumult, and it is scarcely credible how great is the pleasure which the Germans take in these people, who create such a din with their singing, their leaping, and their brawling that they threaten to raise the roof, and no man can hear his neighbor. And yet they consider this to be an agreeable mode of life, and one is obliged to sit up until late in the night.[22]

The "German thirst," as Erasmus implies, calls for more than a wide variety of drinks; it also calls for the right mood, the right atmosphere, in which to drink. In this connection Hermann Glaser speaks of the *"altdeutsche Saufgemütlichkeit"* (the "Teutonic camaraderie of the bottle"),[23] and he goes on to designate coarseness, fondness for drink, and love of roistering as specifically German character traits. This is in line with Max Bauer's observations on the German "beer thirst": "The comforting beer dulls the body and the brain but it rouses *Humor,* that age-old German something, which, like *Gemütlichkeit,* is a condition known only to the German people and which only the German language can express." [24] When a German drinks, he needs more than alcohol; he also needs music and song, he needs a band to create an atmosphere and put him in the mood for the beer concert.

What these people are looking for is "atmosphere." But the social tone which prevails on such occasions is not one of natural gaiety. When a German feels good, he sings *"Ich weiss nicht was soll es bedeuten, dass ich so traurig bin"* ("I do not know what is the reason, why I should feel so sad"). And then there is also the exuberance, the intoxicated mood, which is often forcibly induced but which still represents, albeit at a low level, something of the holy zeal of noble minds.[25]

When the Rourkela Germans were in an intoxicated mood and felt the urge to sing, they gave vent to their feelings with renderings of German songs, which reached their customary climax when the strains of *O, Du Schöner Westerwald* ("Oh, you lovely Westerwald" *) and *Es zittern die morschen Knochen* ("Now the rotting bones are trembling") issued loud and strong from a chorus of beer-drenched throats. Just as "the riotous behaviour of drunken white sailors in the seaports of the world" was never calculated "to

---

* Forest land east of the Rhine and south of Siegen.—TRANSLATOR.

demonstrate the particular excellence of the white race," [26] so too the roistering German thirst is an attribute that is unlikely to gain sympathy for Germans in India, a land whose religion and laws are opposed to alcoholism and to whose inhabitants the insistent gaiety of the extroverted reveller is almost entirely alien.

Knowledge of Languages

By and large the Germans who went out to Rourkela had very little knowledge of English. Even the superintendents and senior engineers frequently revealed a deficiency in this respect. Like many of the fitters they were able to give essential technical instructions and advice with the aid of a few odd phrases, but only too often their command of the language was insufficient to permit them to enter into a discussion of technical or other problems. But settling technical details or working arrangements with their Indian colleagues was not very important for a large section of the Rourkela Germans and also presented them with less of a problem, as we have already pointed out. Where the real difficulty lay was in trying to clear up and iron out misunderstandings, not only in the technical sphere, but above all in the wider sphere of working relations. In very many instances the Germans were unable either to recognize and evaluate the undertones and nuances in the statements of their Indian colleagues or to frame carefully-weighed remarks or apt allusions on their own account. Even if we disregard personality factors, the gift of allegory, which can be so important in Asia, was denied to the majority of the Rourkela Germans simply by virtue of their linguistic deficiency.

By and large the construction personnel had less difficulty with the language problem than the operation personnel. Many of the fitters had learned some English on previous overseas projects or while working on foreign construction sites and in the course of their careers had gradually improved their knowledge until it was adequate to their personal needs. However, they also found difficulty in establishing private contact with the Indians. There is, after all, a considerable difference between explaining to an Indian colleague how to work a machine on the site by means of a limited vocabulary, assisted by sign language and practical demonstrations, and sitting with him in the evenings trying to conduct a conversation. Who can blame the fitter if, after a tiring day's work, he no longer feels inclined to struggle with the English language in order to converse with his Indian colleagues? But a certain percentage of the construction personnel seemed nonetheless to have been well aware of the necessity for acquiring a knowledge of English; in 1959, for example, the number of men attending the twice-weekly evening classes in English language rose to as many as 150.

Where the operation personnel were concerned, things looked less propitious both in respect of their initial knowledge and of their participation in the language courses. One of them once declared: "Calcutta was a catastrophe! Amongst other things I couldn't even leave the hotel, because, being unable to make myself understood, I just didn't dare." Of 28 members of the production personnel interviewed before their departure for India, 16 spoke no English at all, 3 spoke serviceable or good English, while the remaining 9 said that they knew "some" English, "a few phrases," "just a little." Another inquiry carried out in Rourkela among a group of 35 members of the operation staff revealed that 12 spoke "no English," 11 "some English," 10 "quite good English," and only one "perfect English." Of the 35 only 4 were trying to improve their English by attending the language classes. From the way in which the answers were given and the circumlocution employed in certain cases it was clear that the assessments of the 11 men who claimed to know "some English" were based either on quite inadequate knowledge or even on no knowledge at all, a circumstance which they had evidently felt ashamed to admit. Nearly all of them, however, were persuaded of the necessity for being able to speak English.

Very few of the Rourkela Germans knew Hindi, the principal language of the non-English-speaking peoples of Northern India. But it soon became clear that their knowledge, quite apart from providing them with an additional and valuable means of communication, also placed them in a special relationship to the Indians. The fact that a German speaks and understands Hindi is regarded by most Indians as proof of a very special interest on his part in India and its people. Considered within the general framework of collaboration between Europeans and Indians, just a few words of Hindi appropriately interspersed may well prove a valuable acquisition.

In this connection the "concert" given in the German Club in Rourkela following a sports meeting, to which some thirty Russians from Bhilai [*] were also invited, provides an interesting commentary. Each national group was called upon to perform: the German fitters formed a mouth organ trio and played German folk and pop songs; the Russians sang—with great feeling and extremely beautiful voices—Indian folksongs in Hindi. The effect on the Indians in the audience was indescribable: the tears welled up in their eyes— and this despite the fact that they well knew they could not have conversed with the Russians either in English or in Hindi. In this way even the most superficial knowledge of the native language, provided it is correctly applied, can make an important contribution to understanding between peoples.

Prejudices and Stereotypes

This is an important chapter in our inquiry into the disposition of the Rourkela Germans, for it poses the following questions: How did the Germans who signed on for Rourkela regard "the" Indian and how did they assess him before their arrival in India? What ideas did they have about India? How were those ideas formed? Could they—insofar as they proved false—have been corrected or even banished by the provision of more accurate information?

The concept of "the" Indian, which was used by all the Rourkela Germans, is in itself a dangerous generalization whose untenability

---

[*] Bhilai is a town in the Indian state of Madhya Pradesh. An Indo-Soviet steel plant was erected there, which was as large as the Rourkela plant and was built at the same time.

is clearly demonstrated by the vast extent of the Indian state, by the diversity, indeed the contrariety, of the individual regions and by the multiplicity of racial, religious, and language groups which make up its population: the difference between an Indian from the North, for example a Punjabi,* and an Adivasi† from the territory of Chota Nagpur, near Rourkela, is at least as great as that between a Swede and a Sicilian. And yet, before he even sets foot on Indian soil, the German who intends to go to Rourkela has firm ideas about India and about the external appearance, the properties, and the peculiarities of "the" Indian.

These ideas come within the context of prejudices, which are here understood in the general sense as ideas, views, opinions, and assessments that are formed in the absence of any objective proof, that is, before the information on which they are based has been subjected to systematic scrutiny. From this sphere of general prejudices we wish, however, to isolate one particular type of aggressive social prejudice, whose import is pejorative, if not indeed spiteful.[27] Certain categories of people, especially certain ethnic groups, are frequently regarded in a stereotype light, that is, as if all members of the group were identical in all essential respects.[28] Thus we are told, *inter alia,* that the (i.e., all) Turks are cruel, the (i.e., all) Scots are mean, the (i.e., all) Indians are backward. The term "stereotype" was coined by Walter Lippmann, who used it to denote the images which characterize the symbols and labels employed in social thought. For example, if somebody meets a Turk, a Scot, or an Indian he will react not so much to the individual as to a symbol that is fashioned by the qualities of the stereotype.[29]

The stereotype most frequently dealt with in American social science literature is that of the Negro, who is characterized—from the viewpoint of the white Americans—as superstitious, lazy, religious, and musical.[30] An image such as this, even if it is distorted or false, will influence the behavior of the person caught up in it to an inconceivable extent. An example of stereotype thinking (or cliché thinking), which bears a strong resemblance to both the

* Inhabitant of the Punjab, a state in northern India.
† Original inhabitant.

attitude and the terminology of the Rourkela Germans with regard to the Indians, has been reported from Africa. A European mining employee gave vent to his feelings in the following words:

"The Africans have no brains. They can never be civilized, not even in a thousand years. They walk into my office without knocking. An African had the cheek to tell me I made a mistake. The educated Africans are the worst—they do nothing but imitate the Europeans; did the Kaffirs ever invent anything? They can learn nothing; if you gave them a palace they would use it as a lavatory. The only good Kaffirs are the old men in the bush and the dead ones; when the educated native goes back into the bush, he reverts to type and goes wild and is just like a baboon." [31]

Such an extremely negative and aggressive outburst cannot be explained simply in terms of the prejudice which the speaker clearly has about the Kaffirs. There are other motivations as well, but these we propose to investigate later in this study. The observations made in Rourkela suggest that the stereotypes operative there should be divided into two main groups: those which the Germans had before they went to India and those which they formed during their stay. We might call the first group "second-hand stereotypes" and the second "first-hand stereotypes." The second-hand ones, which may well have existed before the men concerned ever thought of going to India, are usually quite unspecific. From conversations and a few small-scale inquiries carried out in Rourkela it would seem that the men's ideas about India were extremely varied, extremely fragmentary, and in some cases even fantastic. It was all the more surprising, therefore, to find that the great majority of Germans had formed a somewhat negative and pejorative assessment of "the" Indian, which, although it was never formulated in any detail, nonetheless placed him somewhere within the general category of the "underdeveloped," of the "blacks"; he was probably "dirty," perhaps even "smelled" and—to sum up their feelings in a single negative word—he was a Kanaka.*

---

* Kanaka (Hawaiian for man) is a term of abuse for a simple, rustic person. Originally the name of the earliest inhabitants of the Polynesian Islands, this term was subsequently extended to the whole of the indigenous population of those islands (see Ludwig Kapeller, *Das Schimpfbuch* [Herrenalb, 1964], p. 94).

This word "Kanaka" is also used by German seamen to describe all dark-skinned people, especially Asiatics. It seems highly appropriate that a second-hand stereotype, which does not really mean very much, should be expressed by this foreign word, Kanaka, which sounds mysterious and vague and certainly does not suggest any clear-cut images or ideas.

The first-hand stereotype, the image of "the" Indian acquired by the Rourkela German during the period spent in the company of Indians, was not a new creation; it undoubtedly utilized elements which were already present in his second-hand stereotype. It was really more of an amalgamation, made feasible in the first instance by virtue of the fact that the second-hand stereotype had been so little developed and consequently lent itself to further entrenchment and mutation. As a rule, fully developed and firmly entrenched stereotypes are virtually immune to external influences, since prejudices afford a valuable support to every individual by providing him with a means of orientation in an unknown, completely strange, and consequently uncanny environment. In this way they acquire value as a relieving factor. They relieve the individual of the complete uncertainty which may assail him in situations in which he is obliged to make decisions or adopt attitudes without having a prior opportunity of forming a thorough assessment. This is also where the danger of the stereotype lies for relations between individuals of different categories, peoples, or races, for by virtue of its "function as a relieving factor the stereotype—and this is the crucial point—automatically blocks any chance of adopting an individual attitude based on understanding in the widest sense of the word." [32]

How do these stereotypes of ethnic groups come into being, especially those which are formed before the individual concerned has come into direct personal contact with the members of such a group? Although it has often been stated by competent authorities that the problem of the origin and emergence of such schematic yet precise ideas has as yet scarcely been touched upon by researchers, and although it is also maintained in America that we are not yet in a position to say very much about the way in which these predominating criteria have acquired their importance, we should not overlook the great significance of the second-hand knowledge, which is primarily imparted to the individual through the agency of the so-called mass media, but also through the reports and descriptions of third parties.[33]

There were two principal aspects of the Germans' image of India as demonstrated in Rourkela: firstly an exaggerated sense of the exotic, prompted primarily by the land itself, and secondly the above-mentioned "Kanaka" attitude, which of course concerned "the" Indian. The only conclusion to be draw from a comprehensive analysis of the information propagated by the German mass media between 1958 and 1964 is that the traditionally stereotyped German image of India has been perpetuated and strengthened by certain newspapers, illustrated magazines, and scandal sheets, with their use of such captions as "holy cow," "cremated widows," "fakir," "Indian rope trick," "tiger," "snake," and so on. It is far more difficult, however, to say anything about the origin of the Kanaka attitude. One is inclined to think that the color of the Indians' skin may have triggered a mental association with either an original German or possibly an acquired Negro stereotype, that racial prejudice will certainly have played its part, and that the tales told by Germans who had worked with Indians and failed to get along with them will have given rise to further dangerous generalizations. An English writer who has been associated with India for many years clearly demonstrated the dangers of such generalizations when he wrote, "How easy to pass from saying, 'The Indians, who are coloured, have a civilisation inferior to ours' to the thought 'The Indian civilisation is inferior because Indians are coloured.'"[34]

Off to India Unprepared

A newspaper reporter who visited Rourkela in the summer of 1959, commenting on the impressions he had gained from numerous conversations and observations, wrote:

"Young fitters from the 'Kohlenpott'* . . . sit . . . in the German Club . . . and play "Skat." Unfortunately, neither their firms nor the

* Ruhr-area in Western Germany, center of heavy industry.—TRANSLATOR.

governments concerned have bothered to tell them where they are. Perhaps that would be asking too much. You would have to learn so much here before you even began to understand: the whole of the Indian Pantheon and the caste system, climate and history, the old Colonial Empire and the young autonomy." [35]

The Cologne sociologist René König goes one step further: "Neither the workers, i.e. the German fitters, nor the German engineers had the faintest idea what they were going to have to contend with —and not only them, there were others besides." [36] Another author with really expert knowledge of India and Rourkela has said much the same thing: "The German fitters failed to appreciate that things in Rourkela were not the same as in the Ruhr. . . . Nobody had taken the trouble to tell them the difference in customs, deriving from centuries-old tradition." [37]

Apart from attending a few introductory courses run by a number of the German firms for their own workers, most of which were inadequate, the German construction personnel really did set out for a minimum tour of eighteen months in Rourkela without any knowledge of India and its inhabitants. The fitters' ideas as to what awaited them were predetermined either by positive or negative stereotypes or—in the most favorable cases—were quite undefined and permeated by fantasy images.

By and large the only preparation given to the Germans prior to their departure consisted of the regulation number of injections and a medical examination to determine their fitness for tropical duties, which, incidentally, was far from strictly supervised in all cases. In terms of tropical medicine that is scarcely good enough. Under a sensible system of health checks *every* worker setting out for India and *every* worker returning home from India should be subjected to a thorough medical examination. Steps should also be taken to ensure that the men are given all necessary information to enable them to lead sensible lives in Rourkela. This would involve detailed explanations as to what constitutes correct conduct in a tropical climate: ensuring good food of the right kind, acquiring suitable accommodations and clothing, checking supplies of drinking water, lavatory installations, and drains, supervising servants, never going without shoes, and many more precautions. Many of the Germans who came to Rourkela had no idea that it would be difficult in a Hindu-Islamic land to obtain beef or pork in sufficient quantities and in the prime condition to which they were accustomed. Nor had it occurred or been suggested to them that it would be preferable to eat less pork in 100 degrees of heat and that "Schnaps" was not to be recommended for breakfast. One fitter who passed the Schnaps bottle around on his birthday during the breakfast break—as he would have done at home in Germany—was not a little panic-stricken to find that he had to report to the medical officer with acute disturbance of vision.

But even more serious was the failure to inform the men about the fundamental problems of India and to advise them of the need to show understanding for the complexity of those problems, which are not restricted to economic and technical matters alone but, on the contrary, involve far wider and more deeply rooted questions of a general cultural and social nature. Even the most comprehensive financial and technical aid programs on the part of the industrialized countries are senseless and in certain circumstances may even provoke hostility unless the aid is accompanied by a sympathetic understanding of these underlying problems and circumstances. From the difficulties experienced by the Rourkela Germans, who had come to India quite unprepared, in acclimatizing and adapting to Indian social and working habits, it is clear that a world as alien as India is not going to reveal itself to the foreign technician of its own accord. On the contrary, it may in some cases grow even more alien.

The crucial consideration here is the extent to which the new arrivals from Germany are initiated into the culture and society, the religious rites, and the attitude of mind to which these have given rise, in their host country. A thing which should never have been allowed to happen, for example, was the occasion when one of the more senior of the Rourkela Germans punished his Muslim driver for some minor irregularity by placing him on extra duties on the second most important holiday in the Muslim year. "Inadequate knowledge of cultural detail" is what the Americans would have said about this sort of thing. Having had their own bitter experiences in technical assistance they are constantly pointing out, and quite rightly so, that the success or failure of a whole project may well depend on such knowledge.

All authorities on the developing countries who have had experience of the human side of development aid are agreed on this point: "Those who arrive 'out there' with a sound knowledge of local conditions are received very differently, especially by peoples who are proud of their homeland, from the novices, who are also exposed to the additional danger of tactlessness, however unintentional." [38] "Those who form disparaging assessments of foreign institutions simply because they are unable to discover their true significance, or who make offensive and critical remarks about them are rightly regarded as uncivilized ignoramuses." [39] "Things which we classify as 'primitive' are not infrequently things we know nothing about or even more probably things we do not understand." But ignorance and intolerance are near neighbors; "occasionally that . . . vicious circle is formed, in which intolerance is constantly reinforced by ignorance." [40]

Suitability and Selection

The last and the most important points to be considered in assessing the qualities which the Rourkela German has to offer are the question of suitability and, as a corollary to this, the question of the criteria which govern his selection.

The least disputed and also the most important criterion—always assuming that it is possible to establish priorities within this context—is that of medical fitness. It is not difficult to demonstrate to all concerned that, if relatively large sums of money are to be spent on sending workers abroad, a good state of physical health —and, where appropriate, fitness for duty in the tropics—is a necessary prerequisite. There is also the further fact that the doctor's assessment is based on positive criteria, namely the results of objective tests; it is this assessment, backed up if necessary by a second medical opinion and presented in the form of a medical certificate of health or of fitness for tropical duties, which determines whether a given applicant may be sent overseas or not. Once a certificate has been issued to the effect that a particular man is medically unfit, both he and his employer will normally be obliged to respect it.

In the case of Rourkela, however, this principle was not always observed. Whether it was that individual fitters or their relatives found some way of getting around the regulation that required them to produce a certificate of fitness for tropical service or, alternatively, to submit to an examination by the firm's doctor to establish their fitness, or whether, in view of the excellent medical services provided in Rourkela, the health requirements outlined above were not strictly adhered to, must remain an open question. What is quite certain, however, is that in a number of cases German workers had to be sent back home again by the German medical officers in Rourkela immediately or very shortly after their arrival because they were unfit for tropical service. Since doctors are bound to silence by their medical code it is not possible to give details of such cases. By the same token the doctors themselves were unable to take any action against those concerned. Nonetheless, it was common knowledge that German wives had come out to Rourkela in a pregnant condition without having been vaccinated against typhus, smallpox, and cholera and, upon proving unfit for life in a tropical climate, had had to be sent home again, still without having had their vaccination, since this was precluded by their condition.

It was also an open secret that these women appeased the authorities in Germany with a certificate of vaccination that they had bought on the black market in Calcutta for a few rupees, and thus they constituted a risk for their home environment as potential carriers of disease. This one example must serve for a whole series of similar incidents that illustrate the irresponsible behavior of all those who came to Rourkela or who sent personnel to Rourkela without taking the relevant health precautions.

But, for all that, the problem of physical fitness is far more easily solved than that of temperamental suitability. On the one hand, practitioners of tropical medicine rightly insist that anybody intending to live and work in the tropics should subject himself to a searching self-examination well in advance with a view to determining whether he is, both physically and psychologically, the right man for the job. On the other hand, the service department or firm concerned also bears a responsibility and should first carry out a careful test of the worker's total personality before sending him abroad. The experience gained in Rourkela would suggest that Ernst Rodenwaldt, an authority on tropical medicine, is entirely right when he demands "a thorough examination of the worker's standard of life and personal conduct" and designates "self-control and self-discipline" as essential requirements both in the workers themselves and in their wives; [41] he is in favor, incidentally, of allowing wives to accompany their husbands. Further details of the author's experiences with the Rourkela Germans will be presented under the heading "The Climate and its Effects," but at this point it should perhaps be added that, in the opinion of medical men and in accordance with the observations made in Rourkela, the men selected for tropical service should not be too young. In physical terms twenty-year-olds are of course as fit as anyone. But one of the most important facts learned from the overseas posting of European troops in both world wars is that they give up more readily than older men when subjected to heavy physical work in a tropical climate.

But what have those responsible for sending workers overseas to say about the question of suitability and selection? Understandably enough the industrial firms concerned are primarily interested in completing their delivery and construction programs on schedule and according to the terms of their contract. In the traditional view the way to do this is to ensure, above all else, an adequate supply of skilled men. But recent experience—in Rourkela and doubtless elsewhere—has undermined this traditional view and prompted the realization, which is gaining greater and greater currency, that the character and human qualifications of the men working in the developing countries are also a factor to be considered. This is evident from the attitudes adopted by a number of industrialists who work in the foreign branches of various large German concerns and were interviewed in an inquiry carried out by the Institute for Foreign Relations in Stuttgart: "'Pure technicians' . . . are not suitable for the construction department, since our men have to be able to adapt themselves to a very considerable degree." "The choice of personnel is based primarily on technical and personal qualities." But unfortunately the mere fact of knowing what the right man looks like is not enough in itself, for, "as far as selection is concerned, it would doubtless be true to say that this varies according to the rise and fall in the demand for labor at home." This last remark probably offers a partial explanation for the fact that in a number of cases there simply was no process of selection. The example of the fitter who was sent back to Germany by one firm only to be reengaged for Rourkela by another is doubtless a case in point. "A man who is offered genuine opportunities at home is . . . not so easily persuaded to go abroad as one who stands in the shadows. Although such circumstances are not always a yardstick of ability, when personnel are in short supply they may occasionally produce a negative selection." [42]

But quite apart from the exigencies and problems of selection it is as yet by no means generally recognized that a fitter of only moderate ability but who has understanding for Asians is of greater use in Asia than the best fitter in the firm, who loses all patience every time a native worker is "careless." On the one hand, the firms feel that to insist both on the great importance of professional and technical competence and on the even greater importance of certain human characteristics in their overseas personnel is asking too much of them, since men of this caliber simply are not available. On the other hand, however, there are those who still hold an opposing view, as is evident from the following quotation from a pedagogical work:

Unlike the colonial official, the development adviser is invited to the territory and consequently is not expected to display the same high degree of dexterity in public relations; he is there on account of the project for which he was brought there and not in order to exercise psychological or any other form of power.[43]

In Rourkela it was not because of technical deficiencies or criticisms of their work that the German construction personnel came into a certain disrepute between 1959 and 1961 but purely as a result of incidents caused by a number of Germans whose personalities rendered them quite unsuitable for employment on such a project. The disproportionate influence exercised by these negative elements—who usually banded together into cliques—on the German community as a whole will be described and investigated in greater detail under the heading "The Rourkela Germans as a Social Group." The kind of men needed on construction sites abroad are men of reliable character. Malcontents are as much out of place there as apathetic or overly sensitive persons. A healthy sense of adventure is no less necessary than the ability to exercise effective self-criticism at all times on the basis of a sober and accurate self-assessment.

In the experience that the hanseatic mercantile companies have acquired over long years of trading in foreign parts and which was borne out by events in Rourkela, even Germans of comparable technical skill "differ widely in their ability to adapt to a given environment. One may be suitable for South America and nowhere else, another will be better able to come to terms with the people and conditions in India than in Black Africa." [44] And so it was that fitters who were said to have got along particularly well with the native workers on construction sites in other parts of the world failed to live up to their reputations for human contact in Rourkela. By contrast, a number of Rourkela Germans whose previous records had given grounds for concern as to their behavior developed a particular interest in their environment and so took the most important step towards establishing a positive attitude to both India and the Indians.

One of the basic facts learned from the experience in Rourkela is that suitability and selection constitute a particularly important aspect of the planning and preparation of industrial projects undertaken by an industrialized country in a developing country.

Our economists must be made to realize that today, unless human contacts are established, there is no business to be done. The colored peoples regard such contacts as genuine proof of our good will as partners. It is as working colleagues that we will best be able to persuade foreign peoples that a superficial knowledge [of technical matters] is not enough and that omissions of long standing cannot be made good within a single generation. We will succeed in this task only if we are able to provide qualified persons, who are both technical experts and "psychologists." [45]

2/ THE INDIANS IN ROURKELA

Origins and Composition

To speak of "the" Indians where Rourkela is concerned seems particularly unsatisfactory, both in view of the limitations placed on this concept by German prejudices and stereotypes and also because of the great diversity of the regional groups who lived together in this district and whose attitudes to "the" Germans were by no means identical. We will consider the Indian population, therefore, under three main headings.

Original inhabitants: The Adivasis

Rourkela lies on the southeastern border of a mountainous and well-wooded district previously known as the province of Chota Nagpur. This territory, which was called Jharkand ("the forest region") by early Muslim authors, still has some three million original inhabitants, who were gradually forced back into the forests and mountains by more highly developed immigrants in the large-scale population shifts that took place over the course of history. These original inhabitants (the Adivasis), are not Hindus but animists. Some are also said to be totemists. They all live in firmly structured tribal communities and support themselves by a primitive form of agriculture in which stakes and primitive hoes are their only tools, by growing rice with the aid of a wooden plough, and by keeping a few animals (goats, pigs, chickens, cows). To some extent they also still follow their traditional occupations of hunting, fishing, and collecting wild berries and roots.

These people have developed their artisan skills only minimally. In those spheres where they have tried their hand (pottery, basketmaking, spinning, and weaving) their work shows no real sense of method and its products are intended primarily for their own use. Village markets are for the most part run on the barter system.

And yet there have been forces at work—especially since the beginning of this century—which, although scarcely noticeable further afield in the Rourkela area, have nonetheless constantly promoted the development of the Adivasis. Small industries have started up, largely as a result of the discovery of minerals, and by employing individual Adivasis as laborers these have introduced elements of change and progress into the villages and tribal communities.[1] Christian missions have been located in this territory for several generations, and their members have taken a particular interest in the Adivasis, primarily in the sphere of education and social work.

Principal inhabitants: The Oriyas

Apart from the Adivasis, who make up about 17 per cent of the total Orissa population of 17,565,645 [2] and who have a special significance within the Rourkela area, the other inhabitants of Orissa are known as the Oriyas. The overwhelming majority of these Oriyas are Hindus, the few exceptions belonging to minority religious groups such as the Muslims, the Christians, the Jains, the Buddhists, and numerous others.

With its per capita income of 190 rupees, as compared with the Indian average of 294 rupees (in 1957), Orissa is economically one of the most backward states of the Indian Union. This is no doubt due in part to its geographical position, which has kept it isolated for centuries. Screened from the rest of India to the west, the north, and the south by chains of mountains and uninviting, dense forest and jungle territories, and protected in the east by the waters of the Bay of Bengal, Orissa was far less exposed even to the irruptions of the Muslims than other parts of the subcontinent.

Consequently, although today it is often visited as a rich source of Buddhist and Hindu antiquities and art treasures, it is still very much cut off from the economic progress being made in the rest of the country.

It is therefore scarcely surprising that the Oriyas should also have developed little inclination for economics and technology. For this reason the few industrial concerns operating within the state (iron and metal processing; paper, cement, and textile manufacturing), while employing Oriyas (and a few Adivasis in subordinate positions), fill all key posts with immigrant workers from other parts of India.

Immigrant workers

A similar situation developed when work began on the Rourkela steel plant. Technicians and skilled men poured in from every part of India to offer their services. This influx was not due simply to the inability of the Adivasis and Oriyas to provide the large numbers of qualified men needed for such a gigantic project but also to the fact that the Indian government, as the central authority responsible for the distribution of work, was obliged to ask for tenders from Indian contractors in all parts of the Union. The successful applicants all brought their own staff of skilled men with them; this in turn prompted others to follow.

It was not long before regional groups from the Punjab, from West Bengal (Calcutta), from Bombay, from southern India and other parts of the country had settled both on the construction site and in its environs.

Regional differences

The first stage in erecting the steel plant called for a particularly large number of workers. Due to the fact that the Indians used what were for the most part extremely antiquated working methods, forty to fifty thousand Adivasis, both men and women, were employed as unskilled laborers during the period of major earthwork and concreting for the foundations. They arrived every morning from their villages in the surrounding countryside and in the evenings, after a full day's work, they set off again, tramping home along jungle tracks for several miles. A few made temporary dwelling for themselves in reed or tin huts on the edge of the site. Their daily rate of pay was the equivalent of 35 cents for women and 40 cents for men. This was enough to entice them from even the most distant villages.

The better jobs, which required higher qualifications and consequently carried higher rates of pay, were taken partly by the relatively small number of Oriyas, but more especially by the immigrant workers, among whom the Punjabis were both quantitatively and qualitatively the dominant group. This gave rise to envy and constant unrest amongst the workers in Rourkela.

The nationwide problem of regional and religious differences commonly referred to in India as "communalism" or "regionalism" was already particularly oppressive in Orissa due to the special conditions—already apparent in historical times—created there by the territory's isolation. This problem was rendered even more critical by the rivalry for employment in Rourkela. Time and again during the early years of the construction period there was public discussion of the alleged injustice whereby the inhabitants of Orissa were denied the right to work in a steel plant being erected within the borders of their own territory. This led to bloody clashes between the inhabitants of Orissa (both Oriyas and Adivasis) and members of other regional groups (from the Punjab, Madras, Bengal).[3] Detailed accounts of such incidents, many of which had religious implications, will be considered in the light of their effect on the Rourkela Germans under the heading "Exotic environment."

The Indians' Attitude toward the Germans

According to the personal impressions formed by the Germans who arrived in Roukela in 1957 there was little to suggest that the vast majority of the Indian population was well disposed towards them. At most, occasional "lip service" was paid to the idea of friendship on official occasions, in speeches and in print:

We Indians will always remember that Germany was the only great power in Western Europe never to have made territorial claims to our country and that of all the European powers only Germany supported the Indian revolutionaries in their struggle for freedom. The Germans sought contact with India because they wished to discover our ancient cultural heritage. Thus the association between our two countries, which has existed since the days of Max Müller and Paul Deussen, is a purely cultural one based on mutual respect.[4]

Although this kind of attitude may have been adopted by a few intellectuals, the great majority of Indians in Rourkela certainly did not think along such lines.

Indian attitudes toward Western economic aid

Since no opinion polls were taken among the local inhabitants as part of the general planning for the Rourkela steel plant, it is not possible to make any precise statement about their attitude to the Germans or to "their" industrial project. But we can form some idea by considering the findings of an inquiry carried out among the Adivasis in connection with another project immediately prior to the commencement of work on the Rourkela site. These Adivasis lived at the Hirakud Dam, about two hundred kilometers from Rourkela, which meant that both groups were in roughly the same Adivasi area. The inquiry was carried out by Nitu, the Indian anthropologist, at the suggestion of members of the American Friends Service Committee in India, who were helping with the removal and relocation of villages in the area and also advising the villagers living below the reservoir about the system of artificial irrigation that was soon to be initiated. The purpose of the inquiry was to discover the motives attributed by the Adivasis to the Indians and Americans engaged on this village development scheme. The American development workers commented on the findings of their survey as follows:

> Some of the people say that we will acquire the best lands of the area and start a farm.
> We will change the caste system and make everybody equal. We will change the religion of the people.
> We have acquired the area of Barpali from the Government of Orissa as it could not pay off the loan taken from the American Government

for the purpose of constructing the Hirakud Dam Project. We are permanently settling here and will rule them.

We are very high officers delegated by the Government of Orissa to settle and rule the people of this area. If this is not a fact then the Government people would not have built buildings for us and the great officers such as Deputy Commissioners and members of the Board of Revenue would not have come to us to pay homage to us. (The visits of high Government officers to us makes them believe that we are concerned with the Government and make us higher in position than those who visit us.)

Some believe that we are going to change the way of life from individual families to community living. Under the conditions of community living we will ask them to have a common kitchen regardless of caste, creed and nationality, and they will have to live under one roof. They need no longer take care of their children as their children will be taken care of by us in our maternity center. As soon as a child is born in the village, the parents will be asked to hand it over to us.

Some of the villagers are under the impression that we will not allow the leper patients to live in the area of Barpali. We will either shoot them or take them away from this area and keep them in a leprosy hospital.

We have come here to influence the people politically in order to gain votes.[5]

From his own experiences in Rourkela and its immediate environs the author discovered that the people living in the Rourkela district are to this day haunted by ideas similar to those expressed in the findings of the Hirakud survey; they regard the steel plant and the events and changes to which it has given rise with incomprehension, if not with aversion.

No opinion polls were taken among the other inhabitants of Rourkela either, (the Oriyas and the immigrants). Consequently their attitude to Western economic aid can only be deduced from the personal experiences of the Rourkela Germans and from the attitude of the Indian population as a whole, about which a certain amount of information has been supplied in the relevant literature or can be inferred from it.

It is not surprising to find that on innumerable occasions and for many reasons Indian official spokesmen have expressed their country's sincere gratitude for the economic aid afforded by the richer nations to the Indian Union and have also appealed to the magnanimity of these nations for further support in the future. At the same time, however, there is a real fear—especially on the part of the government—that this economic aid will prejudice India's hard-won independence. But this fear of dependence is not only felt in the political sphere; it also extends to the personal sphere of the individual Indian.

He wants to live in his own way and to seek happiness according to his own ideals; he is certainly not prepared to give up his customary way of life in exchange for foreign aid. This attitude is prompted on the one hand by feelings and reactions which are pretty generally known, for unfortunately it is not infrequently the case that a sense of gratitude for gifts and assistance is transformed into aversion and annoyance simply because people do not like to feel dependent. On the other hand, however, it is also based on a genuine fear of political dependence, which promotes a frame of mind in which all foreign aid is regarded as a necessary evil for which there is not a single good thing to be said and which prompted Nehru to describe the need for such aid as "the plague of the underdeveloped peoples." This attitude is adopted toward all the richer nations, whether they belong to the East or the West. A further result of this attitude is that, despite the far greater economic aid afforded by the Western nations, India is no more sympathetic toward the West than toward the East. However, she is far from unequivocal on this point:

> On the one hand they [the Indians] have a positively fanatical longing for the doctrines and achievements of these peoples and are prepared to imitate them quite blindly; on the other hand they harbor resentment of their superiority, of their arrogance, and are fearful lest, despite their national independence, they should be unduly influenced by them. Consequently they place innumerable obstacles in the way of Western contractors, although their need of them grows in direct proportion to their determination to enter into the modern world.[6]

The first of the German technicians, who came to Rourkela in 1957, were made to feel both the opposition and the ambiguity of the Indian attitude.

But there are other reasons for the Indians' reservations about foreign aid, most of which derive from their colonial past and find expression today in various forms of sensitivity. One such form is that of mistrust. In the first place they mistrust one another; a German fitter once remarked that "the reason why they need so many more people is that they have more supervisors than workers. And every supervisor has to be supervised." But their mistrust does not stop there. It is extended both to development aid as such and to those who bring it to them. An American visitor to Rourkela recognized this and formulated it in terms of a general requirement for Western development workers: "Recognize that the natives of these countries are apt to distrust, or even resent, foreigners who come in to do jobs they themselves are unable to do." [7]

Mistrust is to be found at all levels of society. In the case of the ordinary working man it finds expression in a stereotype of the older colonial epoch, namely the composite image which has been formed of the "master race." In the case of the intelligentsia it extends to every conceivable sphere, even to the point where it is believed that the Christian missions in India are merely a cleverly disguised attempt to realize neocolonial ambitions.[8] "This feeling that 'you foreigners are here to do something to us' is a feeling which runs very deep." [9] From conversations with Indians in Rourkela the author learned that certain of the Indian workers had repeatedly voiced the opinion that the Germans had delivered inferior, second-hand machines for use in the steel plant and that they had only offered aid in Rourkela so as to be able to export their own unemployment problem—an accusation which was also made elsewhere about American development aid—or in order to sell their surplus production to India because they were no longer able to dispose of it in Germany. When the German construction firms engaged on the Rourkela project found that they would also be required to provide operation and maintenance personnel—more than they had originally contracted for—they had no option but to re-engage as members of the maintenance staff a number of the men who had already worked on the building of the steel plant. This prompted Indians in Rourkela to remark that these men were retained so that they could cover up any faults which might subsequently emerge in the installations and so carry the firms in question safely through their guarantee period. These and similar expressions of a vigilant mistrust were constantly encountered throughout the construction period and were later also to be found in certain articles in the Indian press.

The ordinary Indian worker, accustomed to the old traditional ways, scarcely knows what it is to feel disgruntled or envious. But the first generation of the newly educated Indian intelligentsia are finding that they are constantly obliged to fight for the right to equal pay in their professions. And, because they are having to fight, the Indian engineers, who have been trained at Indian training centers and universities, do not see why they should be financially so much worse off than their foreign colleagues. Many of them are of the opinion that it would be preferable for India to forego the help of such foreigners rather than pay them inflated wages—even if this were to mean that the country suffered temporary setbacks. Their attitude is understandable, especially when we consider that even an Indian undergraduate engineer earns only a third of the wage paid to the German fitter (skilled worker) working alongside him. The comparison with American skilled workers is doubtless even less favorable to the Indians and must really foster any disgruntled feelings they may possess.

The great admiration felt by the Indians for the high standard of technical development achieved in the industrialized countries is often accompanied by an attempt to compensate for their own inferiority in respect of technical ability by demonstrating their superiority in other spheres. By exaggerating in both respects they create inferiority complexes and feelings of superiority that, in their different ways, prejudice the Indians' attitude to foreign aid.[10] From the observations of the Indians in their relationships with the Germans and Americans in Rourkela and with the Russians in Bhilai, and also from further observations made elsewhere, it would seem that the Indians are more prone to unconscious inferiority feelings vis-à-vis Westerners than vis-à-vis the Soviets.

It is interesting to note that many Indians are unaware that the technical and industrial superiority of these foreign countries is set against a background of corresponding intellectual and civilizing processes. They seem to think that they can isolate the technology, the machines, the experience of the industrialized countries from a general setting they regard as largely useless and import them as they stand. They want to take over the functioning of Western civilization ready-made, that is, its products and the processes by which they are produced—in a word, its "know-how." This is reflected in India by various strange regulations, such as that limiting the tax exemption granted to foreign technicians to a period of three years. At the end of this time the "expert," as he is commonly called, is liable to pay taxes in full, and no authority in the land, not even the central government, can release him from his liability. The reason given for this regulation is that by the end of three years India would have got "full value" from the expert, which means that he would then be valueless and could go home again, leaving behind for the Indians all the know-how he once possessed. It is in keeping with this attitude that, by virtue of their long and proud cultural heritage, the Indians should feel themselves to be fundamentally superior to these simple exponents of know-how. They consider that they themselves have something of great value to offer, which puts everything else, everything which comes from outside, in the shade.

By compensating in this way for their own technical and, in part, unconfessed inferiority, the Indians create conflicts that must be regarded as being closely linked with the immature forms of nationalism that have become virtually symptomatic in many of the developing countries and which frequently constitute a source of grave danger. This point is also made by Klaus Mehnert, an expert on Asian affairs, who draws attention to the endeavors of those Asian peoples who have recently acquired their independence "to overcome the sense of inferiority instilled in them as 'coloreds' by the 'whites' and to regain the self-respect that they had lost under the oppression of their white colonial overlords." [11] This kind of endeavor was aptly expressed by the title of a newspaper article on the fast-growing steel plant in Rourkela: "Re-Awakening India." We may say with the German historian Gerhard Ritter that

nationalism is never the expression of a national consciousness that is calm and assured but of one that is agitated, somehow startled, whipped up to alarm or resentment. The more strident its tone, the more probable it is that there is an ultimate, inner uncertainty at its core. As a lasting attitude it is a sign of dangerously morbid conditions . . . above all: it obscures only too easily the good sense of healthy and sober government.[12]

Wherever he goes the foreign technician in India must expect to encounter the repercussions of this nationalism, which obscures not only the "good sense of sober government" but even more often the common sense of the individual, "whipping him up to such a frenzy" [13] when certain ideas or schemes are mentioned that it is impossible to discuss with him their worth or worthlessness, their advantages or disadvantages, in moderate and objective terms. This nationalism is of recent vintage in Asia and reveals a positively frightening youthful virulence. It begins by intruding into the sphere of daily work in quite simple ways and ends by interfering with the schedules for the starting of new works, which are frequently fixed not in accordance with technical, industrial, and economic requirements but out of considerations of domestic prestige—themselves determined purely by the dictates of nationalism. Whether the newly erected works are made to suffer in the process is not normally taken into account.

Although foreign advice and foreign capital are needed and although this need is often quite clearly recognized, the foreigners are nonetheless driven out. We find transitional stages, in which countries and governments which have been freed from "colonialism," instead of solving their social and political problems, "live off nationalism," whereby nationalism is primarily understood as aggression to foreigners.[14]

It may perhaps be realistic in terms of African countries for Kai Uwe von Hassel to assert that the peoples now gaining their independence have "meanwhile recognized that their construction programs will be far quicker and far more stable if they take place within a 'multiracial' framework, i.e. not in opposition to the white or Asian races but in collaboration with them." [15] But in India this is certainly not the general case. And when Hassel goes on to stipulate that "those who expect our collaboration should be prepared to give a friendly welcome to the collaborators" he is certainly being completely unrealistic since this requirement takes no account of nationalism in the young countries of Africa and Asia.

As a political phenomenon nationalism is easily explained: it is an indigenous structure that is formed in order to oppose either Western or Eastern attempts to exercise influence.

It is triggered off by the encounter with a technically and consequently often politically superior culture. This produces feelings of inferiority and arouses compensatory forces. Those particularly prone to this process are . . . the members of the rising social strata who have been uprooted and whose emergence and rise were only made possible in the first instance by the social crisis which their nation has undergone, by the transformation of its economic methods and structure, due—in many instances—to industrialization and a sudden increase in population.[16]

The relevance for our inquiry into the Indians' attitude to foreign aid of nativism (which is the name given to one of the component elements of nationalism in recent sociological writings) is more difficult to assess. The Heidelberg sociologist Mühlmann understands by nativism "a collective course of action prompted by the urge to restore the sense of group identity, which had been shattered by a superior foreign culture, by means of a massive demonstration of the group's ability to make 'a contribution of its own.'" He also regards Gandhi's "Quit India" revolution as an "expression of widespread nativistic attitudes" and goes on to say:

The nativistic aspects of Gandhi's movement were the concepts of political autonomy (*svaraj*) and of economic autarchy (*svadeshi*), both of which also implied a state of inner self-determination, inner freedom from foreign luxury, and both of which were linked with a powerful desire to reject foreign technology and its products. *Svadeshi* is virtually synonymous with *moksha*, i.e. with the concept of release, of emancipation (from Western civilization of course).[17]

It is by no means fanciful to refer to such matters within the context of present-day India, for even in the higher social strata, indeed precisely there, we still find large numbers of Indians whose sense of tradition is sufficiently powerful for them to cling to the kind of conceptions put forward by Gandhi and thus to declare themselves open enemies of the modern technology being imported from abroad. It is not even unusual to find these traditional attitudes among the older members or the wives in families in which the younger men hold important posts as engineers or managers within the field of modern technology and economics. This was also true in some cases of the Indians engaged both on the construction site and subsequently in the steel plant in Rourkela.*

From this example we see how close the alignment can be in India between traditional concepts and modern thinking, between mythical conditions and actual experience. It should not surprise the reader, therefore, if we suggest a comparison, from the viewpoint of Hindu India, between the modern construction personnel working under the auspices of development aid and the former, low-caste itinerant craftsmen referred to by Max Weber, the grand old man of German sociology. It seems that after inviting these craftsmen to come to their territory in order to exploit their skills the Hindus set up "ritual barriers" against them because they considered them to be "tainted by magic."[18] Weber has spoken in a similar connection (in 1921) of "pariah peoples" and "guest peoples." In the light of this comparison it does not appear inapposite when Mühlmann says of these people:

their skill was highly esteemed and consequently they were helped to develop it, but they themselves were kept at a distance, they remained

---

* This transitional problem between the India of yesterday and the India of tomorrow has been dealt with most impressively by the Indian author Bhabani Bhattacharya in his novel *Shadow from Ladakh* (New York, 1966), in which the action also centers around the construction of a steel plant.

strangers; for the magical, mysterious aura which surrounds strange and incomprehensible gifts ["know-how"], coupled with the ritual mystification openly indulged in by these privileged exponents, provokes constant mistrust towards the "royal craftsmen"; they are never really trusted.[19]

This statement is equally applicable to the Rourkela Germans and to the other foreign technicians working in India today.

How does the Indian see the German?

To the best of the author's knowledge there is no available information on which to base even an approximate assessment of "the" Indians' opinion of "the" Germans during the period 1956–1957. The only facts relevant to the earlier period of German collaboration are those to be gleaned from a collection of seventy-nine unpublished letters written by Indian trainees living in Germany in the year 1960. For the following two years, 1961 and 1962, however, we have the findings of two surveys that reveal clear traces of the impact of the Indians' dealings with the Rourkela Germans in the preceding years.

The letters of Indian trainees in Germany

At the end of 1959 the Verein Sozialbetreuung Rourkela in Essen (Association for Social Welfare in Rourkela) organized a public competition in which Indian technicians resident in Germany were invited to submit an essay on the subject "My Impressions of Germany," with special reference to any unusual experiences and to the value of the knowledge acquired in Germany for their future careers in India. There were seventy-nine contributors to this competition. The value of these essays for our present inquiry into the Indians' view of the Germans is of course strictly limited, but in their introductory remarks a considerable number of the contributors did deal with the ideas which they had formed about Germany and the Germans prior to their departure from India. We may assume that these ideas were not presented in their original form, for at the time of their formulation they were in many instances already several years old and will have been overlaid—at least subconsciously—by personal impressions. However, we may say, generally, that these ideas were largely based on stereotypes, which, as we have already indicated, do not readily lend themselves to change; and they were so different or even opposed to what the Indians actually encountered upon their arrival that they tended to stand out in their memories as "remarkable" or curious phenomena, for which reason, of course, they acquire a certain value for purposes of our study.

What emerges from these letters is that by and large these young Indians, like students from other developing countries, had come to Germany "without any concrete conception of the Federal Republic and in some cases quite uninformed." [20] Many of them described Germany as the land of their youthful dreams, as the land of promise—especially for the young technician—but few presented a reasoned case. Of the 79 contributors only 18 defined their ideas in any detail—by explaining, for example, that their early interest in Germany had been due to the proverbially high quality of German goods, the tag "Made in Germany" being quoted by no less than 9 of them. Seven more felt attracted by the Germany of the composers and philosophers, whereas only 3 mentioned negative memories of the war in connection with their preconceived ideas about Germany. Taken as a whole, the image of Germany formed by these young Indian technicians before their departure from India seems to have been a positive one.

But this image grew rather less favorable after they lived for a while within the Federal Republic, a fact which is also of interest for our study since a number of these young Indians subsequently came to work in Rourkela, where they contributed to the attitude adopted by the Indians to the Germans in general and to the Rourkela Germans in particular. In fact, they came to exercise a strong formative influence since, quite understandably, particular attention was paid to the opinions of men who had had experience of "the Germans" in their own country. Surprisingly the thing which annoyed the greatest number of contributors (22) was something of which they themselves were also guilty: ignorance of the other man's country. In castigating the "uneducated Germans" they quoted various examples ("Is Calcutta your biggest village?" "Do you also have tea in India?") and announced with great pride that in response to the many questioners who had asked, "What's it like where you come from with all those tigers?" they had always maliciously replied, "Oh, they always wait for the lights to change before crossing the street."

Nine of the trainees mentioned unpleasant incidents arising out of color prejudice, but for the most part these were reported without rancor. German hospitality received high praise (18) and was illustrated by many really astonishing examples. Invitations to spend Christmas Eve with German families were numerous and were described in most impressive terms. The Germans' punctuality and industriousness were considered to be exaggerated and consequently disagreeable. The Indians also had little understanding for the strict segregation of work and leisure ("when they work, they work—when the enjoy, they enjoy"). "German materialism" was pilloried in many letters ("man and wife both work, save their money, and then spend it all on electrical household appliances, furniture, pictures, a motor car . . ."). A number of criticisms, which may well have been prompted by the dichotomies of Indian life (caste system, regionalism, and so forth), were concerned with the split between the religious denominations in Germany and also with particular antitheses between North Germany and Bavaria ("they are either Catholics, Protestants, Bavarians, Berliners, or Hamburgers, and they all have their own idiom"). A few of the Indians observed that the Germans were "very much home-centered." Several implied and one actually wrote, "The characteristic features of Germany are: briefcases, rubber trees, Frankfurters, and detours." All in all we may say that there was no antipathy and certainly no aggression in these letters. On the contrary, although they made a number of justified and—in rare cases —unjustified criticisms, they were all basically friendly.

The Indian view of development aid:
The findings of a 1961 survey

At the beginning of 1961 the Studienstelle für Entwicklungsländer in Bonn (Study Center for the Developing Countries) coordinated the findings of three representative surveys that it had carried out in collaboration with the EMNID Institute for International Market and Social Research in Bielefeld and the Indian Institute of Public Opinion Research in New Delhi, and presented them in the form of an inquiry.[21] The surveys were based on interviews with 100 members of the Indian Parliament, 200 community leaders and 1,000 members of the lower middle class who had received either a school or college education. The value of the survey was greatly augmented by the fact that it was carried out by Indians among Indians and that even the interviewers were unaware of the identity of the German agencies by which it had been commissioned.

The most important result of this inquiry for our immediate purpose is the enormous importance attributed to the "human climate" in a combined operation, on which the success or failure of German development aid in India depends to a very considerable degree. The Indian Members of Parliament (with 42 per cent not replying) regarded the Soviets as the most sympathetic helpers, followed in second place by the Americans, then by the Germans and English. Among the community leaders the Americans topped the poll, followed by the Soviets, Germans, and English, while the middle class (with roughly one-third not replying) again placed the Soviets in the lead, with the Americans, Germans, and English following them. These ratings were based on assessments of the behavior of the foreign helpers and the level of their technical ability.

In order to discover the predominant Indian stereotype, those interviewed were asked on various occasions to give a character sketch of "the" German. The findings would seem to suggest that their conception of the German had been strongly influenced by a first-hand stereotype—the impression Germans had created in India. The predominant Indian view of the German was that of an authoritarian, domineering person. Asked to name three positive characteristics in the German, the majority of the community leaders and the members of the lower middle class said that he was hardworking, capable, and disciplined; the second largest group saw him as very practical, brave, and courageous; others spoke of his honesty and candor. Answers to similar inquiries as to the German's negative qualities mentioned his domineering nature, his racial superiority complexes, his warmongering, aggressiveness, chauvinism, Hitlerism, and dictatorial attitude. Sixty-three per cent of the first and 77 per cent of the second group listed no negative qualities.

The key question asked the community leaders and members of the lower middle class what pleased them best about the West German. The answers emphasized his scientific and technical skill, his hard work, his industriousness, and also his general ability. Germany's economic recovery after 1945 also received recognition.

The members of the middle classes were asked to assess the German against the following list of requirements: scientific ability; economic progress; past contribution to the dissemination of knowledge about India's cultural heritage; honesty in business or honest intentions; positive attitude to India; technical knowledge; German character as compared with the character of other nationals. Technical knowledge, individual ability, and scientific development were assessed as "very positive." Honesty in business and the German character received only an indifferent assessment and there were many abstentions. The Germans' attitude to India was said to be "positive within limits." The members of the lower middle class were even more reserved in their assessments.

The Indian Members of Parliament assessed "the" Germans, as opposed to "the" English, as follows:

Germans	%	*English*	%
Hardworking	85	Very practical	64
Brave	53	Honest	56
Thorough	43	Thorough	38
Very practical	37	Hardworking	37
Amiable	17	Amiable	32

The community leaders and the members of the lower middle classes were asked: "What effect is West German aid likely to have —for example, on the Rourkela plant?" Their answers are given in Table 1. It should be borne in mind that the questions were framed in such a way as to permit only a positive answer or an abstention. Nonetheless, 89 per cent of the one group and 82 per cent of the other voiced an opinion.

Table 1. The effect of German aid in India
(responses are expressed in per cent)

Effect	Lower middle classes	Community leaders
Promotion of Indo-German understanding	53	49
Higher opinion of German technology on the part of Indians	38	34
Increase in the flow of German capital to India	18	10
Improved market for German goods	7	7

An interesting light is cast on our inquiry by comparing Indian assessments of the three steel plants then being erected in India: Rourkela (German-aided), Bhilai (Soviet-aided), and Durgapur (English-aided). The Indian delegates' assessment is reported in Table 2. The responses of the community leaders and the lower middle classes were much the same, although the assessment of the Soviets within these two groups was even more favorable by comparison with the Germans.

Table 2. Indian assessments of foreign-aided steel plants
(responses are expressed in per cent)

Answers	Rourkela	Durgapur	Bhilai
Very good	10	9	35
Good	32	30	43
Satisfactory	14	20	8
Critical	24	16	2
Don't know	20	25	12
Total	100	100	100

The image of Germany in ten different Asian countries: The findings of a 1962 survey

In 1962 another survey was carried out by the Studienstelle für Entwicklungsländer in collaboration with the EMNID Institute in

Bielefeld;[22] one of its objects was to establish the nature of the Indians' "image of Germany." The survey was based on a group of 500 people who were able to read and write and on a further group of 100 representatives of the educated classes (journalists, officials, economists, businessmen, teachers, professors, free-lance workers, politicians, and so forth). The survey was intended to cover ten Asian countries and its findings were tabulated accordingly; we have abstracted the figures relevant to India and listed them in Table 3. It is noticeable that, although industriousness is still listed as the German's principal characteristic, in this assessment he certainly does not lag behind the American and the Rus-

Table 3. Character assessments of various nationalities
Question: I will show you a list of qualities. Would you please tell me which *three* of these qualities, in your opinion, most aptly describe a *typical* Englishman, a *typical* American, a *typical* German, and a *typical* Russian? Answer by placing a check beside the qualities chosen.
(I = educated class; II = persons able to read and write.)

Quality	English		Americans		Germans		Russians	
	I	II	I	II	I	II	I	II
Honest	37	32	16	11	20	11	18	10
Industrious	33	28	42	37	42	35	40	36
Thorough	17	14	7	7	19	19	5	9
Philosophical	7	8	4	2	17	13	3	3
Fanatical	3	3	11	10	10	4	20	7
Generous	7	10	31	31	1	4	1	4
Brave	21	17	10	7	22	25	20	19
Amiable	18	17	17	15	8	3	5	5
Educated	17	19	7	8	6	7	3	7
Self-seeking	8	12	4	5	–	2	6	7
Domineering	9	11	9	8	12	10	11	13
Intellectual	14	22	6	13	22	25	5	15
Practical	21	16	19	14	19	14	21	24
Helpful	8	5	29	16	10	5	9	9
Dishonest	1	5	3	2	–	1	3	1
No. of statements	221	219	215	186	208	178	170	169
Persons making statements	68	67	65	61	62	58	59	57
Persons declining to make statements	32	33	35	39	38	42	41	43

sian in other respects either. Here too, however, we must bear in mind that the answers were also preformulated and allowed dissenting statements only to a limited extent.

What attitude had the Germans to expect from the Indians upon arrival?

The attitude of many of the Indians in Rourkela to the new arrivals from Germany underwent a considerable change between 1957 and 1964, although the nature of this change, which was occasioned, above all, by personal experiences with the Germans, varied greatly from case to case. Consequently we can only hazard a very general statement as to the corporate Indian attitude, a statement which has been arrived at by abstracting all relevant data from the two previous sections and considering it in the light of the special conditions in Rourkela.

Among the Adivasis there was relatively little prejudice toward the Germans. Their tribal laws do not demand such strict allegiance to the requirements of the caste system, according to which all strangers are "tainted with magic" and are to be kept at a distance by the erection of "ritual barriers." Thus the Adivasis' attitude was determined by a healthy mistrust, coupled with timidity, a certain deference (influence of white missionaries), and also curiosity. But the really basic factor was their relative lack of bias, which made collaboration between Germans and Adivasis an uncomplicated affair even in the early years of the construction work in Rourkela. It must, however, be pointed out that the direct work-contacts between Germans and Adivasis were relatively few because the latter were employed only in subordinate positions and also because communication was difficult (the Adivasis speak tribal languages and only very few of them know any English).

Thus from the Germans' point of view—which is the one with which we are concerned in this section—the attitude adopted towards them by the Adivasis offered no serious problems. If this attitude subsequently changed for the worse, then the reason for this was to be found in the dubious experiences which the Adivasis, and especially the Adivasi girls, as we shall see, had with the Germans.

But the attitude of the rest of the Indian population constituted a far greater problem, principally because the Germans found it hard to believe that the same Indians who had asked them to come to their country to perform tasks which they themselves were quite evidently incapable of accomplishing nonetheless treated them with extreme reserve and even disapproval, making little secret of their conviction that the best Germans were those who were going home. The underlying reasons for this attitude have already been fully discussed: mistrust, fear of dependence, envy and disgruntledness, an admixture of inferiority complexes and feelings of superiority, nationalism, nativist and traditionalist promptings—all these factors combined in Rourkela to set up an invisible barrier in front of the Germans. It was invisible because the Indians' inbred sense of hospitality blunted the edge of their antipathies so that these remained largely subconscious. This meant, however, that the Indians' attitude was quite incomprehensible to the Germans, who knew nothing about the underlying factors or the cultural climate which had produced the attitude. Nor had anybody taken the trouble to explain to them that in the innermost recesses of their souls the Indians could scarcely rejoice at the German presence, since this was a constant reminder of the painful truth that foreigners were carrying out in their country complex tasks which as yet they were unable to accomplish alone.

But when Indians and Germans have to live and work together such feelings and attitudes are of great consequence, for although the Germans did not grasp their full implications, they certainly sensed the reserve and in some cases the rejection that they encountered in many Indians, especially the more educated ones. "Indians are Asiatics; when you talk to them they smile, and when you turn around they call you a dog." This was how one German fitter put it, and although his drastic language may have been prompted by some momentary irritation, it nonetheless reflected a view which was shared by many Rourkela Germans.

3/ THE GERMANS IN ROURKELA

The Climate and Its Effects

Acclimatization

The first really powerful impression of being in a new and strange country, one which assails the German as soon as he sets foot in India, is caused by the climate with its high temperatures and—depending on the season—a degree of humidity to which he is quite unaccustomed. There are of course many other strange impressions, but it is the climate which poses a major problem for the new arrival and to which he has to accustom himself. This process generally goes under the name of acclimatization, but the concept has not yet been coherently formulated by the relatively new science of tropical medicine. Scientists have so far failed to provide a great deal of substantial information in certain areas that, although not strictly a part of tropical medicine, would nonetheless be of interest within the context of events in Rourkela.

The possibility of a successful but purely personal adaptation to a foreign climate—which is referred to as relative or individual acclimatization—is discussed in complete isolation from the possibility of transplanting large numbers of people from a climate which suits their race to one with totally different conditions for purposes of resettling a corporate national group.[1]

Considered in these terms only "relative or individual acclimatization" is applicable to the Rourkela Germans and consequently of interest here. The relativity of this process requires special emphasis, for

if we . . . understand by acclimatization a process whereby a particular type of person or group of persons adjusts to a foreign climate, while at the same time retaining all their known physical and psychic properties, then we must reject this concept as Utopian. In practical terms the only thing to be done is to try to retain to the greatest possible extent those predispositions and properties which appear to be good, useful, and advantageous for the particular type in question.[2]

This view is in complete accord with the observations made in Rourkela: those Rourkela Germans who insisted on leading precisely the same mode of life to which they had been accustomed at home had little prospect of adapting to the climate. Grober, a German physician, made a revealing comment in this connection when he wrote that "acclimatization is not an anatomical test, one that is specifically concerned with tissues and organs, but a general test of a person's functional ability, the outcome of which may be approximately—but also wrongly—assessed and which consequently can never be accurately predicted even by the most experienced physicians."[3] In what follows the concept of acclimatization will be considered as "relative or individual acclimatization," in the terms advanced by Rodenwaldt, a specialist in tropical medicine. This specification is necessary if we are to distinguish between acclimatization and adaptation, which is here understood as a supraordinate concept embracing the whole process whereby an individual reorients himself within a different social, cultural, and physical environment. Acclimatization forms one part of this process of adaptation; the interdependence of the parts, however, is quite marked, with the result that when we come to consider adaptation problems and the reasons underlying the failure of a given individual to adapt, we find that the number of cases with complex motivational structures frequently exceeds the number of cases capable of monocausal explanation.

Acclimatization in the period between October and March presented no particular problem to the Rourkela Germans. From the figures given in Table 4 we see that the average temperatures for this period correspond to what might be expected in Germany in the course of a fine summer, and the amount of rainfall is considerably less than the German average. Although the humidity levels in Rourkela are very much higher than those in Germany through-

Table 4. Temperature and humidity in Rourkela [*]

Date	Max. temp. in °C		Min. temp. in °C		Rel. humidity in % [†]	
	Max.	Ave.	Min.	Ave.	Max.	Ave.
1960						
Oct.	36	32.8	20	24.5	97	88.2
Nov.	31	28.3	13	17.9	99.5	92.6
Dec.	30	26.8	11	15.4	97	90.7
1961						
Jan.	29	26.3	10	14.6	99	90.2
Feb.	31	26.2	11	15.1	100	88.7
March	38	35.8	14	20.3	83	67.2
April (until the 15th)	42	36.9	21	24.1	87	69.9
May	–	–	–	–	–	–
June	45	36.3	24	28.4	99	79.6
July	40	33	25	26.9	100	90.5
Aug.	38	34.6	26	27.5	98	89.8
Sept.	36	33	25	26.5	99	87.5
Oct.	34	27	20	22	99	76.5
Nov.	29	27	12	16	98	93.2
Dec.	26	23.7	6	10.6	100	92.1
1962						
Jan.	28	24.7	7	10.8	100	91.1
Feb.	32	29.1	12	16	98	87.7
March	39.5	33.9	15	19.9	96	68.7
April (until the 15th)	41	38.7	23	25.7	70	58.4
May	–	–	–	–	–	–
June	46	38.1	24	27.8	100	83.2
July	39	34.2	25	27.7	99	91.9
Aug.	37	33.8	26	27.1	100	91.2
Sept.	36	33.5	24	26.8	97	90.8

[*] Measured 1 m. above ground level.
[†] Measured at 07.00 hours local time.

out the whole of the year, the climate in these months could scarcely be said to be humid in view of Rourkela's geographical position (almost 400 kilometers from the Bay of Bengal and 235 meters above sea level).

In the months of April, May, and June, when temperatures reach 110 to 120 degrees in the shade during the day and seldom drop below 85 degrees even at night, humidity levels are very much lower, which produces a dry heat. High temperatures in dry areas are far more tolerable than less high temperatures in humid areas. The kind of climate which, more than any other, makes life in tropical climates difficult or even impossible for Europeans is one in which high temperatures combine with high levels of humidity. However, in the hot season even the dry heat became oppressive for the Rourkela Germans. Conditions are similar to those in Germany after a protracted spell of warm weather in midsummer: people grow irritable and feel disinclined to work; they tire more easily, lose their appetite, sleep badly, and awake feeling absolutely exhausted.

As a rule the hot season in Rourkela comes to an end in the middle of June with the onset of the monsoons. When the rains come, often intermittently at first, the tension which has been building up during the hot season is immediately relaxed. During these initial downpours the accompanying increase in humidity is not felt to be oppressive because the heat stored up in the baked earth is greatly reduced by the effect of the rain, and this brings an immediate measure of relief. But the monsoons normally go on until September, and during this time the tension among the Rourkela Germans again gradually builds up, prompted and continuously promoted by such unaccustomed quantities of rain, by the flooding of the bungalows that frequently ensues, and by the constantly high level of humidity. The oppressive, sultry atmosphere makes heavy demands on the individual's capacity for acclimatization.

Most of the Germans arriving in Rourkela started work at once. More experienced colonial peoples, such as the English, the French, and the Dutch, have long been aware that Europeans arriving in a foreign climate, no matter whether they are soldiers, officials, or emigrants, should not be required to plunge into their new duties immediately but should be allowed an appropriate period of leisure in which to acclimatize. All the evidence points to the fact that acclimatization imposes a very considerable strain on the human body. Of course the time of year plays an important part. The most favorable time to arrive in Rourkela was December or January—the cool season—because this gave the body a chance of "chiming in" with the seasons, of passing through a certain stage of acclimatization in the months preceding the period of extreme heat and the monsoons.

What further emerged from the experience in Rourkela was the great difficulty of predicting how a given individual would in fact acclimatize. Many passed through this process relatively quickly and without complications; others suffered from temporary ailments quite clearly caused by the climate and were unable to achieve their normal output until several months had elapsed. These "acclimatization ailments" may well be of a very general nature and may not appear to be directly connected with the climate. Grober has said in this respect that "these events do not always [take place] beneath the threshold of perception. The strange feelings of 'malaise' with which so many new arrivals in a foreign climate have to contend are a clear indication that such is the case." [4]

Fitness for life in the tropics

More traditional authors still point to the great dangers of living in a tropical climate, still refer to "the hell of Calcutta," still compare "years spent in the tropics with years spent at the front" [5] as far as health is concerned, and insist that white settlers in the tropics must live either on the coast or at a minimum height of 1,300 meters above sea level,[6] but the large numbers of Germans who have lived and worked in Rourkela in recent years have shown that such views are quite outmoded. After five years' experience of conditions in Rourkela the medical officer in charge of the German hospital, Dr. Kurt Bergter, said that "the risk entailed by a stay in the tropics that existed some forty years ago has today been considerably reduced for healthy persons." [7] Other physicians working in the field of tropical medicine hold a similar view: "Now that we have succeeded in combatting tropical illnesses to the point where they are no longer unavoidable . . . the maxim, 'years spent in the tropics count as double,' has lost its meaning." [8]

By the same token the criteria previously applied in determining the fitness of Europeans to live in tropical climates have also become outmoded. In the technical literature on the subject we still find a great variety of opinions, although these tend to take the form of questions and suggestions rather than specific statements based on substantiated facts.[9] The spectrum ranges from the view that once Europeans have reached a certain age they should no longer be sent to the tropics (with the rider that the effect of the climate on younger Europeans is by no means beneficial) to the assertion that people between 23 and 40 and between 55 and 60 years of age are those best able to acclimatize, to the modern conception that all healthy Europeans between 20 and 60 years of age could live under the kind of conditions normally enjoyed by Europeans resident in the tropics without running any health risk essentially greater than that to which they would be exposed in Europe, provided the possibility of an outbreak of specifically tropical diseases is restricted or eliminated. We shall come to see that this provision was fulfilled in Rourkela.

There is a similar diversity of view regarding the capacity for acclimatization of women and children. A number of practitioners of tropical medicine are very skeptical on this point,[10] while others are distinctly in favor of married men taking their wives and children with them. Some go so far as to say that if infants and young children living overseas are protected against infectious diseases such as malaria, dysentery, and ancylostomiasis, they are likely to grow up with fewer problems than in Europe.[11] From the observations made in Rourkela it would seem that Rodenwaldt is also right in this respect. The many hundreds of German women who brought their children with them to Rourkela or gave birth to them there (there were 107 confinements between July 1, 1958, and June 30, 1963) bear him out. But Rourkela did not provide quite such a happy home for older children and adolescents; the principal reason for this was presumably that they were not kept sufficiently occupied, a general observation which is also confirmed by other authors.[12]

Medical welfare

The relatively good capacity for acclimatization revealed by the Rourkela Germans was due primarily to the fact that it proved possible to avoid or limit the incidence of tropical diseases. To this end the German firms engaged in building the steel plant had sent out a German doctor with the advance party of construction personnel in the early months of 1957. This doctor set up his surgery in one of the bungalows and took care of any accident cases which occurred on the site; within a few months, however, he had adapted another of the bungalows for use as a temporary hospital. Meanwhile work was started on the construction of a solidly designed forty-bed hospital. This was fitted out with all necessary technical and medical equipment, specially imported from Germany, and was opened in the following year with a staff of two German doctors and one German dentist. Thus the medical welfare provided for the Rourkela Germans, which was such an important factor in enabling them to acclimatize to Indian conditions, was far more comprehensive than is customarily the case on construction sites overseas.

It nonetheless remains undeniably true that in their case "the chances of catching an infection . . . were still very much greater than they are in more moderate climates," [13] especially in view of the fact that of all the states in the Indian Union Orissa is the one in which tropical fevers (including malaria), intestinal diseases, and smallpox are the most common causes of death.[14] The following list provides a conspectus of the work of the German hospital in Rourkela between July 1, 1958 and June 30, 1963.[15]

This list of cases merely reflects the general pattern of illness prevailing in Rourkela and observed in the German hospital, a pattern in which tropical diseases simply formed a complement to "the spectrum of illnesses met with in the normal [i.e., European] environment." In the cases of death the causes were sepsis, typhus

Persons treated	No.
Male patients	3,047
Female patients	1,092
Births	107
Deaths	5

Cases of sickness:

Dysentery (bacillary)	2,593
Mycoses	1,017
Amoebiasis of the intestines	574
Lichen tropicus	410
Lambliasis	264
Amoebic cyst carriers	203
Hymenolepis nana	14
Malaria	13
Heatstroke	10
Ancylostomiasis	9
Amoebiasis of the liver	7
Typhus abdominalis	3

Injuries and wounds caused by:

Industrial accidents (slight)	1,667
Industrial accidents (severe)	211
Road accidents	30
Dogs with rabies	28
Dogs without rabies	18
Monkeys	16
Scorpions	3
Snakes	1

abdominalis (typhoid fever), fractured skull resulting from a road accident, encephalitis, and arsenical poisoning caused by an overdose of Neo-Viasept tablets. There were five other deaths which were not entered on this list because they did not take place in the hospital. Two engineers died of a thrombus, a young fitter was involved in a fatal accident in the plant, another was killed by an electric shock from his refrigerator, and an infant suffocated in its bed.[16]

There was one further death—an engineer who died of a

thrombus—but this occurred before the report was drawn up. Thus the total number of deaths among the Rourkela Germans up to the end of June, 1963, was eleven.

Bergter observed an increase in the number of persons reporting sick in the summer and monsoon months.[17] This increase was not restricted to cases of infection but applied equally to accidents of all kinds, from which it would appear that the tensions that built up during the periods of intense heat and rain promoted accident-proneness. Certain works on the subject, as well as Europeans with "tropical experience," constantly assert that Europeans grow more prone to such tropical diseases as malaria, yellow fever, cholera, and plague the longer they stay in the tropics.[18] There is also frequent mention of the European's diminishing "tolerance" of heat and humidity. On the basis of self-observation a number of the Rourkela Germans claimed that "the hot season became more difficult to endure from year to year." Hellpach speaks of acute or tropical asthenia in this connection and considers that the nadir of this condition comes in the second or third year of a person's stay.[19] But the occasional statements made by the Rourkela Germans can scarcely be regarded as furnishing reliable information. The available data on this subject has yet to be subjected to a systematic analysis.

For the year 1959, in which an average of 1,250 German men, women, and children were in Rourkela, the German hospital reported 26,810 consultations involving an examination of the patient. This does not mean, however, that the average German in Rourkela consulted and was examined by his doctor more than twenty-one times in the course of the year. The population figure is misleading, for on a construction site of this kind the personnel are constantly changing. Fitters who have completed the particular task for which they were engaged are sent home again; others come out to take their places. Clearly, therefore, the number of Germans who spent some part of 1959 in Rourkela was considerably higher, and although this duplication will scarcely have affected more than half of the population figure quoted as the annual average, this would still mean a rise in the number of potential patients to approximately 1,875. This, in turn, would mean a drop in the average number of consultations to fourteen—still a very high figure indeed. Even if we make allowance for the fact that, for very good reasons, medicines were obtainable in the German hospital only on prescription—which of course considerably increased the number of consultations—we are still forced to the conclusion that the Rourkela German visited his doctor unusually often.

There were two principal reasons for this. First, the Rourkela climate produced more illnesses among the Germans resident there and consequently provided them with more reasons for visiting the doctor. Of this there can be no doubt, even if we consider only the dysentery, the amoebic dysentery, and the mycosis cases. The second reason, however, is less obvious and requires special consideration: it was the fear of illness. A large number of Germans in Rourkela lived in constant fear of catching some "uncanny" and "virulent" tropical disease and so tended to visit the doctor quite unnecessarily. However, this attitude does not appear to be peculiar to the Rourkela Germans for we find references to similar conditions in the relevant medical and sociological literature: "The fear of such illnesses alone has a depressing effect on the activities and general behavior of the men." [20] Rodenwaldt states that "in the tropics every disturbance is taken more seriously, produces greater anxiety, and consequently has a greater effect on the individual's general psychological state." [21]

This fear produced in many of the Rourkela Germans a marked degree of instability, which not only sent them running to the doctor with imaginary or exaggerated symptoms but also gave rise to a fundamentally depressive outlook that had strong repercussions on their general psychological state. External factors such as the death of a fellow countryman, indications of an epidemic among the Indian population of Rourkela, or the statistics of cholera deaths in Calcutta that were published daily in the Indian newspapers throughout the summer months were enough to send these less stable people into a depressive condition, which was often difficult to cure.

In the majority of cases such psychoses were accompanied by a general inability to adapt to the outside world. Thus the fear of illness, which sometimes induced the individual concerned to seek refuge in an imaginary or even a simulated illness, was at the same time symptomatic of a sense of discordance whose original source lay elsewhere. In Rourkela it was extraordinarily difficult to convince these people that their fears were groundless. They kept going to their superiors and above all to the doctors in the German hospital with new complaints and new (imaginary) illnesses, insisting that they should be sent back to Germany at once. One fitter who had been struggling with his neurotic symptoms for days came crying to his supervisor, declaring that he was going mad and could no longer accept responsibility either for himself or his actions: "the Indians" had just torn up a working drawing he had given them and had used the pieces to roll cigarettes; that was the last straw; his nerves were shattered and he demanded to be sent home at once. These words were accompanied by hysterical wailing. The supervisor—who had acquired a kind of shrewd wisdom from his long experience on construction sites—found himself obliged to adopt a somewhat unorthodox remedy: he slapped the man's face with considerable force; this brought him to his senses and consequently back to work.

But in the majority of cases the solution was not so simple. It cost the German doctors, especially the specialist for internal diseases, a great deal of time and patience to talk these men out of their bouts of instability. The shock triggered by the death of a fellow German, especially when the cause of death was one of the "uncanny" tropical diseases, was always protracted. Similar reactions have been described by English colonial officials in India, who also stressed the suddenness and the uncanny effect of such deaths: "I know not when I have been so shocked as I was last evening to have Mrs. Newnham's death announced to me. She took Tiffin [lunch] here last Thursday, had an attack of fever that night, expired last evening. Here people die one day and are buried the next. Their furniture sold the third and they are forgotten on the fourth." Or to quote another example: "We heard this morning with awe and horror of the death of poor Mrs. Wilson, only 32, a most amiable excellent woman; she was only unwell a few days, and ill only 36 hours. These deaths make one tremble." [22]

These descriptions aptly reflect the feelings released in the Rourkela Germans by the death of one of their fellows. In their case, however, there was an additional factor at work, for the members of the German colony were far more intimately concerned with such matters than they would normally have been back home in Germany, save in the event of family bereavements. If a dead person's remains were to be taken home to Germany, then for protection from the climate the zinc coffin had to be soldered and sent on its way within a matter of hours. This meant that the German hospital was obliged to call on the services of a number of German fitters. But even when a German was buried in Rourkela, German workers had to dig the grave with all possible speed and also help with the actual funeral. (For religious reasons the Indians were not prepared to undertake such work.) All these factors contributed to the great sense of shock felt by the Germans upon the death of one of their number.

With some the fear of illness was so disproportionate that they would go to almost any lengths in their precautionary measures; everything within reach had to be disinfected, and they scarcely dared offer their hand in greeting.

Errors of diet

On the other hand there was a widespread tendency to disregard the more reasonable precautionary measures, which Western people living in tropical countries are well advised to observe. Above all, the Germans' readjustment of their diet to local conditions left much to be desired. Surveys carried out in the Federal Republic have shown that 45 per cent of the population regard meat as a necessary part of their midday meal even on weekdays.[23] It should not surprise us to find, therefore, that most of the Germans in Rourkela considered a meal without meat to be no meal at all—and this despite the fact that good-quality meat was virtually unobtainable (especially in 1957 and 1958) and beef and pork were supplied (by Muslims and Hindus, respectively) from the most obscure sources. Whether the thermometer showed 85 or 110 degrees in the shade was also a matter of complete indifference. Not only the German doctors in Rourkela but many other experts on tropical countries have insisted that the regular consumption of meat in large quantities is not to be recommended for Western people acclimatizing to conditions of extreme heat. It is also considered advisable to limit the consumption of canned meat, because in such conditions all animal products constitute a greater hazard than eggs and dairy produce.[24]

There were a number of Germans in Rourkela who paid their respects to local eating habits by demonstrating a preference for Indian dishes and for the wide variety of indigenous fruits, many of which had been quite unknown to them. They fared well on their diet.

The Rourkela Germans were warned time and again not to drink water without boiling it. Their rooms were also equipped with a special water filter. A German-operated soda-water machine that boiled and filtered the water and also sterilized the empty bottles was installed in 1958 in order to ensure a supply of pure mineral water.

Consumption of alcohol and general license

Alcohol deserves a chapter on its own where acclimatization is concerned. Quite apart from the partial or total prohibition in force in India and the Indians' religious attitude to alcohol, both of which militate against the drinker, medical opinion has also come out very strongly against the consumption of alcohol in hot climates. The ethnopsychologist Hellpach has recognized the interconnections between heat and alcoholic tolerance,[25] a recognition which impressed itself on nearly every one of the Rourkela Germans in very real terms. This tolerance diminishes in a hot climate; it is subject to fluctuation and is difficult to assess in advance; it also promotes excitation symptoms (which were already present in a latent form in the majority of the Rourkela Germans). The climate seems to combine with a number of other factors to free the European from his inhibitions, thus inducing a certain degree of license for the duration of his stay in the tropics. This state is by no means peculiar to the Rourkela Germans. Drascher, an author with considerable experience in the tropics, has made a similar observation: "When Dutch ships crossed the equator [homeward bound] there was a great celebration, in the course of which the Europeans were reminded that they must readjust their behavior to the customary European norms." [26] Hellpach considers that it is primarily their unsuitable habits, especially their drinking habits, which make Europeans lose control and indulge in so many different forms of license.[27]

Following a series of unpleasant incidents perpetrated by men who were drunk at the time, it was discovered that these men had suffered total amnesia and were genuinely horrified to learn what they had done. There were some, of course, who had a predisposition to violence and agitation that was reinforced by the effects of alcohol (induced more quickly in Rourkela's climate). The following incident is a case in point: On a June evening toward midnight a German man gate-crashed a party that was being held in the front garden of one of the German bungalows, and to the accompaniment of apparently meaningless exclamations, such as *König Oedipus, wo sind die Römer?* ("King Oedipus, where are the Romans?"), started hitting out without the slightest warning and for no obvious reason at a dancing couple. It proved impossible to calm the man and in order to protect the company from his furious onslaughts the host and occupant of the bungalow, aided by several of his guests, knocked him down. As the man lay on the ground with blood trickling from his head, one of the company drove off to consult with the German doctor.

Meanwhile the man recovered consciousness; the rest of the company then tried to persuade him to go home quietly. This he did, but not without having first issued further threats and curses. As he was making his way home two other Germans who saw him from their car stopped and asked him, in view of his blood-stained appearance, whether he was in need of assistance. The man reacted as before: one of the occupants of the car received a violent blow and had great difficulty in defending himself against further attack, whereupon both decided that it was preferable to drive off in search of medical help.

The next morning the man reported for work as usual and told his general foreman that he thought he really ought to apologize for something that had happened the night before but apart from a few bits and pieces he couldn't really remember what it was.

As a rule the same "types" inclined to drunken orgies—with all that these implied—and often appeared in cliques. They constituted only a small proportion of the total number of Rourkela Germans, but there were always others who, instead of keeping themselves at a distance or trying to call their intemperate comrades to order in a friendly fashion, allowed themselves to be infected by them and consequently to become involved in disagreeable incidents. In a hot climate the "brake" of self-discipline has to be applied before the second bottle of beer has been downed; otherwise it may well be too late.

In this connection, Rodenwaldt has quite rightly said, "We must not forget that the chief attraction of life in the tropics is the generous standard of life, but if he is to enjoy it a man must have the right outlook." [28] The observations made in Rourkela bear this out. Probably the most important task of those responsible for the conduct of Germans overseas is assessing whether or not they have the "right outlook." Normally this will have to be done on the spot, for it is usually impossible to form an adequate assessment in advance, that is, in Germany. It is only when the men are actually on the job, when demands are being made on them, that it is possible to decide whether a man has temporarily "gone off the rails" on account of the unaccustomed climate and various other environmental influences or whether he just has the wrong "outlook." In the latter case experience has shown that exhortations and threats of punishment are quite useless; the man simply has to be sent home before he "seduces" others. To the best of our knowledge the hope that in time such a man will eventually acclimatize is always illusory.

This tendency to bad behavior in a tropical climate, especially when alcohol is consumed, has also been attributed to the English, which means that it is by no means typically German. One reporter, in summing up his experiences, did say that the Germanic races were particularly susceptible, while the French, the Spanish, and the Portuguese, for example, inclined far less to drunken behavior in tropical countries.[29] In one of the biggest restaurants in Calcutta, which is situated on the second floor of a large building on one of the city's main thoroughfares, the story is still told to this day of how a group of young English officials once threw a grand piano out of the window in the course of a party. In the early days of the English colony in Nairobi, we are told, the English would shoot up the saloons on a Saturday evening and hold rickshaw races on the main street of the town.[30] We also learn from another source that it was quite customary for the English in India to shoot bread pellets at one another at dinner and to throw plates all over the place.[31] In view of this it is hardly surprising that there should also have been a number of Rourkela Germans who behaved with a similar lack of restraint in public places: at the end of one particularly joyous evening in the German Club several of the waiters were flung into the swimming pool, followed by their trays and glasses; an Indian family with a goodlooking, unmarried daughter had the door of its bungalow "garnished" with rifle bullets by nocturnal snipers. Drunken brawls—usually among Germans but sometimes involving Indians—were by no means rare. Although all of these events were determined to some extent by the effects of the climate, there were of course other motivating factors, which we will deal with in the section, "In-Group: We-Feelings". Many of the Rourkela Germans will no doubt have felt inclined towards license, but by and large only a small number of them actually indulged their inclination.

To make generalizations on the basis of such individual incidents and to present them as typical of the behavior of "the" Germans in Rourkela, as did the international press on various occasions, is unfortunate. At the same time, however, we should not overlook the fact that the behavior patterns induced by the effects of climate in even a small number of men may well have implications and give rise to dangers that could have considerable political significance.

The Germans' Way of Life

Living accommodations

When the first large group of Germans came to Rourkela in 1957 there were only enough bungalows for the senior employees. All the other Germans lived in the two-storied "trainees' hostel" in rooms which they rented through their firms from the housing department of Hindustan Steel Limited (HSL), a state-owned company founded for the express purpose of administering the construction of the Rourkela plant. The German fitters—all of them bachelors, or "temporary bachelors" who had come out without their families—lived two to a room on long corridors. Nearly every pair of rooms had a communal, narrow, covered veranda. With nearly 400 fitters living in a density that would be considered quite unusually high in Germany, living conditions were very restricted and in such a climate they can only be regarded as critical, despite the exceptional circumstances and the obvious need for improvisation. The unpleasant consequences of living at such close quarters made themselves felt at once. In many instances a number of fitters, usually various sets of roommates, joined together into household groups, employing servants on a group basis and taking their meals together, but this form of communal living did not turn out at all well. There were also a number of groupings among the German fitters that were described at the time as "clique formations." The members of these cliques tended to stick together in a way that went beyond the bounds of normal comradeship. Their camaraderie* was incapable of distinguishing between right and

---

* "Camaraderie is not friendship; it is a distortion of friendship, often merely an association of confederates who have seen one another in a special situation as naked beings, who know too much about one another." (Freiherr Friedrich August von der Heydte and Karl Sacherl, *Soziologie der deutschen Parteien,* [Munich, 1955] p. 303).

wrong and saw its fulfilment in blind allegiance to the group; it was particularly noticeable whenever there were disputes or brawls and whenever the members of a particular clique had broken any of the German or Indian regulations. These cliquish communities, which sprang up at the very outset of the construction period—or, to be more precise, were already in existence at that time, since they were based on the concept of common membership of a given firm—immediately incorporated all eligible new arrivals. Whether the new arrivals belonged to the permanent staff of the firm or had merely been recruited for the Rourkela project and whether they were personally known to their colleagues in Rourkela or not were matters of complete indifference.

A further and far less rigid system of grouping arose from the fact that the trainees' hostel consisted of three largely similar buildings, two of which were placed at the permanent disposal of the Germans and were called "Fitters' Hostels I and II." Fitters' Hostel II was situated between Fitters' Hostel I and the third building of the complex (part of which was also rented to the Germans on a temporary basis and called Fitters' Hostel III). Now it happened that the largest number of disputes, brawls, and other unpleasant incidents involving either Germans alone or Germans and Indians took place inside or in the immediate environs of Fitters' Hostel II. This gave rise to a distinction in the qualitative ratings accorded to Fitters' Hostel I and Fitters' Hostel II. This distinction may have been fortuitous, it may have been imaginary, and it has certainly been exaggerated; but the fact remains that when the Rourkela Germans—not only the members of these two groups but the whole German community—referred to "the men from Fitters' Hostel II," the expression had a faintly pejorative connotation, while any reference to "the men from Fitters' Hostel I" had a slightly positive ring.

The groups mentioned so far appear as a common series, and might be represented as horizontal to distinguish them from other kinds of associations that were formed without regard to any existing groupings, on the basis of the common interests of their individual members. These may be termed vertical series. The most striking example of vertical association was provided by the football teams, whose members sometimes came from the same firm, sometimes from different firms, but who all developed a particularly strong sense of team solidarity—indeed, they almost gave the impression of being bound to their confraternity by solemn oath.

It soon became apparent that the great disadvantage of the fitters' hostels was the fact that the men were obliged to live in such close proximity. Despite the installation of reading and table tennis rooms and the provision of badminton courts and a football field in the immediate vicinity, the prevailing atmosphere in the hostels was that of a camp or barracks, for which reason they were commonly referred to as the *Bullenkloster* ("Bulls' cloister"). The restricted accommodations, the primitive nature of the "household arrangements" (the narrow verandas usually had to serve as both kitchen and dining room for the household communities) and the impossibility of finding, let alone maintaining, a certain degree of privacy were factors which imposed an additional burden on the German fitters, who were already having to cope with the problems of living in a foreign country. The superintendents of the German companies and the German Social Center (GSC), which had been specially set up by the German firms engaged on the project to provide social, cultural, and medical care for the German community, soon realized that the fitters' hostels were a hotbed of discontent and strife, and in collaboration with HSL, they did their utmost to ensure that this kind of communal accommodation was replaced as quickly as possible by the self-contained quarters then under construction.

These self-contained quarters already accommodated the engineers and the small number of fitters who had either brought their wives with them or had sent for them shortly after their arrival. They consisted mainly of single-story buildings of soft brick with flat concrete roofs; each contained a living room, a bathroom or shower, a toilet, and between one and four bedrooms. They were built in numbered groups of twenty in various parts of the town—called "sectors" in Rourkela—and they were all surrounded by sufficient open space to enable the tenants to lay out a garden, if they so wished (see the Town Plan of Rourkela in this section). In some cases a number of adjacent bungalows would all be occupied by Germans; in other cases Germans often had an Indian engineer or technician as their neighbor. The order of allocation was largely fortuitous and was determined primarily by the growing need to accommodate the Indian and German workers who were arriving in Rourkela in ever increasing numbers. As a rule the size of a bungalow allocated to a family was based on the number of people in the family. Often four bachelors or "temporary bachelors" would share a two-bedroomed bungalow, which meant that each paid a

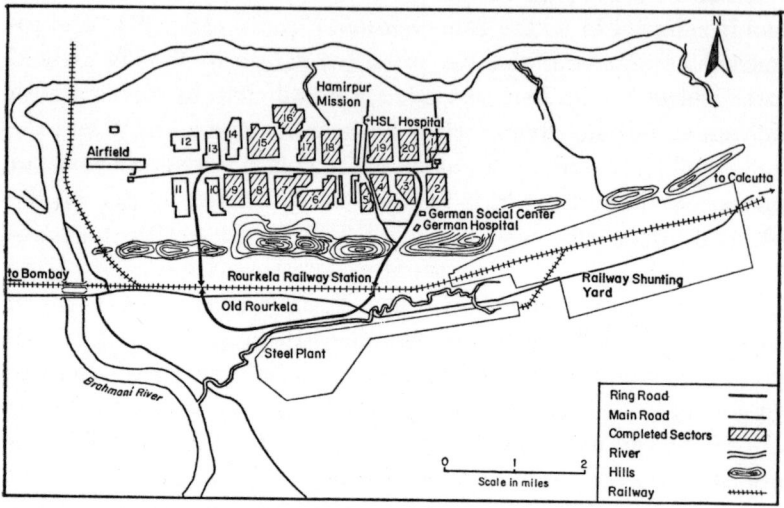

Town Plan of Rourkela

very much lower rent. A number of the Austrians, who were well-known for their frugality, did not care how restricted their living conditions were; they would even sleep three to a room in order to economize. Among the Germans, on the other hand, there were also a number of individualists who preferred to live alone in one of the smallest bungalows with their own bedroom, living room, shower, toilet, and kitchen, even though this did mean a somewhat higher rental.

The ground areas of the three main types of dwelling were as follows: a one-bedroomed house, 45 sq.m.; a two-bedroomed house, 99 sq.m.; and a three-bedroomed house, 157 sq.m.[32]

As a rule the German site offices would take the houses over from HSL immediately upon completion, the actual transfer usually being arranged through the German Social Center, and would then equip and furnish them themselves. But since nearly all the firms purchased furnishings from the local market, or occasionally the Calcutta market, the various rooms in the German bungalows had a sort of standard equipment which seldom went beyond the following articles:

Living room: 1 suite of furniture, consisting of 1 bench and 2 easy chairs, together with 1 low table (all made of bamboo or local timber with plaited cane seats and backs and fitted with padded or soft cushions), 1 standing or wall cupboard or 1 sideboard, 2 dining chairs, 1 dining table, 1 sisal carpet, curtains for the windows.

Bedroom: 1 wooden bed (with wooden or cane base [i.e. without bedspring], kapok or foam rubber mattress, pillows and 2 woolen blankets), 1 bedside table, 1 wardrobe, 1 table, 2 chairs, 2 rugs (cane) or 1 sisal carpet, 1 lamp, curtains for the windows.

Further general equipment: 1 refrigerator (usually among 4 persons), 1 air conditioner (usually between 2 persons), plain crockery and kitchen equipment including cooking utensils, 1 kerosene cooker, bed linen, table linen, 1 ceiling fan in each room (installed as a permanent fixture by HSL).

If the tenants wished to make their rooms more comfortable and more attractive, it was up to them to do so from their own means. In the course of time a number of Rourkela Germans, especially those who had brought their families out and had fairly long-term contracts, acquired tapestries, carpets, standard lamps (mostly Kashmir ware), small pieces of furniture, pictures, carvings in wood or ivory, and various other articles, many of which they bought from itinerant merchants who came knocking at their doors, and which they subsequently took home with them to Germany.

Most of the engineers and especially the superintendents, who were the principal representatives of the German firms abroad, had larger bungalows, which were usually far better equipped. But these men had to do quite a lot of entertaining in connection with their work and also used their bungalows for meetings.

The rents paid for the rooms in the fitters' hostels and for the bungalows, which included the cost of electricity and water, were calculated on the basis of 3.80 rupees (80 cents) per square meter.* Subsequently meters were installed and both electricity and water were paid for according to the amounts consumed. An additional charge was made by most of the German firms for the use of furniture, refrigerator and air conditioner. By and large the German fitters paid between 120 and 220 rupees per month for rent and all services, which amounted to about 10 to 20 per cent of the allowance paid out to them in local currency. After 1962 most of the Rourkela Germans paid higher rents.

In the course of time it became apparent that this more flexible system of housing in bungalows scattered over a number of different sectors (at first the majority of Germans lived in sectors 3, 4, 5, and 6 but subsequently in sectors 2, 19, and 20 as well) was a happy solution. It confirms the view of the specialist in tropical medicines who said that in the tropics "the European who understands where his interests lie will prefer to live either in a single or a scattered settlement." [33] Another specialist has also insisted, in the light of his experience in Africa, that

where possible everybody . . . should be given the chance of setting up his own self-contained and snug little home by being allocated a small villa similar to those in use in India, where they have been a considerable factor in protecting the settlers from moral depravity and from the danger to health which ensues from excesses of Bacchanalia and venery." [34]

By comparing the behavior patterns and the modes of life pursued by the Rourkela Germans in the overcrowded conditions of the fitters' hostels with those which emerged after the process of decentralization had been completed it was quite clear that once they were living on their own or in small groups, the Germans

* Indian rents, which were subsidized by HSL, were considerably lower.

were considerably more composed and more amicable. After they had adopted the bungalow style of living the orderly and peace-loving majority were able to isolate or keep themselves at a distance from the disagreeable elements among their own community to a far greater extent than had been possible within the narrow confines of the hostels. Old group formations, such as those based on common membership of a particular firm, were still maintained despite the physical separation of many of their members. New neighborhood groups came into being although a distinction must be made between "weak" and "strong" neighborhoods: weak neighborhoods are those in which people simply live next to one another but do not have social intercourse with one another; in strong neighborhoods the people behave in a really neighborly fashion and maintain numerous social contacts. Most of the neighborhoods created in Rourkela as a result of the bungalow style of living are weak.

At this point the question arises as to how much consideration the planners (primarily HSL but also the German planning bodies and firms) had given to the problem of accommodation and living conditions for the German personnel before construction began in Rourkela. In the light of what has been said so far it should be evident that those responsible were simply concerned with "providing accommodation" for the new arrivals from Germany, although it is not possible to say whether the failure to plan more appropriate living conditions for the German construction personnel was due to lack of experience or lack of foresight. However, the fact that in 1963—four years after it had finally proved possible to resettle the last of the Germans from the fitters' hostels —a large number of Germans were again concentrated in newly built two-story houses with four three-roomed flats would indicate that even by this late stage no real thought was being given to the question of living conditions. All that mattered was that accommodation should be provided so that the new arrivals would have a roof over their heads. But just to be given accommodation, to have a roof over your head, is not at all the same thing as actually "living" somewhere. Accommodation is provided because it is necessary, because "the man can't be left standing on the street." But this is mere expedience, an administrative act.

To live somewhere is quite different; it is a condition of social interrelationship:

> consequently everything that has to do with living [i.e., as a social condition] must always be regarded in the light of the individual's relationships and of the group's or groups' relationships. In this respect, however, there is only one factor which can establish these relationships for [the social condition which we call] living and that is the [individual's or group's] living experiences.[35]

We shall have to consider these "living experiences" because they were an important factor in determining the behavior patterns of the Rourkela Germans. If a worker feels dissatisfied with his living conditions he will come to work "in a bad mood." For all manner of good reasons, which we need not go into here, this is not going to benefit either the (Indian) client or the (German) firms. In the particular case of Rourkela, however, the men's dissatisfaction with their living conditions posed additional problems, for it had a negative effect both on Indo-German collaboration and on the Germans' ability to adapt to their new working conditions, which in themselves were not always felt to be very attractive.

Satisfactory living conditions, or satisfactory "living experiences," on the other hand, raise the morale and by providing home comforts may also have the effect of cutting down on the consumption of alcohol. The point to be considered here is that in the tropics Europeans develop a particularly urgent need for a "home," and if this need is not gratified they may only too easily turn to drink as a palliative. There could be no better illustration of this than the following letter, written by two German fitters to the management committee of the German Club:

> We are sorry to say that due to excessive drinking we behaved in the club in an unseemly manner. We sincerely regret having done so. We realize that we must now offer to surrender our club membership cards. If we should have personally offended other club members, we would like to offer them our apologies. The reason for our excitable condition

was that for some time now one of our colleagues has had to live in a bungalow that is equipped with nothing more than a table, a bed, and a chair. Despite all our efforts we have so far been unable to prevail upon the department concerned to improve upon these wretched conditions.

We appeal to your understanding, although we have no right to expect it.

It should be explained that, when construction or operation and maintenance personnel were engaged directly by HSL and not through the agency of one of the German site offices—a practice which became virtually standard during the operation period—HSL was also responsible for fitting out their bungalows. But this particular responsibility was one which HSL did not always take terribly seriously and a new arrival might immediately find himself in the sort of situation described above.

For the Rourkela Germans—especially the new arrivals—the prospect of building a home where the atmosphere would be European and where they could enjoy living conditions that were both familiar and satisfying promised some kind of protection from the extremely alien world in which they found themselves. The accommodation in the fitters' hostels was not calculated to meet such requirements. By comparison the bungalows were a considerable improvement, although even these were in many cases unable to provide a satisfactory home environment. Certain restrictions and irritations were, of course, unavoidable: there was no television and hardly any radio; * from July to September (the monsoon months) the damp often penetrated the walls and, owing to the combination of high rainfall with high levels of humidity, forced its way into every nook and cranny in the bungalows and even between the pages of books; it spread a musty odor and caused short circuits. The power supply in Rourkela in the early days was not very good; water supplies were restricted to a few hours daily and

---

* By and large radio reception was limited to Indian transmitters, whose programs were of little interest to the majority of the Rourkela Germans. There was also Radio Ceylon (which transmitted European music) and, when conditions were favorable, the German short wave. But most people considered it hardly worth while to buy a radio for such limited purposes.

were sometimes cut off for days on end. But there is nothing to be done about this sort of thing in a young construction town in the Indian jungle; it simply has to be endured. Meanwhile, however, conditions have greatly improved.

Although the modern German certainly regards radio and television as necessary parts of everyday living, his desire to fashion a home for himself according to his own tastes and his own ideas as to what constitutes domesticity and *Gemütlichkeit* is doubtless a far stronger and far more developed need. But since their relatively short stay made it scarcely worth while to the majority of the Rourkela Germans to attempt to give practical expression to such desires, the German firms and HSL could perhaps have done rather more than they did to embellish the extremely bleak and purely functional furnishings in the German bungalows. A German simply does not feel happy in a setting which, although perfectly hygienic, creates an impresion of coldness and frugality. On the contrary! A statement made more than thirty years ago on the style of furnishing most favored in Germany is probably still largely applicable today:

Not infrequently the furnishings have a somewhat jumbled and overladen look, which creates an impression of homely intimacy. Many of the articles in the German dwelling are overdraped and cluttered with objects. In the poorer-class dwellings with their knickknacks, prints, Renaissance furniture, tavern-like cheerfulness, stuffed animals, earthenware jugs and poker work there is an air of miscellaneous good cheer that is unmistakenly German.[36]

In Germany we are "still being made constantly and painfully aware of the fact that in newly built flats . . . the same sickly *Kitsch* is to be found;" [37] by the same token we have to accept that the famous "sofa" is ineradicable and continues to enjoy its status as a place of honor for invited guests, thus acquiring "social significance, even when there are no guests in the house." [38]

It is clear from surveys and conversations that the Rourkela Germans both felt and deplored the lack of comfort and warmth in the bungalows. This was particularly the case with the operation personnel, partly because the furnishings supplied by HSL were particularly meager and partly because they had higher standards. While the operation personnel were constantly complaining about the poor quality of their accommodations, the construction workers chose other ways of expressing their displeasure. Their complaints were to be heard in the humorous but outspoken verses of the various songs which they composed for carnival celebrations, social evenings, and similar occasions. The verses which follow were taken from two such songs:

> But first we had the dysentry and then we had the rain.
> It flooded through the bungalow, then flooded through again.
> You couldn't go to bed at all without an umbrella,
> Imagine paying such high rents for living under water.

> > One of these days we will all go home:
> > We'll take our fill of television,
> > Enjoy our German civilization,
> > Look at the pictures in our apartment
> > And think of India, "land of enchantment." *

Servants

In India it is customary for a household to employ one or more servants according to its size. This custom was adopted by the Rourkela Germans. The Soviet Russians in Bhilai—acting presumably on orders from above—did not employ Indian house servants and did not ride in rickshaws. This was then publicized (with the Rourkela Germans particularly in mind) as being indicative of a close Indo-Russian relationship based on equality. Although this version was unquestioningly accepted by part of the international press, one reporter, who had a sound knowledge of Indian conditions and investigated the matter rather more closely, considered that this was a propaganda move on the part of the Soviets, which only had the desired effect outside of Bhilai. The Indians directly concerned, that is, the house servants and rickshaw coolies in Bhilai, had hoped—like many of their fellows in other parts of India—to obtain well-paid employment as a result of

---

* See Appendix for complete texts of songs.

the great influx of foreigners. They were far from grateful to the Russians for adopting this attitude and complained bitterly of their miserliness.

The mass of Rourkela Germans behaved in exactly the opposite way. Instead of seeking advice from Indian families or foreigners who knew local conditions and the correct attitude to adopt to house servants, they automatically agreed to pay the wages demanded of them by those offering their services with the result that by the time the first large group of Germans had established themselves in Rourkela, the wages for house servants had doubled. (The prices of food and other commodities also doubled.) Not only was this practice prejudicial to the Rourkela Germans themselves, since they paid their servants out of their own pockets, it was even more prejudicial to the Indian families, who earned far less and were therefore justifiably annoyed when they suddenly found that it was no easy matter to hold on to their servants. One particularly well-informed reporter said that he had spoken to Indians who had continued to bear the Germans a grudge on this account years after the event, and who maintained that the Germans had paid these higher rates with "ostentatious generosity" and without even bothering to ask their Indian colleagues what the correct rates were.[39] There was a kind of rough justice in the fact that the Germans were subsequently paid back in kind when, in 1961, a group of Americans—the "Coletti Team"—came to Rourkela to operate the wide strip mill, bringing their families with them. They received far higher salaries than the German personnel and were therefore in a position to pay even better wages than the Germans had been paying. This led to a general rise in the rates of pay for Indian servants and on this occasion the Germans were also affected—and suitably indignant.

The principal servant in the German households in Rourkela was the bearer, a sort of "man of all work." Although both the abilities and the willingness of the Indian bearers varied to some extent, by and large they performed all, or nearly all, of the household duties: they tidied, dusted, made the beds, did the shopping, cooked the meals, and served at table. Their wages ranged from 80 to 130 rupees a month. As a rule the bearer was not required to do the laundry or to clean the house; consequently most households also employed a "sweeper" to do all the heavy cleaning, for which he received a monthly wage of 40 to 60 rupees. It was not uncommon for two families to share a sweeper. Laundry was generally done by outside workers. A further member of the household staff was the *mali,* who laid out and tended the garden and received a monthly wage of 50 to 70 rupees, although here again it was fairly common practice for two different households to share one gardener. And finally there was the "ayah," who was either a housemaid or children's nurse or both. Those ayahs who were employed exclusively as children's nurses were said to be very good and reliable helps, which explains their relatively high wage of 120 rupees a month. The housemaids, many of whom also did the laundry and were often able to sew and iron clothes, received an average wage of 75 rupees a month.

Some of the Germans who remained in Rourkela for a number of years kept the same bearer throughout. This was particularly the case with certain of the engineers and superintendents, whose bearers almost became part of the family. Their loyalty and devotion were most impressive. Like their counterparts in Africa [40] they were real "pearls," who proved their worth to quite a remarkable degree and were always concerned for their "sahib's" welfare. In such cases, of course, the concern was reciprocated by the German employer and it was by no means rare for a bearer to be able to show his colleagues in the neighborhood a new wristwatch, "made in Germany," which his sahib had brought back for him from a home leave. In other cases—probably a majority—the Germans changed their bearers frequently, often several times within the course of a few weeks. The bearers were, of course, a mixed lot: some were good, some less good, some bad, and a few even deceitful. It was therefore not surprising that the Germans made frequent use of the power of instant dismissal still enjoyed by the employer of domestic servants in India.

On the other hand we should not overlook the fact that many Rourkela Germans who had had no experience of dealing with servants at home in Germany also contributed to this fluctuation. Instead of retaining their composure and treating their servants justly and sympathetically but with a certain measure of reserve, many of the Rourkela Germans made the mistake of treating their staff as the mood took them—badly one day and well the next. The first of these two extremes could not be better expressed than by the following letter written by a young German when he was in Africa:

I believe that they [the Europeans] would do absolutely anything to one another in the aggressive frame of mind which is induced in them by the climate, were it not for the fact that they are able to work their moods off on the children of this land, whom they treat as doormats. Upon first arriving on this continent nothing impressed itself upon me quite so forcibly as the brash arrogance and even the coarseness of the Germans, especially the younger ones, and, by contrast, the patience and good manners of the Africans.[41]

It can scarcely have been the unaccustomed climate which made the Germans behave in this way, but rather their lack of self-control and maturity. It is of course also highly improbable that this kind of behavior towards native servants would be typically German. We also hear of English housewives in Africa who are no less inclined to work off their moods by using their boy "as a doormat." [42] Here too, one of the explanations given for such bad behavior is that the women in question had never before in their lives been in a position to employ servants.

The other extreme—which was every bit as disagreeable—produced a state of affairs in which Rourkela Germans would strike up friendships with their bearers as between equals. This intimacy sometimes reached such a pitch that they would drink together and even parade their fraternal feelings in public. Such "demonstrations" often ended badly for the simple reason that as drinking companions, the bearers were unable to keep pace with the Germans; as a result they soon became drunk and were then liable to forget themselves. In May, 1958, an incident of this kind very nearly touched off a general riot between Germans and Indians in Fitters' Hostel II. Two Germans were taking an early glass with their bearers when one of these, who was drunk, suddenly went for his companions with a knife. They ran out of the building, where other Germans and Indians intervened, some of them taking sides without even knowing what had actually happened.

Since his attitude towards his servants vacillated over the wide range between these two extremes, the Rourkela German should not have been surprised to find that he was not respected and that the Indians gossiped about him. Thanks to the bush telegraph—also known as "the bearer post"—everybody knew everything about everybody else. But since the Indians seldom mentioned such matters to their German colleagues, many of the Germans fondly believed that they could do as they pleased, at least within their own four walls, without anybody finding out. Many a Rourkela German would have been surprised to learn just how much the Indians knew about the more intimate details of his private life, of his behavior towards his servants, his friends, and the members of his family. This kind of thing was damaging to the reputation of the Rourkela Germans.

But the practice of employing servants, common to virtually every German household in Rourkela, raised another problem, which drew the following comment from one observant woman reporter:

> The role of many of the women in the German Colony seems particularly problematical. In Rourkela they have staff (cook and housemaid at least), but they have never been told how to deal with them. The full working day, to which—as normal German housewives—they had been accustomed at home, drops out. Often they don't really know what to do with their greatly increased leisure, with their "eternal summer holidays." And then the climate makes them listless and deprives them of much of their initiative. Few have intellectual interests. Consequently their experience of life is restricted to a state of "perpetual relaxation" in the Club swimming pool. It would also seem that this life of leisure is not particularly conducive to a composed state of mind. One sees an astonishing number of well-tanned morose young faces among the women.[43]

There is nothing to be added to this, although one might perhaps ask whether it would not have been preferable to have encouraged or even directed the German women in Rourkela to put the leisure they acquired through the employment of servants to better use, rather than to have left them to their own devices and their boredom.

The same point may be made in respect of the German children. Every year on December 6, St. Nicholas would visit the German children in Rourkela, commenting on their conduct over the past year by reference to the entries in his "big book" and then distributing presents. As he stood there, issuing censure and praise and finally gifts, he was surrounded by well over a hundred children who followed his every word with rapt attention. At one point, when St. Nicholas raised his forefinger and spoke in threatening tones, "Hansi, I see from my big book that you never want to put your toys away before you go to bed—you'll have to change your ways from now on," an astonished and indignant little voice replied from the great circle of children, "What, don't you have a bearer in your house?"

In most of the German households in Rourkela the bearer came to occupy an important, central position. But the ayahs, the housemaids, must claim our attention even more.

The woman problem

In the early years, from about 1957 to 1959, apart from the large numbers of German bachelors who came to Rourkela, it was also established practice with the majority of the construction firms to send out married men without their families. It was only after the negative consequences of such a practice had been observed that the firms gradually allowed and helped more and more of the wives and families to accompany their husbands. This, together with the resettlement of the German bachelors in bungalows, greatly improved the situation in 1959 and 1960. Finally, the arrival of the operation personnel created a social structure in which the large majority of Rourkela Germans were married men with families.

From the very beginning it was clear that the easiest and the most discreet way for a single German man to make contact with the local Indian women was by employing an ayah. In the first instance the ayahs were approached through the bearers, who were always the first to be engaged, but subsequently one ayah would follow another. Virtually every one of these girls came from the surrounding Adivasi villages; most of them were Christians and some had also attended the nearby Hamirpur Mission School. It is not difficult to imagine how it was that many of the girls originally engaged as house servants gradually came to be employed "for other purposes" by the single German men for whom they worked; and here imagination is borne out to a considerable extent by the decidedly forthright statements made by some of their "employers" in the course of conversation. It is probable that most of the girls—who had been trained to obedience and consequently had no real will of their own—offered little genuine resistance to the urgent and in many cases no doubt palpable wooing of their German sahibs.

But there is also another explanation for their submission, which had to do with the conditions of Adivasi life. Until ten years ago Adivasi girls were virtually nonentities. They were sold in marriage at the age of fifteen for two or three cows—and they had to obey. Then suddenly German men appeared in the Adivasi villages to hire women and girls as laborers for 15 to 18 cents a day, and the girls' fathers seized upon this chance of acquiring precious money. In many Adivasi villages and families the girls were the only breadwinners. Subsequently, when there was an opportunity of sending the girls into service for considerably more money, this opportunity was also grasped. One of the mission fathers reported in a circular letter of the "Young Christian Workers, Girl Section Rourkela" that in offering his daughter to a European (i.e., a German) an Adivasi had said, "Give me 200 rupees and my daughter is yours for a month." (This offer becomes more understandable if we recall that the Adivasis lived in exceptional poverty.)

Although not all of the Rourkela Germans who kept an ayah will have had them offered for sale in this way, they probably had little difficulty in obtaining them in adequate numbers. Presents, higher wages, and special concessions will then have done their part in persuading the girls to accept their new "duties." From conversations with German fitters it seems that most of the girls remained quite passive during the sexual act and this, together with their background and missionary upbringing, indicates that they had originally undertaken their "housework" in good faith and could by no means be said to have been depraved individuals. The fact that they had been seduced by the Germans gradually became public knowledge both in Rourkela itself and in the surrounding villages and mission stations, giving rise to both latent and active aggression towards "the" Germans. The strongest outburst of such hostility came in 1957, when the relatives of one of the ayahs attacked her employer with the traditional Adivasi weapons; the German fitter in question received a number of arrow wounds.

The missionaries joined with the heads of various Adivasi families in an attempt to prevent the village girls from going to work in the growing town of Rourkela; above all, the girls were strictly forbidden to work for unmarried Germans. One day before the town gates of Rourkela a notice was seen hanging from a neem tree, which read, "Adivasi girls quit the ayah job!" It is said that a number of village elders and tribal chiefs ordered the parents of girls working in Rourkela to bring their daughters home to the villages, threatening to have them "outcasted" if they failed to do so. The missions even sent social workers into Rourkela for the express purposes of caring for the girls who worked for Germans and of trying to bring back to their villages those who had already been, or were in imminent danger of being, seduced.

But not all of the Adivasi girls who worked as ayahs for unmarried Germans were innocent. There were a few, whose talents and inclinations were such as to render them entirely suitable for the occupational sphere that appeared so desirable to a number of the German fitters. Because of their proficiency these girls were soon well known and well loved among the interested parties. They frequently changed hands and are even said to have been "loaned out" on a number of occasions.[44] In the evenings, when they were sitting around their tables drinking beer, some of the Rourkela Germans would brag about their "ayahs," singling out their various qualities for special comment, although it should be added that not all of their listeners found this practice particularly edifying.

A third type of women and girls had nothing to do with the Adivasis; they had come in from outside, mostly from Calcutta and Jamshedpur, to do business in the rising "gold-diggers'" town of Rourkela. Most of these were "professionals" who had been considerably hampered in the prosecution of their trade in the big cities by the prohibition of prostitution in the Indian Union on May 1, 1958, and were consequently looking for business elsewhere. In Calcutta alone the number of prostitutes was said to have been 150,000![45] At first when these women went in search of clients they did brisk business; the author himself saw a number of them going from one German bungalow to another with a sort of order book, asking their customers to make advance bookings and to enter in the exact time for the assignation. There were many such entries. But the boom soon died down when it was discovered that a very high percentage of these women had venereal diseases. The German authorities issued strict warnings against any contact with them.

These warnings found expression in the following verse from a Carnival song composed by the Rourkela Germans:

> The welfare people talked to us, the superintendents too,
> They told us all the things we could and all we couldn't do.
> The big boss came along as well to sing his little song:
> "Those men who keep an ayah here
> Do not stay healthy long.*

But the ayahs who actually worked in the German bachelor households remained, and despite the almost complete absence of verbal communication, they succeeded in extending and consolidating their position until they enjoyed what was virtually the status of a housewife; this meant that they were able to bring a by no means inconsiderable influence to bear on the way of life of their German sahib. Rodenwaldt has confirmed this observation: "The position of the unmarried European in the tropics merely appears to be more congenial than in Europe. He is virtually obliged to live with a colored woman if he is to avoid the risk of

* See Appendix for compelete text.

venereal infection, which would very soon render him incapable of tropical service." [46]

Cohabitation between a German fitter and an Adivasi girl was of course decidedly problematical in view of their completely different backgrounds. It was, for example, by no means unusual for the ayahs to play their German masters off, one against the other, and so give rise to brawls and sometimes quite serious disturbances. To accuse a colleague's ayah of theft was often considered justification enough for an affray, which might well end up with police intervention and an appearance before an Indian court.

The Rourkela "ayah problem"—and in 1958 it really was a problem—gave rise to serious resentment and protests among the Indian populace. Here too the fitters' hostels played a particularly significant part, for it was there that any trouble over the ayahs tended to break out. Moreover, because the buildings were very open passers-by were actually able to observe the ayahs in the fitters' quarters when they appeared both in the open vestibules at the front and on the open verandas at the rear of the hostels; and to this the Indians took exception. It was for this reason that in February, 1958, the management of HSL insisted that the German site managements should expressly forbid the occupants of the fitters' hostels to keep ayahs from that time forth. Since the superintendents and the German Social Center had no means of enforcing such a requirement, they tried to resolve the problem by persuasion and discussion. In this they were only partly successful; some of the fitters maintained that "the Indian women were breaking their doors down to get at them" and that it just wasn't possible to keep them out; they argued that it was up to the Indians to put a stop to it. The upshot was that HSL surrounded the fitters' hostels with a barbed wire fence, leaving only a few entrances, which were guarded.* The German fitters in the hostels, who had been in

---

* It is interesting to note that the same sort of problem was reported in connection with the Italian workers' settlement in the German Volkswagen town of Wolfsburg, where it proved necessary to protect the Italians from the constant "incursions" of insurance agents, salesmen, and the "inevitable ladies of easy virtue" by erecting a fence—"naturally without barbed wire" (Klaus Wiborg, "Eine Stadt für 4,300 Gastarbeiter in Wolfsburg," Frankfort *Allgemeine Zeitung*, September 26, 1962).

an angry mood for some time past because of the shortages and restrictions imposed by HSL, especially the power cuts and the water rationing, regarded the barbed wire fence and the police posts around their quarters as an infringement of their personal liberty, and in the night of March 5–6 they tore the whole fence down.

Following this destructive demonstration immediate negotiations had to be started up with the general manager of HSL in order to pacify the enraged Germans. The fitters' representatives presented their case first. They wanted to know whether there had ever been any instances of force being employed against an Indian woman. They asked the general manager whether the employment of ayahs were forbidden under Indian law. They regarded his ban on the employment of ayahs as an encroachment on their personal liberty and as racial discrimination—in Germany nobody objected when Indians associated with German girls. They told the general manager they intended to inform the German press of his statements and threats and that the men most adamantly opposed to the idea of discharging their ayahs were, in fact, those who had no sexual relations with them. These men were prepared to risk being sent back to Germany by the general manager, and if this happened, it would certainly lead to demonstrations of solidarity. The fitters demanded that the general manager drop his objections and let the fitters decide for themselves whom to employ, especially since, in many cases, the police had given permission for Indian women to go on working in the hostels. The fitters felt that the general manager had greatly exaggerated the whole problem; there had not been a single instance which could even be remotely regarded as constituting an offense in law.

The general manager replied that he knew of no case in which force had been employed against an Indian woman and that there was no Indian law forbidding the employment of ayahs by bachelors. He pointed out that his previous attitude had not been based on considerations of racial discrimination but that he had merely wished to warn the German fitters against associating with the local Adivasi women; he would still advise them not to employ them, even as ordinary servants, although this was no longer to be thought of in terms of a prohibition. If they should choose to ignore his advice, however, then they must bear the consequences. He no longer intended to recommend that Germans still employing ayahs should be sent home. He would raise no objection if Indian, Anglo-Indian, or any other women were brought in from Calcutta and employed in the fitters' hostels under some suitable pretext (secretary, house servant, and so forth), provided this did not cause public annoyance. He was also less averse than before to the idea of opening a brothel in Rourkela.[47]

The really interesting point in this connection is the strong legal position of the occupants of the German fitters' hostels. The Indians were quite unable to get their way, and the German superintendents had no disciplinary powers that would have enabled them to put an end to the "ayah scandal," which was clearly a source of great annoyance to the Indians and did immeasurable harm to the good name of the German colony. All that the superintendents could do was to try to persuade the fitters, in which, as we have already indicated, they were only partly successful.

Some of the fitters were directly persuaded or indirectly pressured to give up their ayahs; others retained theirs. Subsequently it was often reported that bearers were supplying girls on demand—bookable in advance—at charges ranging from 10 to 20 rupees for an evening or a whole night. A number of bearers were said to have specialized in this trade.

The over-all effect of such incidents was to predispose Indian public opinion, far beyond the immediate environs of Rourkela, against "the" Germans and, what was more, to prompt part of the Indian press to take up the story and offer it to a still wider public in an exaggerated and sensualized form. The extract from the following article is fairly typical:

> To the visitor with open eyes [Rourkela] looks like a huge community project for the most shameless prostitution in the world. One sees Christianized Adivasi girls stepping out of German cars and station wagons dressed in silks and georgettes, with flashing lipsticks [and] wearing high-heeled shoes. . . . Seeing the number of nude photographs which the photographic shops process every day, it seems that most of these

women are taken to the riverside and stripped and photographed. And the Post Office in Rourkela is kept busy sending these photographs to various parts of Germany. In fact it is said, although we do not have any authentic proof of this well-founded belief, that at least two of the German contractors regularly send out these nude photographs to Germany with a view to persuade German workers to sign up contracts for work in India.

Already quite a number of new fair-skinned Christian births have taken place and by the time the plant is completed—if at all it is completed in time—Rourkela will have a thriving little community of Indo-German bastards. . . .

In ancient times [the Goddess] Sita went through the crucible of fire to establish her chastity. Today Indian women of Rourkela are heating up a crucible for steel with the fuel of their chastity.[48]

Excerpts from articles such as this were subsequently reprinted in certain German newspapers—often without any critical comment—and then found their way back via friends and relations in the Federal Republic to Rourkela, where they aroused feelings of bitterness towards the "ungrateful" Indians and indignation over the attitude of the Germans at home. Few of the fitters were prepared to concede that such press reports were not *entirely* fanciful and that a number of the Rourkela Germans had actually given grounds for such an assessment. Those who were innocent joined in the general sense of grievance without making any attempt to exercise a moderating influence on their guilty companions. It is interesting to note that those fitters who had a reputation for noisy and disagreeable behavior in other spheres (crimes of violence and alcoholism) were also those who were most heavily engaged in the ayah question—and this despite the fact that in all other respects they would have nothing to do with the Indians, whom they regarded as inferior. The Indians called such men "troublemakers," a word which was soon taken over by the German Social Center and made its way into the German language.

The general annoyance caused by the relations between German men and Indian women in Rourkela was not alleviated until the German and Indian departments joined forces in an attempt to rehouse the occupants of the fitters' hostels in bungalows. Whatever happened in these individual houses, many of which were hidden away in gardens skirted by hedges or palm trees, it was far less obvious to the general public and could at most be observed by a small circle of neighbors.

The general situation was, of course, also greatly improved by the growing recognition on the part of the German firms that it was in fact desirable to allow the construction personnel to take their wives and families with them to Rourkela. The German evangelical chaplain in Rourkela commented on this: "As more and more German families came out and the number of German women in Rourkela steadily increased the riotous behavior which had often marked the initial phase of the project was greatly ameliorated." [49] Doctors engaged in tropical medicine are also strongly in favor of wives accompanying their husbands.[50]

Unfortunately, however, there were indications of objectionable behavior on the part of some of the German women in Rourkela. We are told that a number of Indians regarded the German fitters' attitude towards the ayahs and the prostitutes as "representative of normal behavior patterns in Germany," and one of the arguments which they advanced in support of their view was the fact that the German women in Rourkela frequently appeared in public in clothing which was so scanty as to be provocative by Indian standards.[51] A number of German women have been strongly criticized even by the Rourkela Germans themselves, especially in recent years. For example, one of the German men once said: "Although I like to think of myself as being tolerant, I don't feel particularly inclined to form further friendships here, for there really are a lot of negative types in this place. When you see the way in which the German women try to turn the Indians' heads with their showy dress, then you just don't want to have any contact with them." This and many similar observations on the behavior of the German women were made without any prompting. The fact of the matter was that German wives (but only very rarely the secretaries of the various construction departments, who were in any case only a small minority) were often seen on the way to the club in what were—even by German standards—the briefest of pants and in blouses which were quite a revelation. These same women were of course highly indignant when the "shameless Indians turned and stared at them" or cast "lascivious glances in their direction." [52]

Social life

The surprising thing about the Rourkela Germans was that they did not form social groups on the basis of mutual professional interests; their work in the plant and its attendant problems did not form a natural center for the social life of the colony. Instead this was established by the mere techniques of social intercourse: food and drink (but especially drink), giving parties, going to parties, visiting the clubs—all these things acquired great importance and became the focal point and purpose of social living. This seldom produced real friendships but merely a superficial friendliness similar to the "back-slapping joviality" observed by Han Suyin among Europeans in Malaya, "which, with its forced bonhomie, its insistence that all should be 'good guys,' show *esprit de corps* and rival one another in conformity, which alone offered some relief from loneliness, has something macabre about it." [53] It was only inevitable, therefore, that in the social gatherings in Rourkela one tended to see the same faces or at least the same types of people, who all had similar problems and similar subjects of conversation.

This sort of social life was particularly strong among the more senior men—the engineers and superintendents—who were often visited by important people from outside Rourkela and consequently had frequent occasion to give "a party to meet Mr. X." But the need to provide hospitality was intermingled to some extent with an urge for social recognition, which in some cases developed into a positive obsession for representation. This was particularly so when big official dinners were held. Those not on the list of guests either felt put out or—if they discovered their omission in time—tried in every possible way to obtain a last-minute invitation. Often they would buttonhole a colleague who had been invited and ask him to telephone his host and remind him that so and so had been overlooked. As a consequence the question of whom to invite became quite a touchy business, since nobody was anxious to make enemies, and soon the task of compiling a list of guests involved full-scale conferences, which often necessitated the help of outsiders versed in matters of protocol. On occasions Indian departments would also take part in such protocol discussions. The Indians themselves were usually more generous in this respect. For example, on March 28, 1961, when the wide strip mill was commissioned, HSL gave a dinner, which was attended by Prime Minister Nehru and to which no less than 150 German and Indian guests were invited. However, just a few hours before the dinner was to begin, one of Nehru's security officers decided that only sixty guests should be admitted, which meant that HSL had to cancel the invitations of ninety guests in a great hurry. Although they consulted with the proper German departments, mistakes were still made, and a number of senior Germans who should have been included on grounds of rank were in fact excluded. Those "snubbed" in this way talked about their ignominy for weeks on end.

Gradually the Rourkela parties developed into a positive craze, which many of those concerned claimed to find distasteful but which nonetheless became a self-perpetuating institution because nobody had the courage to be the first to break away. The official parties given by the representatives of the various firms got bigger and bigger until in the end the local catering establishments were not always able to cope with the numbers involved. When this situation arose one Rourkela German suggested that the 340 guests at a party which was then being planned should be served with a first-class stew and the money thus saved given to the poor or to the Red Cross for one of their leper stations. His suggestion met with resistance and a caterer in New Delhi—six hours from Rourkela by plane—was asked to supply the food at a cost of 40 rupees a head, "whereupon," as one Rourkela German put it in a private letter, "some were sickened by the price, others by the bad lobsters." The same writer went on to say:

What a ridiculous business it is, trying to mount formal banquets in the heart of the wilderness, surrounded by mountains of difficulties and dangers, when the chimneys have scarcely even begun to smoke. But heaven forbid that anyone should fail to notice that we senior fitters, foremen, administrative officers, and engineers have meanwhile become the "Herr Ingenieur," the "Herr Resident Administrator," and the "Herr Superintendent."

These official parties, most of which were held as a public relations exercise, took place either in a bungalow or in one of the clubs, depending on the numbers involved. Indians were also invited to such occasions, sometimes with their ladies. But when the parties were of a less official nature it frequently happened that no Indians at all were asked. When they celebrated in private, especially in their bungalows, the Rourkela Germans tended to keep to themselves. Although the language barrier was certainly a factor here, Indian sensitivities were nonetheless offended.

The status mania in the social life of the Rourkela Germans has also been observed among other European nationals and Americans living in Africa and Asia. In a sense this is hardly a surprising phenomenon, since overseas employment always offers young people a chance of professional advancement, which means that they frequently find themselves in more responsible and more important positions than those which they would have been occupying at home.

The two clearly defined classes in Rourkela were the upper stratum of the superintendents and the broad lower stratum of the fitters. Between these two classes there was any number of intermediate grades, but these were far less prominent. The only individuals to stand out from their fellows were, on the one hand, those who felt ill at ease in the upper stratum and renounced their prescriptive rights quite voluntarily and with what amounted to a sense of relief, and, on the other hand, those who seized upon the chance of a lifetime to enter the upper stratum and proceeded to exploit it to the best of their ability and by every means at their disposal. During the operation period this mobility was greatly reduced. Owing—perhaps in part, perhaps even entirely—to the incorporation of the Rourkela Germans into the official system of grading employed by HSL, clear-cut distinctions were established between the various grades, which—in complete contrast to the practices of the construction period—everybody was expected to observe. When questioned about private contacts between the Rourkela Germans, one of the general foremen remarked:

That is unquestionably the most difficult problem we have here. The arrogance of the Germans vis-à-vis those of their colleagues who hold a lower rank under the HSL system of grading is simply unbearable. I imagine that the caste mentality, which the English colonialists must have had, was exactly like this. The social gap which separates a man from his superiors is quite insuperable. In this respect the part played by the German women is about as negative as it could possibly be.

The first social gap to emerge was that between the last remaining members of the construction personnel and the newly arriving operation personnel. All of a sudden there were "old hands" and "new hands." One member of the operation staff once said: "Unfortunately there are two parties here now. That is most regrettable. I myself get on well with the old hands. I have a number of friends and I do what I can to help bridge the gap between the old and the new." When one of the old hands was discussing the same problem he said: "By and large I like to keep to myself. I'm just a fitter, not a stuck-up, holier-than-thou *petit bourgeois* like the rest of the Germans here." This opinion was voiced at a time when the total complement of Germans in Rourkela was only about 600. It appears that as the size of the colony decreased, the antitheses became more pronounced, and social differences were taken more seriously.

Both during the construction period and later, the principal status symbol was the situation and size of the family bungalow; there was a time when to live in Sector 3 was "the thing to do"—and if at all possible in a large bungalow with three bedrooms. It was also considered essential to have a car of one's own, and some even regarded the size of their car as a matter of importance. Many found the title of "Superintendent," which is simply the English equivalent of the German *Bauleiter*, highly desirable and used it on every conceivable occasion on their letter headings, invitation cards, and anywhere it could be displayed.

There was, in fact, a widespread desire to appear as a man of the world, a person of generous habits, although from time to time the signs of a narrower background were not to be denied. A German mother gave the following grounds for refusing to receive the lady teacher from the German school in order to discuss her children's education: "What would the neighbors think, especially since they know I've already spoken to her twice in the school." At Christmas, 1958, the shop in the German Club was accepting orders for poultry. Owing to an error of translation *Fasan* (German for "pheasant") was understood as "capon" and as a result more than fifteen German housewives who had ordered pheasants received capons. Not one of them objected, although normally they would have complained about the slightest trifle. A fitter who was joined by his wife some months after his arrival in Rourkela showed her the German Club and ordered a liqueur for her in the club bar. When the liqueur was served in a heavy water tumbler (for very good reasons the German Club had no delicate glasses) the fitter declared that his wife could not drink from such a glass, for she "wasn't used to that sort of thing." One of the club officials was obliged to remind him that in the course of the past few months he himself had used and wantonly destroyed many such tumblers.

We have already seen from our description of the party craze that the general level of social intercourse was not particularly high, least of all where social gatherings were concerned. Intellectual and cultural interests were present only to a limited extent among most of the Rourkela Germans, especially within the sphere of daily social life. This was probably due partly to the composition of the German colony and partly to the exacting professional demands made on the men in an unaccustomed climate, although it may also have had to do with the fact that while the German overseas grows more practical, his intellectual capacities decline.[54]

Consequently, there was a hint of shallowness in social conversation, unless the subject under discussion concerned the daily work or particular aspects of the plant. Topic number one for a large part of the Rourkela Germans was gossip. The industrious pursuit of tittle-tattle, which usually revolved around their nearest acquaintances, neighbors, colleagues, or rivals, filled the empty evenings and weekends that so many of them found unbearable. Gossiping also made it possible for the German community—especially the underworked housewives—not to think about their isolation from the outside world. The women, of course, needed no fixed social venue to indulge their proclivity, for they could have a chat over the garden fence or in one another's bungalows. The fact that their bungalows had no Yale-type locks, as is customary in Germany, but were usually left wide open, tended to encourage this unconventional practice of just dropping in for a chat. And then there were the daily sessions of idle talk at the swimming pool of the German Club—not to mention the "bearer post," which greatly sustained the need for gossip by furnishing the interested parties with what were often very precise accounts of what went on within the walls of their neighbors' bungalows. The findings of a German inquiry have revealed that, apart from the rearing of children, the favorite topics of conversation among Germans in Germany are the events occurring within the circle of their mutual acquaintances or within their work sphere.[55] But in Rourkela gossip acquired an additional significance as an instrument of information. The Cologne sociologist, König, has reported on an American survey

which describes the proposed replacement in a small American community of a manual telephone exchange by an automatic exchange. The young lady who had operated the manual switchboard was of course listening in to all the calls, which meant that she was the most important source of information in the whole village. In a manner of speaking, she provided the local news bulletins. The automization of the exchange would have put an end to all this. The result was that the whole village combined to oppose the introduction of the automatic system.[56]

The Rourkela gossip probably served a similar purpose.

If gossip is regarded as the most primitive form of communication, then it could be said that with the installation of a bulletin board in the German Club to display notices of all kinds—information about coming events, articles for sale, and so forth—a higher level of communication was established. It should be added, however, that this new form of communication succeeded in meeting the needs of the colony only to a strictly limited extent. The Germans' need for information was not always sufficiently strong for them to make what was in many cases an awkward journey to the German Club. It was only when there was a political crisis, such as the erection of the Berlin Wall in August, 1961, that large numbers of Rourkela Germans gathered in the club to hear taped programs recorded over the German short wave. But even at such times interest would wane after a few days, so it was scarcely worth while to continue the transmissions.

At one point an attempt was made to impose the outside news on the community by running a news tape at the beginning of the evening program in the open-air cinema. This attempt failed: the cinemagoers demonstrated their lack of interest by arriving ten minutes later and in some cases by requesting that the bulletins be discontinued. From this we may assume that they were primarily interested in information about the more restricted world of their own work and social community.

Considered in this light it seems all the more surprising that the attempt to establish a local newspaper, which was pursued over a long period by one of the two German ministers in Rourkela, elicited no great response from the community and consequently did not prove a lasting success. The fact that the paper appeared only at long and irregular intervals presumably meant that it failed to meet local needs.

Structuring of leisure

A number of experts have recommended that all those going to the tropics should pay particular attention to the problem of leisure. Among other things, they are advised not to become too engrossed in the trivial events of daily life but to structure their leisure in interesting and absorbing ways, such as reading, writing, playing chess, collecting stamps, studying the indigenous culture, or acquiring foreign languages. They are warned against the great danger of giving in to the feeling of isolation from their own native culture and are urged to counter this threat by keeping up a close correspondence with friends and relatives at home and by forming groups for purposes of amateur theatricals, choral singing, and any other suitable hobbies.

Observations made over a period of years in Rourkela confirm both the importance and the relevance of such advice. Of course it is easy to give—and probably easy to follow—such advice if you are a cultured person with intellectual interests and are carrying out your duties somewhere in the tropical wilderness of a developing country, where you are thrown back entirely on your own resources. But the situation in which the great mass of Rourkela Germans found themselves was very much more difficult. Even in Germany the concepts of leisure and the structuring of leisure are of fairly recent vintage and still very much in the process of crystallization; but in large areas of India they are so unfamiliar that time and again the Indians felt distinctly irritated by the fact that the Germans appeared to pursue their leisure quite as seriously and as thoroughly as they pursued their work. Those Rourkela Germans who had to negotiate with Indians in the course of their daily work were seldom able to make them understand that although they were perfectly prepared to work for 9 or even 14 hours a day, they did not want to go on discussing business matters in their leisure hours as well. The patience and self-control required of the Germans in this respect was all the greater since they well knew that many of the Indians—still following the timetable introduced by the English—did not normally start work until 9 or 10 A.M.

It is important to know what is meant by the concept of leisure within a given context. On the one hand it may be regarded in its literal sense as the amount of time during which a man does not work, that is to say, the time when he is free from external commitments and can relax; on the other hand it may also be regarded as a social problem of the modern consumer-oriented society.

For purposes of this study the latter conception of leisure is of particular interest. Owing to the impersonal nature of the tasks the modern worker is required to perform and in the absence of the ethical bonds that existed in earlier decades, the worker no longer finds the same measure of fulfillment in his work as was once the case (this of course being equally true of the German technicians in Rourkela, although comparatively less so in the case of the construction personnel). And so, having failed to gratify his desire for experience and satisfaction in his work, the modern working man turns to leisure in the hope that he will find gratification there. The supply of "leisure articles" is then presented to him in a manner that has been aptly characterized by Aldous Huxley in his visionary novel *Brave New World:* "Never put off till tomorrow the fun you can have today." The desire for fulfillment in leisure and the inability to control this desire are two of the characteristics of modern man. As a consequence leisure becomes even more exacting than work. The concept of output is then transferred from the industrial sphere to the sphere of leisure, where it is measured in consumption.

The Frankfort sociologist Alexander Mitscherlich has commented on this phenomenon:

The exhausting but anonymous and often monotonous work leaves the worker with no problems worth thinking about, but it does leave him with a sense of agitation, which rouses a desire in him for contrasting experiences, for a new kind of agitation, which will ease the other. . . . [His capacity] for creating an . . . animated atmosphere is stunted. Even within the sphere of his personal life he adopts an attitude of passive negation, waiting to be provided with suitable fantasy material for diversion and licence.[57]

In his analysis of the young modern worker another contemporary author even goes so far as to speak of "substitute individuality" when discussing the part played by the cinema cult in meeting the cultural requirements of leisure.

Seen in this light the requirements and recommendations of the above-mentioned experts on the tropics, which are undoubtedly correct and relevant in themselves, are not so readily applicable to the problem of structuring leisure in Rourkela. The mass entertainment, the diversions, and above all the canned culture supplied in such abundance in the Western world today are not available in the relative remoteness of a town such as Rourkela. But, since

Western-style leisure has been structured in this way, merely to suggest that a man might replace the mass media by writing letters or playing chess or pursuing some hobby is not going to solve the problem. As far as the use and structuring of their leisure was concerned the majority of the Rourkela Germans felt that they had been transported back to the conditions described at the beginning of this century by Adolf Weber, who said that during their leisure hours, and especially on Sundays, all that the working men in the large towns could do was to "kill time" by visiting "beer palaces" and "whisky bars." "Socialibility" consisted of satisfying the stomach and imbibing great quantities of alcohol.[58]

Those Rourkela Germans who were unable to overcome their passivity when faced with the problem of filling their leisure hours and still opted for the ready-made structure available to them in their environment were obliged to content themselves with whatever satisfaction the social life, their bungalow and garden, or the German Club were able to offer. There were few other opportunities for a "change of scene." But there were some who, either because the problems posed by their work kept them fully occupied or because they approached the question of structuring their leisure in a positive and systematic way, regarded leisure more in terms of relaxation. For them—but unfortunately only for them—there was, therefore, the additional prospect of pursuing their interest in their new and strange environment. Traveling in the territory is difficult, for Rourkela is badly placed for fast communications: to reach Calcutta by train takes 14 hours, by air 2 hours (but there are only three flights a week); Bhubaneswar, the capital of Orissa, can be reached by train, but the journey involves lengthy detours, or by overland bus, which means a 15-hour trip over bad roads. Both towns are too far away for a long weekend. Another possibility is making short trips into the surrounding countryside, but these are only feasible for the small number of Rourkela Germans with personal transport, and the climate is not exactly ideal for rambling. Hunters, on the other hand, have the opportunity of some good sport, but most of the hunters found no difficulty in occupying their leisure hours.

And so the majority were obliged to devise entertainment for themselves within the existing framework of bungalow and club. A number of people did, in fact, organize small discussion groups, record listening sessions, a bible circle, and so on, although it soon became clear that it was advisable for any such undertaking to be planned with a specific aim in view, perhaps a social evening or a play production, for the common aim helped to keep the members interested. But here again it was the "unproblematical" Germans who joined such groups. The others, the great majority, wanted somebody else to arrange things for them; and in this connection it is perhaps permissible to observe that one of the purposes of the officially organized entertainment in totalitarian states (*"Kraft durch Freude"*—"strength through joy") is to fill the leisure hours of the masses to such an extent that nobody gets out of hand.

The German Social Center

Before actually starting on the construction work the German firms concerned had realized that they would need a special welfare center for their personnel. They therefore formed an association, which then proceeded to set up the welfare organization that was to be known as the German Social Center of Rourkela (GSC). The man sent out as head of the center was also the manager of the association (in Germany). He was given a small staff of German employees and instructed to build and administer a hospital and a clubhouse, together with various annexes, to provide medical, cultural, and social welfare. These buildings were constructed between August, 1957, and the autumn of 1958. But during this initial period the GSC was already doing what it could to dispense provisional welfare in the fitters' hostels and this body gradually became the physical, intellectual, and political center of the whole German community, while at the same time serving an important function as a "contact point" for Indo-German relations. Apart from occasional consultations in Germany, which took the form of routine discussions (partly of technical questions but more particularly of problems connected with their terms of contract), the German firms—nearly forty of them—had no form of corporate contact regarding Rourkela save through this communal instrument—the GSC. There was no consortium or anything of that sort. Since HSL had concluded a separate contract with each of the German firms, each firm was a direct contractor of the Indian company.

Although the Rourkela offices of the various German firms collaborated in a very friendly way, helping one another out with tools, materials, equipment, and sometimes even with personnel, the terms of their individual agreements with HSL often differed widely, causing particular difficulties for both site managements and personnel. For example, a number of the German firms had failed to consult one another before fixing the amount to be paid out in expenses to their construction personnel. As a result, fitters belonging to different firms but doing pretty much the same sort of work were receiving different daily rates. The men were certain to point out such matters to one another and this sometimes led to strife. There were similar variations in the rates charged for bungalows and for the rental of furniture, air conditioners, and refrigerators. The attitude of different firms to the question of whether wives and families should accompany their husbands also varied, as did the extent to which they were prepared to help financially. There were even differences in the class of air travel booked for the fitters themselves, although the great mass of complaints—not the least of which concerned the condition of the many fitters who had applied themselves all too liberally to the free drinks dispensed in the first-class lounge—eventually persuaded the German firms to agree on tourist class travel for all.

When the German firms were recruiting operation personnel for Rourkela they found that the only way of ensuring an adequate work force was by offering far higher wages than they had previously been paying to the construction workers, and this immediately gave rise to difficulties. We have already seen that, apart from their basic wage plus overseas allowance (usually an additional 20 per cent), the German fitters received expenses of about 38 to 40 rupees a day. The expenses for engineers, superintendents, and other senior men were correspondingly higher, ranging from 60 to 80 rupees a day. From the outset the operation personnel received at least 10 rupees a day more, as well as a considerable increase in their basic wage. By 1965, however, work was well under way on an extension of the plant to raise output from 1,000,000 to 1,800,000 tons a year; large numbers of construction personnel have again been sent out to Rourkela and men of equal rank are again working side by side for different rates of remuneration. It is likely that this will continue to cause difficulties. During the initial phase of the construction period such matters as the lending of vehicles for public use, which were trivial enough in themselves and could have been dealt with beforehand, were quite enough to cause friction among men living and working at such close quarters. All such matters, which presumably appeared rather unimportant to the responsible people back home in Germany, became the subject of endless debates and complaints and led to bitterness, especially in the hot season, when tempers were raw anyway. In such situations the GSC, as the only corporate instrument of the German firms concerned, gradually came to assume a new function that had little to do with its original duties of affording medical, cultural, and social welfare.

When the site offices had difficulty in obtaining housing for their men the GSC had to set up a central accommodations agency and so became a mediator between HSL, which distributed the housing, and the various German site offices, which were in need of it. The minor practical problems that had accumulated over the course of time between the site offices and HSL needed to be put in order. Whether the German offices were acting jointly to discuss the acceptance of HSL railway demurrages or the introduction of new charges for power and water supplies or any other measures put forward by HSL, it was the GSC which provided a neutral zone where meetings could be convened in the interests of all parties and any problems discussed. The head of the GSC led the discussions but remained impartial.

The individual requests and complaints made by the Rourkela Germans involving HSL or other Indian authorities (about poor water supplies, irregular deliveries of letters, clogged drains, leaking roofs and porous walls in the monsoon period, and so forth) called for consultation and representation at a general level, which was provided by the GSC. This also involved giving advice on the legal rights and the personal behavior of the German personnel within their work sphere in Rourkela, helping them in their correspondence with German service departments, law courts, etc., helping with travel arrangements when workers were going on leave or returning from leave, contacting the Consul General in Calcutta to obtain extensions of passports and documentation, and providing other similar services.

Acting in concert with the German managements the GSC persuaded the personnel of the various construction firms to elect representatives, who then met the executives at more or less regular intervals to submit any requests or complaints on behalf of their members and who were therefore able to influence the structuring of the social life of the colony.

Since any large German colony overseas (in Rourkela there were sometimes as many as 1,800 Germans) is bound to produce community problems both within the national group itself and in its contacts with the indigenous population, it needs a neutral body to act as arbitrator in community questions. And so the GSC also assumed this function and on a number of occasions (in collaboration with the superintendents concerned) even enforced the immediate repatriation of German personnel who had become involved in disagreeable incidents or whose general conduct had been conspicuously bad. And, in 1958 and 1959, when the Rourkela Germans found themselves subjected to massive attacks in the Indian press, the GSC was faced with a new task, one which it was obliged to undertake without delay: public relations.

Club life in Rourkela

Next to the hospital the clubhouse was the most important concern of the GSC. It was opened in the autumn of 1958 and provided the following amenities: a restaurant (for 500 people), a hall (for 230), a roof garden (extending over the whole building and accommodating several hundred), a bar (for 40), a terrace (for 48), kitchen and storerooms, a library (containing about 1,000 books), a children's playground (see-saw, swing, merry-go-round), a swimming pool, a bowling alley, a soda fountain, a delicatessen, an open-air theatre (seating 500) for film and other performances. A soccer field and a miniature golf course were added at a later date; two tennis courts were also laid out on club ground but on private initiative. A bus service was set up by the GSC linking the sectors inhabited by Germans with both the club and the hospital.

The club itself was founded as a society under Indian law. With very few exceptions all of the Rourkela Germans became members. Although the construction and fitting out of the buildings was financed by the German firms through the medium of the GSC, once the club and its various annexes were opened they had to operate on membership fees and the profits from the sale of food and drink. At first the monthly subscription was 5 rupees for men, 2.50 rupees for women, and 1.25 rupees for children; these were subsequently increased to 12, 6, and 3 rupees and were raised even higher when the membership began to drop. The turnover was often considerable. But there is a danger here, which should not be overlooked; the smaller the number of Germans in Rourkela, the smaller the amount received by the club in the form of subscriptions, for there is a natural limit to the extent to which these may be increased. Consequently, when the membership drops, the only way in which the club management can offset its loss is by trying to make its services as attractive as possible, thus increasing turnover and producing higher profits. But the result is that the Rourkela Germans have to consume more alcohol—which we know is the one thing to be avoided.

In 1958 the club received an on-license to dispense Indian beer, imported whisky, campari, vermouth, and various other drinks for consumption on the premises and an off-license for the sale of spirits by the bottle to its own members. At this point it should be firmly stated that this license to dispense alcohol was not granted as a special favor to the Germans in Rourkela, as has been constantly asserted by a number of anti-German propagandists. Orissa is composed of thirteen districts, five of which (Ganjam, Koraput, Cuttack, Balasore, and Puri) are virtually "dry," that is, they either prohibit the consumption of alcohol absolutely or grant licenses only in very rare cases. The remaining eight, however, issue licenses in the normal way; one of these "wet" districts is Sundargarh, in which Rourkela lies. Apart from the German Club there were six other (Indian) houses, either clubs or shops, with similar licenses for alcohol. This situation has remained unchanged.

In addition to the restaurant and bar, the library and the sporting amenities, the club also offered its members an entertainment and cultural program of sorts. A dance band (consisting first of German fitters and subsequently of Indian musicians) played in the hall in the evenings. The open-air cinema showed three German films a week, which were specially flown in, and three English or American films, which were obtainable from the Indian circuit. The library was gradually built up until it was able to offer more than just light reading matter. Its membership was never very high, but this is hardly surprising if we consider that in a representative survey carried out in the Federal Republic 43 per cent of those interviewed admitted that they seldom if ever read books.[59] But the swimming pool was undoubtedly the major attraction in the German Club, although the soccer field was also a very important feature. From time to time the management of the club would arrange large-scale celebrations, the most noteworthy of these being the Munich-style *Oktoberfest*,* which lasted for several days and which, because it was always attended by several hundred Indian guests, acquired a certain reputation even as far afield as New Delhi as an example of good Indo-German relations.

The purpose of the German Club, as originally conceived and consistently pursued by the club management, was to provide a sort of community center where people could meet in a hospitable and cultivated atmosphere and pursue their hobbies or seek relaxation in books, games, sports, discussions, study, or any other form of recreational activity. What the organizers had in mind was to try to compensate for living conditions that were not always par-

---

* Famous Bavarian beer festival celebrated in Munich in October attracting thousands of beer-loving visitors from all over Germany, from other parts of Europe, and even from overseas.—TRANSLATOR.

ticularly congenial and also to bring about the social integration of the Rourkela Germans, who were a pretty mixed bunch, and so cultivate a genuine community sense based on friendly neighborliness. But the Germans themselves soon showed that such ideas were unlikely to work out in practice. Some of them looked upon the club more or less as a public house. They always turned up at their regular time to eat, but more especially to drink, and to seek the pleasure of their own company around their beer table in the club bar. These "pubgoers" made their own rules; they decided who was to sit at their table and who was not, and they laid down the law as to what constituted acceptable behavior. If they considered it right and proper to start singing at nine o'clock at night "so as to bring the roof down," then fifty or more other club members, who would have preferred to read, listen to music, or engage in quiet conversation, either had to submit to the sing-song or quietly leave the premises. The club management was soon obliged to organize a system of wardens in an attempt to enforce at least partial observance of the official rules. But even this proved ineffectual on a number of occasions. Every week several hundred glasses had to be replaced. The repairs to furniture and fittings necessitated by the wanton acts of destruction that accompanied these evening festivities proved more than one carpenter could cope with, and finally the club was obliged to buy steel chairs with metal seats. Peusch, who was the evangelical minister in Rourkela over a number of years, spoke in both this and other connections, of the "pioneer days" in Rourkela, which were "reminiscent of the wild west." [60]

The result of this kind of behavior was that a large number of Rourkela Germans, especially the families and the engineers and superintendents, simply came to the club to do their shopping, to borrow books, to go swimming, or to see a film. It was only on special occasions that all, or at least the great majority, of the Rourkela Germans appeared there together. But on such occasions, when the quieter members turned up in force, it was noticeable that the general level of behavior was much improved. There was, however, a further factor at work here, which should not be overlooked; since these large assemblies were always convened for some specific purpose they enabled the "rowdies" to partake in a socially meaningful gathering, which was in marked contrast to their everyday camaraderie.

Apart from the German Club there were also a number of Indian clubs in Rourkela, but these were intended primarily for the use of the Indian employees of HSL. The only one of these clubs where Germans were ever entertained was the Rourkela Club, patronized by the senior HSL members who occasionally invited the German superintendents to their functions. Tennis tournaments between Indian and German teams were also held there from time to time, just as in the German Club. Another club that played a certain part in the life of the German community was the Brahmani Club. Although this was built on the Indians' initiative, much of the thinking that went into it and much of the finance was supplied by the Germans. At one time it had more than sixty German members. But the club buildings were situated a few kilometers outside Rourkela in very attractive surroundings on the bank of the river Brahmani, which meant, of course, that it could only be used by those who had private transport. For this reason and also because the club was run by an all-Indian management, the Brahmani Club was not really suitable for the great majority of Rourkela Germans. This is quite evident from the following incident, which was by no means the only one of its kind. In September, 1958, a large group of Rourkela Germans hired the Brahmani Club for an evening celebration. The evening passed without incident and the actual party came to an end before midnight, whereupon the organizers and most of their guests drove back to Rourkela. But six of them, for whom there had been no room in the available transport, were left behind with instructions to wait for the return of one of the vehicles.

These men then demanded beer or alcohol of some sort from Mr. Gosh, the Indian club manager, although drinking hours (which are subject to very strict police supervision in India) were officially over. At first Mr. Gosh refused them, but as their mood grew more ugly he gave in and handed each of them a bottle of beer. But this was not good enough for the German fitters, who forced their way into the storeroom at the rear of the bar and removed a full sack of beer (in India beer is often sold by the sack—1 sack = 48 bottles = 200 rupees = 33 dollars), which they carried to the entrance hall and subsequently took with them when their vehicle returned to pick them up. In the course of this larceny the manager, in trying to stop the men, was struck on the head with the result that his face was visibly swollen for days. One of the fitters also trod on the club's record player and shattered the pickup arm. According to the club employees, when the fitters finally drove off, they took with them various small objects such as coasters, a small box of teaspoons, ashtrays, and other things. The next morning the manager made an official complaint to the police. It was then left to the construction management concerned and the GSC, who had been notified by the police, to make good the damage and to trace and punish the offenders.

Later, when the German Club was placed under quarantine following an acute case of smallpox among the Indian staff and had to close for a lengthy period, the management of the German Club rented the Brahmani Club and arranged for a regular evening bus service so that the Rourkela Germans might continue to enjoy their club life. This venture went smoothly from the very start, albeit under the extremely watchful eye of the German Club management.

The remarkable thing about this "supervision" is that it only works when the supervisor is able to take part in the general activity—as, for example, when a group of drinkers are in the process of working up an atmosphere—because then he is able to follow and to some extent direct events *from within.* But if the same man were to try to interfere in a quarrel or a brawl as an outsider (because he had been called in), the likelihood of his succeeding would be extremely remote. It is highly feasible for a man who knows what he is about to intercept a boozing song that is just starting up and to silence it completely with a few quietly spoken words before it has time to develop into the usual deafening roar; but the same man will be quite powerless to quell a massed chorus of *"Es zittern*

die morschen Knochen" ("Now the rotting bones are trembling") *
rendered by countless numbers of enthusiastic revelers already at
full bellow, unless the situation is such that he is able to impose
exceptional sanctions. But there were occasions, usually late at
night, when even the grim threat of enforced repatriation failed to
impose silence.

In general we may say that the principal reason for the kind of
disagreeable incidents outlined above was the lack of trained and
capable full-time personnel. Had such men been available in adequate numbers—social workers for example—they could have
exercised effective control and also fulfilled the preventive role envisaged by David Riesman,[61] acting as "avocational counsellors"
and directing the club hooligans in Rourkela to more profitable leisure activities than boozing, bawling, and violence.

School children and the German school

The first German children of school age arrived in 1958 and were
sent to the English-speaking school at the Hamirpur Mission Station, which is only about 2 kilometers from Rourkela. The schoolmistresses there are Indian Carmelite nuns, who are highly praised
—even by the upper-class Hindu population of Rourkela—as good
teachers.

As the number of German children steadily increased, however,
the parents felt that they would like a school of their own, where
the lessons would be given in German. And so in 1959 the GSC
and the German parents, aided by the various construction departments, set about the task of building a German primary school on
the grounds of the German Club. Eventually it also proved possible to enlist the aid of the German Foreign Office, which sent out a
German primary-school mistress to Rourkela. When the number of
children grew still larger the school was extended; initially a number of the German wives then offered their services as supplemen-

---

* Another well-loved song was *Oh, Du Schöner Westerwald* ("Oh, you
lovely Westerwald"). The marked preference shown for these songs is unlikely
to have had any political significance; it was simply that they lent themselves
particularly well to raucous renderings.

tary teachers, but eventually a second full-time schoolmistress arrived from Germany, to be followed in 1963 by a third. In the meantime the school buildings were further enlarged.

Apart from variations in the academic level of the children in the different classes, which were due partly to their heterogeneous composition and partly to the fluctuation natural in a school of this order, the greatest difficulty encountered by the teachers was the children's unruly behavior, indeed their complete lack of discipline, which was almost unheard of in German schools at home. This may have had to do with the fact that in Rourkela the children were subjected to an "everlasting summer" and were never driven indoors by winter weather, as is the normal German school child, who is accustomed to working with great concentration and discipline throughout the whole of the winter season in order to make good any gaps in his knowledge.

On the other hand, however, this wild behavior is also an expression of the corporate attitude of the Rourkela Germans, which we have already mentioned and will be mentioning again in the course of this study. This was particularly noticeable in the children's relations with the Indians. The Indian Carmelite nuns who first had charge of their education had difficulty in enforcing discipline: the German children would not accept punishments from them; they were impudent and often refused to do their exercises. Subsequently, when they were attending the German school within the grounds of the German Club, where they had their swimming lessons, used the toilets, and occasionally bought things in the shop during their breaks, many of them treated the Indian supervisory staff, who were also responsible for the school grounds, with disrespect and contempt; if an Indian called them to order for some irregularity, they tried to boss him about and swore at him. This sort of behavior tallies exactly with the reports of the behavior patterns of the children of English colonial officials, who were exposed to similar situations:

My impression of the children . . '. was that they took their alleged racial superiority for granted. How could their attitude be otherwise since this was the only one the majority of them knew? Children saw adult Africans only as servants, the "boys" who were to wait on them. One white youngster who came to school without his homework gave as his excuse that the "boy" had forgotten to put it in his school bag.[62]

This calls to mind the little boy at the St. Nicholas celebration in Rourkela. Where can these children have acquired their attitude to the Indians, if not from their parents or, more broadly speaking, from their home environment? Vierkandt, a German educationalist, has commented on this phenomenon:

In certain circumstances likes and dislikes, respect and contempt . . . can be transferred from their originator to his environment. Children are particularly prone to such influences, which, like the overwhelming majority of formative influences, are passed on at an unconscious level. Although reasoned statements as to the merits and demerits of a particular person have little effect on children, the effect of the feelings that impinge on the attitude adopted toward that person and which are made manifest by the way in which such statements are made is all the greater. Consequently children are subject to the tensions within their families long before they are able to understand the reasons underlying the conflicts.[63]

The German teachers in Rourkela frequently complained that they received little or no support from the parents in their attempts to train and educate their children. The validity of their complaints was borne out by observations made at the parents' meetings, which were held at regular intervals and at which the parents—acting in what they considered to be the best interests of their children—expressed views (on education) which were more than liberal. The teachers lost a great deal of time as a result of their numerous differences with the parents, which gave rise to considerable friction and quite unnecessarily distracted them from their proper work. On a number of occasions the teachers were obliged to appeal to the GSC (in its capacity as the governing body of the German school) for support in their altercations with certain of the German parents.

Because of these difficulties the German school in Rourkela was unable to exercise the kind of cultural influence normally brought to bear both on the members of the German community and the members of the indigenous population by the really good German schools overseas. The best of these offer a meeting place for the children of different nationalities, who are sent there by their parents precisely because these schools, with multiracial foundations, have a unique opportunity of cultivating interpersonal relations and social intercourse among young people of widely differing backgrounds.

The churches

During the early years of the colony the Rourkela Germans of both Protestant and Roman Catholic faith had to make do with a simple room in the fitters' hostels, which was fitted out as a temporary church and which served for divine service as well as all other church activities. But in 1961, thanks to the initiative displayed by both the Catholic and the Protestant ministers, a small church was built on the grounds of the German Club. The two ministers had agreed that one church would be sufficient for the needs of both congregations; an altar was built at both ends, and by the simple expedient of reversing the seats, the church could be converted from a Protestant to a Catholic place of worship and vice versa.

Both clergymen organized church societies, which met either in their own bungalows or in those of the various members; apart from religious exercises and bible readings, general discussions and leisure activities were also pursued at these meetings. Attendance tended to fluctuate. Sometimes these religious groups extended their activities beyond the immediate locality of Rourkela by making excursions under the leadership of their minister to various parts of the surrounding countryside, usually to Christian villages. The behavior of the Germans who took part in these excursions was not always satisfactory. Both of the ministers were engaged on the construction of a new church for the Indian Christians of their denomination outside Rourkela, and to this end they called on the services of various members of their own German communities. One of these churches took rather a long time to build and so for months on end a relatively large group of Rourkela Germans were kept happily engaged in the jungle scrub of Orissa during their weekends.

Unfortunately, however, such activities were not without their problematical side. This undertaking had the undeniable merit of having kept a large number of Germans occupied in a good cause and consequently out of mischief, but the Indians are extremely dubious about all missionary work, because for many of them the missions are still a symbol of colonialism and neocolonialism. Quite apart from the foreign missions, the tensions between the different indigenous religions and sects in India already pose a nationwide problem that at times threatens the integration of the state. Consequently, in districts where religious differences abound, the Indian authorities oppose all attempts to stress these differences with the object of preserving a sort of balance of power. Accordingly HSL asked the German firms to refrain from all missionary activity; it also forbade the building of new temples or mosques in Rourkela in order to prevent the various and in some cases strongly contrasting religious groups from creating further outward symbols of their disparity before a more or less homogeneous Rourkela population had had time to develop. Although the activities of the German religious communities took place outside Rourkela they nonetheless ran counter to the general thinking underlying these provisions.

But there was a further reason why the members of HSL adopted a suspicious and in many cases even a negative attitude towards these new buildings. It was rumored that a part of the construction material had found its way to the churches from the Rourkela construction site, where it had mysteriously disappeared. In this way the good intentions of the religious communities subsequently came to appear in a somewhat dubious light. This incident shows very clearly just how carefully religious matters have to be handled in a developing country. The principal lesson to be learned from Rourkela in this respect is that church activities should, wherever possible, be restricted to the spiritual welfare of the development workers.

Special Problems of Adaptation

If we are to believe the great majority of earlier authors,[64] the German, when he goes to a foreign land, displays an exemplary capacity and zeal for adaptation. Even Goethe said in his conversations with Eckermann that it was in the German's nature to appreciate everything alien in his own way and to accommodate himself to foreign characteristics. The German businessman was usually singled out for special commendation in this respect and was said greatly to excel his English counterpart in his ability to attune himself to the mentality of foreign peoples both in business procedures and the forms of social intercourse. Leopold von Wiese, the famous German sociologist, was able to report as proof of the German's adaptability the fact that prior to 1914 German businessmen in Bombay had adopted the local custom of visiting the merchants in their houses on the Hindu New Year's Eve and wishing them well for the coming year. The German's willingness to acquire the local language is also cited as evidence of his ability to adapt. Werner Sombart, the well-known political economist, even explained Germany's superiority in the world market as the result of the German entrepreneur's conformist tendencies. The philosopher Max Scheler also spoke of the German's "tireless adaptation to the customer's requirements", although he called this type of adaptation "famous *cum* infamous" and regarded it as a sign of a "servile character," which has earned the German great hatred in the world (from his rivals).

But modern sociological writers—especially those in England and America—who deal with recent events in the developing countries have come to realize more and more that the question of adaptation on the part of development workers from the industrial countries of the Western world to the conditions of underdeveloped territories is extraordinarily difficult and poses an enormous problem. This problem often remains unsolved because it simply is not possible to expect these workers to subject themselves, out of pure idealism, to what are very often extremely harsh conditions.[65] But for the fact that this kind of problem has become the focal point of international and especially American investigations, we would be obliged to form a very bad opinion of the Rourkela Germans, many of whom adopted an extremely negative attitude to the local environment. In point of fact, however, in the course of just a few decades conditions have changed to such an extent that in all those areas of the world that we now call developing countries the degree of adaptability demanded of people arriving from the industrialized countries is considerably greater than ever it was in the past—and this despite the fact that, as we have already shown, acclimatization has now been made very much easier in a majority of cases.

But let us return for a moment to the earlier sociological writers and their contention that the Germans had a particular gift for adaptation. It should be pointed out that the Germans they had in mind were either entrepreneurs in their own right or men connected with business undertakings, for whom personal success in dealing with foreign customers meant advancement and, above all, profits. This hardly applies to the German fitter in Rourkela, who also has infinitely less personal responsibility and consequently little incentive to strive to adapt at all costs.

In addition to these general observations and those discussed earlier, we now propose to deal in greater detail with a number of factors that proved particularly significant in Rourkela in determining whether people adopted a negative or a positive attitude to the question of adaptation.

Homesickness

On the center strip of the 3-kilometer highway linking the plant with the new town of Rourkela there was a steel signpost pointing northwest and bearing the surprising inscription, "Wilhelmshaven 10,000 km." All the Rourkela Germans passed this way several times in the course of each day when going to and from work. What must their feelings have been on seeing this signpost, erected by a native of Wilhelmshaven? Certainly such a sign cannot be dismissed as a mere joke but must, on the contrary, be regarded as a symbol of homesickness. In Rourkela the keen observer was able to note many such phenomena. A number of Rourkela Germans decorated the entrances to their bungalows by painting the coat of arms of their home town on the whitewashed wall; one painted an enormous glass of foaming beer on the white stucco of his porch, which was almost plastic in its effect, and wrote underneath it, "Krombacher Pils." Yet another named his bungalow "Haus Essen." Although these "artistic" activities were doubtless inspired by a variety of factors, one of their motivations was certainly homesickness. Nor should it surprise us to find that Germans so far from home suffer from homesickness. There are many authors who contend that Germans are particularly prone to such feelings and they point out in support of their argument that the word *Heimat* * cannot really be translated into foreign languages.⁶⁶ This is not the place to inquire into the validity of such contentions; we merely wish to observe that there were some "pretty tough" fitters in Rourkela to whom homesickness did not appear to be entirely alien. Rodenwaldt has said that "home leave means as much to a European living in the tropics as demobilization means to a soldier"; ⁶⁷ certainly this was true of the Germans living in Rourkela. The last verse of one of the numerous "Rourkela songs" provides an apt illustration of this point.

> The stink of cooking fills the bungalow,
> The ayah's fixing *khana* laced with mango,
> The *mali's* catching snakes out in the garden
> While I sit here and write a letter home.
> Oh, Erika, I can't believe it's true,
> In six short months I'll be back home with you;
> We'll sit together underneath the moon
> Upon the bench in our dear little park.
> Rourkela, Rourkela, Rourkela,
> On the distant plains of India,
> You will never want for construction crew,
> For my heart delights at the thought of you.
> Dear little girl in Germany,
> In our little town in Germany,
> Just wait a little longer,
> For soon we shall be home.†

And yet often enough the same people were perfectly happy to return to Rourkela. With them the feeling of homesickness was not

* Home, home district, homeland, according to context.—TRANSLATOR.
† See Appendix for complete text.

enduring, as was the case with large numbers of the Italian immigrant workers in Germany, who were literally driven home by their longing for Italy after only a few weeks or months on their work sites abroad. The Germans' homesickness was not of this order; instead of actually driving them home, it exhausted itself in dreams and fantasies about home; [68] and indeed the Rourkela Germans would often give expression to their wish-dreams in quite specific terms, such as longing for *Deutscher Löwensenf* ("German mustard") *deutsches Bier* ("German Beer"), or *Wiener Würstchen* ("frankfurters"). Distance, as always, made the German heart grow fonder for such things.

It is to be assumed that to some extent homesickness will have inhibited adaptation, whereas the failure to adapt will have promoted homesickness.

Exotic environment

The emergence of homesickness was closely linked with the strangeness of the exotic environment. This is clearly expressed in one of the Rourkela songs:

> One of these days it will all be forgotten:
> The beat of the drums in the jungle night
> And the jackals' cry in the bright moonlight.*

The Germans in Rourkela found themselves in an environment which was vastly different from the one to which they had been accustomed at home and which contained a large number of entirely novel features (new varieties of trees, flowers, animals, different-colored earth, an alien people, a new way of life and patterns of living). In Germany they had not had to watch out for snakes in the garden or scorpions in the bathroom. When, at the end of the day, instead of the evening stillness descending, the air was alive with the chirping and buzzing of countless insects, it all seemed so different and aroused strange sensations in them. There was something uncanny about this alien world—like the uncanny tropical illnesses which could lead to death—and many were

---

* See Appendix for complete text.

afraid. But their fear was not normally directed toward a specific object; it was much more diffuse and only became concentrated when some external cause—often an imaginary one, a mere rumor for example—set it in motion; then, however, it frequently revealed deep-rooted anxieties and even naked horror. One of the strange things about rumors is that those who pass them on unconsciously tend to reject and consequently to suppress, or at least weaken or distort, all those aspects of the rumor with which they themselves disagree. But in Rourkela things went much further than this: because they were afraid of their unknown and uncanny environment many of the Germans were quite prepared to believe the most far-fetched tales, which had absolutely no substance in fact. These people had little or no real contact with one another and so they felt isolated; their need for security was not gratified. Those most exposed to the feelings of insecurity induced by the exotic environment were, of course, the wives, for, unlike the men, they had no regular work with which to fill their day, and this made adaptation more difficult.

In this connection we must now mention a series of incidents that—like the cases of tropical illness and death among the members of the colony—combined to increase the general sense of fear and insecurity. What we have in mind are the strikes, the unrest, and the religious disputes among the Indians, which often led to bloodshed. The first major incident of this kind occurred on March 6, 1958, when seven Rourkela Germans saw nineteen Sikhs * attacked and very nearly beaten to death by a large number of Hindus outside one of the German bungalows; the police did not try to intervene. In August, 1959, large-scale disturbances broke out both in the plant and in the town between different regional groups: first between Oriyas and Punjabis, then between Oriyas and Madrassis, and finally between Oriyas and Bengalis. All work came to a stop for days on end.

The Rourkela Germans wisely kept well clear of these clashes. But in February, 1964, things became very much worse; the Muslims living in the Rourkela district were persecuted and there were

* Members of monotheistic sect founded *ca.* 1500 in Punjab.—TRANSLATOR.

not enough policemen available to protect the local inhabitants. Several hundred Muslims were killed, their corpses lying for days on the streets; Germans who took steps to protect their Islamic house servants were also threatened by the howling mob, although no Germans were injured. Nonetheless, the situation was considered so dangerous, even for the non-Indian inhabitants of Rourkela, that the U.S. Embassy in New Delhi decided to fly out the members of the American colony (who numbered less than 50) until the riots had subsided. No such action was contemplated for the German colony, which was of course very much larger. Since that time, the Indian authorities have evolved contingency plans to protect both the Germans and the small number of Americans still left in Rourkela if similar riots should break out again in the future.

However, despite these precautionary measures such incidents are bound to increase the Germans' sense of insecurity and to sustain their vague fears of this "uncanny and exotic land," thus militating strongly against successful adaptation.

Interest in the environment

But a number of the men in Rourkela, especially those there during the construction period (1957 to 1959), were actually attracted by this uncanny and exotic atmosphere because it whetted their sense of adventure and prompted them to set off on voyages of discovery into the surrounding countryside. Unfortunately, however, we have no detailed information as to how many of the Rourkela Germans got to know their environment in this way. A small-scale inquiry carried out in 1963 among 35 members of the operation and maintenance personnel, all of whom had been in Rourkela for several months, revealed that 16 had frequently visited the surrounding countryside and 8 had made occasional trips, but the remainder had never been out of the town. Some of these 11 men said that they had had "no opportunity," while others openly conceded that they just were not interested; the rest complained that it was difficult to get hold of transport. The overall picture which emerged from these interviews was that although the men would quite like to have seen something of the surrounding country, they were not prepared to go to any great trouble or to spend very much money in the process. The most positive attitude to this question was in fact adopted by those who had been invited to make a journey in somebody else's car (pastor, Indian colleague).

From the statements made by these men we may draw the tentative conclusion that the Rourkela Germans were not really terribly interested in getting to know more about their environment. The names of the neighboring villages were quite unknown to the majority, as was made abundantly clear in the course of conversation. In the early years a number of groups made excursions on their own initiative. Most of these consisted of people interested in photography or hunting. But when the German Social Center tried to organize bus trips further afield they were unable to attract a sufficient number of passengers for the enterprise to pay its way. Perhaps the journey appeared too strenuous ("It's so bumpy on those bad roads." "If you take something to drink with you, you can't keep it cool." "What are you going to put in your sandwiches with all that dust and heat?") or too expensive (although none of the trips offered for Saturdays and Sundays cost more than twenty dollars), or perhaps it was simply that they could not "find the energy." At any rate, there was not enough interest, and the journey was too uncomfortable.

As for the Indian population, the Germans were probably even less interested in them than they were in their country. But that is not altogether surprising, since by and large people are more inclined to visit "landscapes and places of interest . . . etc. than the people who live in them. . . . We have to recall the language barrier to realize just how insoluble this problem is." [69] But in this particular respect there seems to have been a considerable difference between the construction personnel and the operation and maintenance personnel. The great majority of construction workers certainly made no private contact with Indians. This they left to the engineers and superintendents—and sometimes even laughed at them when *they* did so. On one of the rare occasions when a German fitter did strike up a friendship with an Indian his colleagues took grave exception, and the only explanation they could find for his behavior was that he must have been trying to please his superintendent. To men of this kind words like "Hindu" and "Adivasi" were meaningless; in their eyes all Indians were just "Kanakas." But with the arrival of the operation personnel this attitude receded and the Rourkela Germans began to take a somewhat greater interest in their Indian colleagues—not only because the operation personnel had a different outlook, but also because they had relatively little to do with the lower-class Indian workers. It is difficult to assess the extent to which the preparatory courses held in Germany by the Deutsche Stiftung für Entwicklungsländer (German Foundation for the Developing Countries) may have provided a stimulus, but a survey conducted in 1963 revealed that of thirty-five members of the operation and maintenance personnel, fifteen often met Indians in private, eleven had occasional contacts, and nine had no contacts at all. When asked what the Indians were like, one foreman gave a very telling reply:

Just go and have a look at Shiva * some time, if possible in one of the Indian temples, where he sits in front of a mirror. All those arms and heads that you'll see, the Indians all have them. Which is just another way of saying that they are so difficult, so intricate and complex, so impenetrable, that with all the good will in the world you scarcely even begin to understand them.

But what is particularly regrettable is the fact that so few of the Rourkela Germans concerned themselves with their Indian environment at a really profound level. Not only did they rarely display any great interest in the underlying causes and ramifications of the various incidents and events which came up for discussion in the normal course of conversation, but they also opposed all attempts to enlighten them, with the result that the lectures and seminars that were arranged to bring a positive influence to bear on a wide public came to nothing. Even a series of popular lectures, which had been specially adapted for presentation to the

* One of the three principal Gods of the Brahmin pantheon, revered as the destroyer of the world, always represented with four arms.

general public and were given by a German Indologist (who had studied under Glasenapp) was able to attract no more than 2 per cent of the Rourkela Germans. The reference books in the club library stood on their shelves for years on end without betraying any visible signs of having been consulted. A group of thirty-five members of the operation and maintenance personnel were asked whether they had actually read the literature on India and Rourkela provided by the German Foundation and whether they had continued to refer to it during their stay in Rourkela. But the findings of this inquiry were difficult to evaluate, since there was no possible means of discovering whether those answering in the affirmative were actually telling the truth or merely being polite. Only six of those interviewed openly confessed that they had never even looked at the literature; seventeen admitted that they had not referred to it in Rourkela (some of them excusing themselves on the grounds that the baggage restrictions imposed by the airline had obliged them to leave it behind). If these answers were truthful (which the author regards as highly unlikely), then the findings of this survey would speak very favorably for the operation personnel, especially by comparison with the construction personnel.

The German yardstick

Interest is the first step toward understanding and understanding is a necessary precondition for positive adaptation. There can be no successful collaboration where there is a lack of interest and consequently a lack of understanding on the part of development workers for the developing country and its peoples. Both in their physical environment and in their dealings with the Indians the Rourkela Germans encountered so much that was strange. Why could they not have simply accepted this for what it was, namely "something different"? After all, they came up against these differences nearly every day in one form or another: when the Indian means "yes"—according to the Germans—he shakes his head; when he speaks of "the day after tomorrow," he does not mean that specific day, but sometime in the future; the word "thank you" is not often used in India and in certain Indian languages it does not even exist. There are many such differences, which simply have to be accepted and—if necessary—learned by rote. For foreigners living and working in India such matters should form a normal part of everyday living; they should not really have to be thought about. It is understandable, though, that a man with a fanatical love of order and logical thought processes may find it hard to bear when the Indians—as they frequently do—construe our "either/or" concept in terms of their own "both/and." For example, when an Indian who was engaged on approval was dismissed at the end of his probationary period, not only was the man himself dumbfounded but all his Indian colleagues considered his dismissal to be unjust. This simply means that in India an employee who gives his signature to a probationary clause will at the same time confidently count on its never being used against him. And sometimes in India people will decide on an immediate and urgent course of action in order to avoid some quite specific and undesirable consequence and will then first take a cup of tea together before hurrying off to implement their decision. When this sort of thing does happen it is senseless to fall into a rage; the only profitable thing is to try to discover the underlying reasons for such behavior, to discover the "whys and the wherefores."

The majority of Rourkela Germans did not bother to do this. They criticized. They made comparisons with home. They applied the good old German yardstick in order to decide what was better, whiter, blacker, cleaner, and dirtier. Margaret Boveri, the Berlin authoress, visited Rourkela and held lengthy conversations with the Germans there; she subsequently posed the question in the Frankfurter *Allgemeine Zeitung* as to whether we Germans are not blinded to our own deficiencies by the arrogance of our attitude towards others. Are the Germans particularly prone to judge everything they see, no matter where, according to their own criteria? A West German observer who had travelled widely in the East German Democratic Republic spoke of the embarrassment caused by visitors from Western Germany, who will keep drawing comparisons, even in personal matters. "That offends people's sensitivities," he rightly observed, adding that those who insist on making such comparisons are tactless.[70]

This German vice was dealt with as early as 1788 by Freiherr von Knigge in his famous book on correct behavior: "By all means let people think that what they have is best! Yet I must confess that this often leads to intolerance: that loyalty to the native custom sometimes makes for injustice towards those who depart from it in minor respects, be they of behavior, clothing, fashion, dialect, or gesture." [71] The Rourkela Germans were very intolerant, and it is understandable that the Indians should complain on this account. One Rourkela German, who was interviewed in the course of a survey, remarked quite innocently: "Yes, two of our Indian colleagues drop in on us quite regularly of an evening. The funny thing is that in our conversations we nearly always criticize them. We ask them the reason for all this dirt and misery and why they have so many cows, that sort of thing." It had not occurred to this man that the two Indians might have regarded such criticism as discourteous, especially since it implied a comparison with Germany.

Lily Abegg, who is considered an authority on many Asian countries, has written on the subject of intolerance towards those of a different race:

The servants, who come from quite a different milieu and can scarcely be expected to know how an efficient European housewife wants things done, are all too easily dubbed as lazy, incapable, and even deceitful. The food which is bought for the household is often declared to be bad, unhygienic, and inedible, simply because it is unfamiliar. The onions and the parsley have to be precisely the same as the European varieties. The climate is too hot, a mosquito has had the temerity to buzz, and there was a snake in the garden. The men, who have their work, are usually less affected by all these things, but many of the women grow irritable and soon long to go home. It has often been said, and with some justice, that it was not the Englishmen who lost India, but the English wives! [72]

For the Rourkela Germans a difference in kind would seem to be indivisible from a difference in value. They tend to equate "different" with "inferior." They lack what Mitscherlich has called "social accomplishment," [73] namely the critical ability to observe and to recognize the difference between themselves and other people and on the basis of such recognition to enter into a living relationship with them without making constant comparisons using German criteria.

The wives

Harlan Cleveland, who flew around the world with a group of American scientists in order to study the behavior patterns of Americans in a large number of different countries, has reported that the success or failure of American overseas projects often depends on the attitude of the American wives: "[the American] wife will usually make at least half of the family's decisions on going; she will cast the deciding vote on whether to stay; and in many cases she will make or break her husband's career." [74] Cleveland further observes that the only way in which the American wives really demonstrated their ability to adapt to the conditions in the developing countries was by their willingness to employ any number of house servants at a moment's notice. However, the American authorities have long since adopted the practice of testing and preparing wives who are to accompany their husbands on overseas projects before their departure; this is a practice whose importance has not yet been sufficiently appreciated in many parts of the German Federal Republic.

The influence of the English wives in Colonial India is also said to have inhibited adaptation. The English author Percival Spear writes:

By another irony the same influence which improved the morals of the settlers increased the widening racial gulf. As women went out in large numbers, they brought with them their insular whims and prejudices, which no official contact with Indians or iron compulsion of loneliness ever tempted them to abandon. Too insular in most cases to interest themselves in alien culture and life for its own sake, they either found society and a house amongst their own people, or in the last resort returned single and disconsolate to Europe. . . . So with the advent of women in large numbers a new standard was introduced. . . . The attitude of airy disdain and flippant contempt had the background of fear which an unknown and incalculable environment is liable to excite in everyone. For the men the establishment of English homes in place of the prevalent zenanas withdrew them still more from the Indian ways of thought and living, and the acquisition of homes and families gave them something to lose which they had never had before, and thus made them the victims of the same fear.[75]

There are similar reports concerning the behavior and the attitude towards adaptation of Dutch wives: "Inevitably, their presence exerted a pressure against mixing with the natives. Whatever may have been the reason, it appears to be true that when European women joined their men in the colonies, the community withdrew into itself." [76]

Novelist Han Suyin has described how in Malaya the arrival of European women also slowly but surely prompted the European men—and not only the married men but some of the bachelors as well—to break off their contacts with the native population. Unlike Spear, she offers no explanation for this change, but the picture which she draws is very similar to that provided by both of the authors quoted above, although in her case the ideas are put into the mouth of one of her characters: "with a wife from his own race life would move backwards and forwards between the club and the bungalow like a yo-yo and he would mix almost exclusively with his fellow-countrymen." [77]

We have here three largely similar descriptions by authors of different nationalities of the same basic phenomenon, namely the influence brought to bear by European wives on their husbands' adaptation to local conditions in foreign lands. In the light of these descriptions it is extremely interesting to consider the patterns of behavior of the German wives in Rourkela and the extent to which they influenced their husbands' attitudes.

We have already stressed the fact that contacts between the great majority of Rourkela Germans and the Indian population were not very good and not very close, which meant, of course, that however much the German wives may have been inclined to disrupt Indo-German relations, in actual practice, since there was so little to disrupt, they were unlikely to cause any great harm. Apart from a few isolated cases, unimpeded social intercourse— what is known in India as "free mixing"—was to be found only among the superintendents or engineers in Rourkela, although business considerations and knowledge of English were important factors here. There was no evidence to suggest that this free mixing was impeded by the German women and the author knows of no case in which contacts were broken off following the arrival in Rourkela of a German wife.

What is certainly true, however, (as is implied in the above quotation from Lily Abegg's article), is that the German women were more easily depressed by the great number of minor problems and mishaps of everyday life. When, for example, the water supply was cut off at the precise moment when the German housewife stood under the shower covered with soap or when the electricity gave out just as she was receiving the first of her guests for an evening party, such mishaps, which occurred frequently, took a greater toll on the wife's nerves than on her husband's, who was accustomed to far worse things than this on the site and who consequently tended to regard such setbacks as being all part of a day's work. Friedrich Plehn, a nineteenth-century physician for tropical medicine, has stated that women living in tropical climates frequently develop a nervous condition,[78] which is presumably triggered off in the first instance by the lack of adequate amenities in their daily lives and subsequently aggravated by the heat or other climatic influences. It should not surprise us to find, therefore, that many of the men in Rourkela refused to extend their contracts because their wives wanted to go home.

Seen in this light the thesis that wives inhibit adaptation is also valid for the Rourkela Germans, for no man could put up with a nagging and scolding wife for any length of time in a place like Rourkela. Slowly but surely he would succumb to his wife's negative attitude or—and in Rourkela this was more frequently the case —the negative aspects of his own attitude to both the country and its people would gradually harden, thus precluding all possibility of successful adaptation to the environment.

New arrivals

Dieter Danckwortt differentiates between four phases of adaptation: observation, coming to terms, consolidation, and dissolution.[79] The phase of dissolution is of only subsidiary importance for this present study; the phase of observation was the most evident. The new arrivals showed themselves to be extremely receptive to all new impressions and appeared only too eager to adapt. We propose therefore to deal with this initial phase in some detail in the present section, while the other phases will be reserved for treatment at a later point.

For most of the Germans who came to Rourkela this initial phase of observation embraced three crucial encounters: first with Calcutta, which provided them with their very first impression of India; then with Rourkela (or, to be more precise, with the superficial view of Rourkela received on arrival, which was conditioned largely by the manner of their reception and the style of their accommodation); and finally with the "old hands"—the experienced Rourkela Germans.

The first confrontation with Calcutta, especially the one-and-a-half-hour journey by car from the Dum Dum airport to downtown Calcutta, gave most of the new arrivals a "Calcutta shock." "When I saw Calcutta I was ready to fly straight back home to Germany." "I was genuinely shocked to discover that such things actually exist." "Although I had been told what to expect, Calcutta was still a nasty shock." This kind of answer was given by new arrivals when asked about their first impressions of India. This sense of shock has been known to continue for months on end and in some cases to have extended over the whole period of a man's stay in Rourkela. It was particularly strong in those who had the additional misfortune of being subjected to administrative incompetence. A group of new arrivals from Germany might be dropped off by the airline at their hotel in Calcutta and left to sit there for twenty-four hours. Without anyone bothering about them, without any money, without a word of English between them they were quite helpless, simply because there had been a breakdown in the reception arrangements. The result of such treatment was often an enduring sense of bitterness.

The same sort of thing happened in Rourkela. Germans would arrive at the railway station to find that nobody had come to meet them, and since they did not know where to report, they would spend several uneasy hours on the platform; this also gave rise to unpleasant memories. If, in addition to this, their accommodations were not ready for them—because their flat or bungalow had yet to be completed or because there had been a hitch somewhere along the line—then the negative impression formed at the station could well be aggravated to the point where the men would mouth their first oaths and the women shed their first tears over Rourkela.

Experiences of this kind upon arrival in both Calcutta and Rourkela were quite common among the operation and maintenance personnel. During the construction period they had been virtually precluded, because the departments had taken good care of their men. Subsequently, however, the reception of personnel was taken over by HSL, and the German departments were no longer responsible.

The new arrival's third encounter is with the "old" Rourkela Germans. As far as adaptation is concerned this is the crucial meeting, because the newcomer seeks—and usually finds—orientation from his more experienced colleagues.

The influence of the group of fellow countrymen already present [in the new environment] is all the greater if the newcomer has no contact with the native population in the early days and weeks of his stay, for then he is obliged to seek help from his fellow countrymen, to fit in with their ideas and adopt their patterns of behavior.[80]

Time and again in the course of conversation with Rourkela Germans it became clear that their negative attitude to their Indian environment had been strongly conditioned by these initial encounters, especially when, having arrived with every intention of trying to adapt, their good will was immediately sapped by disagreeable incidents.

Press and politics

Both in India and in Germany Rourkela received very unfavorable press coverage from the outset. After having had a great deal of trouble with the three large English-language newspapers in

Calcutta, HSL set up a Public Relations Office, but unfortunately this was not as successful as had been hoped. For their part the German firms tended to avoid the press in the early years of the project. By and large they adopted the view that until the whole plant had been completed there was no reason for supplying the press with information and that the quality of their work and the success of their undertaking would be the best form of publicity; they also considered that it was the Indians' responsibility to deal with public relations. It was only in 1959, by which time the isolated attacks previously mounted by one specific section of the Indian press had developed into a vigorous campaign, that the German construction departments began to supply the Indian newspapers with press releases. Subsequently an Indian journalist was employed as public relations officer and then, in 1960, a German Industrial Press Office was set up in New Delhi to look after the interests of the Rourkela site and a special press representative was sent out by the Federal Government and attached to the German Consulate General in Calcutta. But these measures only began to produce results after the damage had been done. Today it is generally recognized that the public relations work should have been started at the beginning of the construction period, if not earlier; both the Russians and the English set up press offices for their projects at the very outset.

The harm done by German reporters was not too serious, provided their exaggerations were restricted to the exotic aspects of life in Rourkela, as, for example, in the following piece:

Soon the crocodiles in the Brahmani river will feel the waste from the coke ovens and the gas cleaning plant flowing over their scaly bodies. And when leopards and Bengal tigers, attracted by the glow from the foundries and blast furnaces, slink about the industrial quarters at night, the fumes from forges and blast furnaces will fill their nostrils." [81] *

But it was much worse to have macabre nonsense and downright untruths reported under such headlines as "German Entrepreneurs

* Between 1957 and 1964 *one* crocodile was observed by local villagers in the Brahmani river and was subsequently shot by a German medical officer.

Build Their Own Tomb in India," "The Stalingrad of German Industry," or "A Tragedy in Iron and Steel." One report, for example, maintained that when an Indian worker was killed in the course of his work, the Indian firm responsible would pay out compensation to the widow only if the dead man's body was produced in evidence; because this practice allegedly resulted in the production of one and the same corpse in substantiation of different claims, the Indian authorities, upon payment of compensation, were said to cut off the corpse's left ear, which they then kept by way of a receipt. There were also many instances of tactlessness on the part on the part of the press; for example, cultured Indians were referred to as "natives" in picture captions and the contribution made by Indians to the communal project was often completely overlooked. And finally, reports in the Indian press in which German fitters were said to have misbehaved were subsequently taken up by German reporters without any attempt to check the facts.

This state of affairs could never have arisen if such calumnies had been energetically repudiated in the first instance. As it was, however, the charges made in the Indian press had gone unchallenged over a long period. When they had finally subsided, they were then rediscovered by certain German newspapers and reissued with great success in both Germany and India. Whereas any reference to the "rival" works of the Russians and the English was studiously avoided in the press releases in Rourkela, the Soviet Embassy in New Delhi thought nothing of belittling the achievements of the Germans and the English. In Rourkela it was never doubted for one moment that this Russian source was partly responsible for the defamatory articles appearing in one particular section of the Indian press. All the more reason, therefore, why the German newspapers should not have restricted their comment to the bad aspects of life in Rourkela. Constructive criticism, which could and did lead to the abolition of malpractices and the correction of errors, was practiced by only a part of the German press. And yet there is ample evidence to show that Indian newspapers are quite prepared to accept such criticism in the spirit in which it is intended and—where applicable—to tell their own countrymen necessary home truths.

The "bad press" which Rourkela received in Germany, especially in 1959 and 1960, finally persuaded various high Indian officials and a number of German journalists to put the record straight by furnishing an objective account of the actual conditions obtaining there.[82] The well-known weekly *Christ und Welt,* for example, gave a four-page report on Rourkela which closed with the following comment:

Many critical things have been said about Rourkela in the press. Before ending this report we wish to state quite categorically that the Germans in Rourkela have stood their ground under the most extreme living and working conditions and that their great achievement calls for gratitude and recognition. Those who have seen the steel plant and who understand the enormous potential which it offers to India would be petty and narrow-minded indeed, if they still insisted on carping over a few minor mishaps.[83]

Die Welt wrote:

In a conversation which he held with the head of the Economic Department of the German Embassy in New Delhi, Boothalingam, the Secretary of State in the Indian Steel Ministry, regretted the fact that it had recently become fashionable in Germany to subject the Rourkela steel plant, which was erected by a group of German firms, to sharp criticism. In certain newspapers, events that had long since lost all relevance were given "great prominence to no useful purpose." The critical opinions which had been expressed about Rourkela were not shared by the Indian government, which was "entirely satisfied" with the Rourkela steel plant. Minor technical faults were unavoidable in the construction of such an enormous and complex plant. But these were not only to be found in Rourkela; they also occurred in the Bhilai plant, which was being erected by the Russians, and in Durgapur, where the English had started operations.[84]

This must now suffice as a description of the general situation. We are not, after all, concerned with the question as to how the public relations work for a project of the size and importance of Rourkela should be handled (although this would certainly be a worthwhile subject for a study) but merely with the effects of the press coverage on the Rourkela Germans.

One of the ways in which the Rourkela Germans were made to feel these effects was in the letters they received from friends and relations at home. Often enough the men were asked what they were "up to" in Rourkela for the papers to be saying such things about them; at times the questions took an accusing tone: didn't the men themselves think they were "carrying on a bit too much out there"? The German newspapers had also written about the high wages and the "luxury life" of the men in Rourkela and many wives at home in Germany became suspicious and began to wonder whether their husbands had been telling them the truth about their earnings. Reports about the ayahs also caused anxiety in many German homes. Eventually things reached such a pitch that a number of the German men in Rourkela either applied to the GSC for a certificate of good conduct or asked their pastor for a signed statement itemizing the standard and cost of living, daily expenses, and so forth. A wave of indignation swept through the colony. The press was roundly cursed and threats were uttered: "If we catch another of those newspapermen here, he'd better look out!" Some of the fitters swore that they would beat him up the moment he arrived at the station.

The press coverage had a further, albeit an indirect, repercussion, which remained largely subliminal, was not recognized as such, and so provoked no affective response. Nonetheless, the Rourkela Germans gradually came to feel that all work was not necessarily equal, that the erection of an installation in Rourkela was quite a different thing from the erection of an identical installation in Rheinhausen. The German blast furnace operator in Rourkela was astonished to find that a breakdown, which in Germany might perhaps have been reported to the shift engineer but more likely would simply have been brought under control by the shift foreman, was a matter of immediate concern to the whole plant management, was reported next day in all the newspapers, and eventually led to questions being asked in the Indian Parliament. Slowly the Rourkela Germans came to realize that their work and their private lives were being accorded a degree of importance that they themselves found unpleasant because of the unaccustomed repercussions to which it gave rise. They considered the Indians far too "pompous," they were irritated by the unaccustomed interest taken in them by the general public and felt mistrustful as a result, even though they were not always conscious of the fact. Although their mistrust was not concrete, that is, it was not directed towards a specific object but, on the contrary, remained diffuse and—insofar as it was symptomatic of a more general insecurity—tended to embrace one and all, it was nonetheless present and was revealed in their conversations. A member of the Federal Parliament who visited Rourkela in September, 1959, with a number of his colleagues and who was eager to enter into conversation and discussions with the Rourkela Germans in their club was not a little surprised when he was made to feel this mistrust in unmistakable terms. Instead of reacting with pleasure at the thought of having a member of Parliament in their midst, the Germans were so hostile that the delegate was forced to abandon his intention and leave the club premises.

But quite apart from the feelings of hostility engendered by mistrust the Rourkela Germans also found, to their great distress, that they were utterly exposed to the special "importance" that was accorded to everything they did. Nobody appeared to take their side or was able to present a positive defense on their behalf, which, had it been done, would have brought relief from the state of continuous tension in which they found themselves. And so both the direct and the indirect effects of press coverage released feelings of frustration and aggression among the Rourkela Germans, which also served to inhibit adaptation.

Collaboration in the Plant

Although it would exceed the bounds prescribed for this book to enter into a detailed discussion of conditions in the steel plant and to show how these developed in specific areas, it nonetheless appears desirable to provide a brief synopsis of the conditions obtaining during both the construction period and the initial phase of the operation period, in as far as they cast light on the behavior patterns of the German personnel.

The steel plant was erected by German and Indian firms on the authority and under the supervision of Hindustan Steel Limited. The delegation of authority within HSL was based on a somewhat cumbersome system and it was not always easy to establish which department was responsible for a particular process; this may be explained by the fact that HSL also controlled the Indo-Russian plant in Bhilai and the Indo-English plant in Durgapur, and the administration for this whole tripartite undertaking was divided between Ranchi and New Delhi, both of which towns were one or two days from Rourkela by rail and air. There was also a further complication in that the management of the Rourkela undertaking was constantly changing in the early years of the project. Between 1956 and 1965 there were eight different general managers. Since HSL was a nationalized body and was, moreover, administered primarily by civil servants, it was subject to a considerable measure of control by the Indian Finance Department. The departmental system was time-consuming and in the early stages failed to answer the needs of a modern industrial concern. Personnel organization suffered from the fact that appointments were frequently made and workers' disputes settled in accordance with the requirements of party or regional politics. Security of office and lack of discipline, which are common features of many nationalized industries throughout the world, are not calculated to meet the needs of modern production processes. The technical training of the engineers was often inadequate, especially in the early stages, and the few capable men who were available were often wrongly deployed. Personnel management was not well organized in as far as the responsibilities and powers of the various departments were not clearly defined. The morale of the workers, especially in the lower wage brackets, gave grounds for criticism. Carelessness in servicing the machines in the various plant units was a constant problem and led to breakdowns and loss of production. The supply of tools and spare parts was not properly regulated, the stores did not permit easy checking, and deliveries of materials were painfully slow. Such, briefly, were the conditions in the plant during the early years of the construction and operation periods.

A special light is cast on these conditions by the following quotations from Indian newspapers:

> The troubles at Rourkela that have general application include . . . inadequate devolution of responsibility and absence of requisite autonomy at plant and departmental levels, "over-bureaucratisation" (a headquarters staff four times larger than that necessary to run a comparable European plant), very poor maintenance, and what the Minister for Steel recently admitted as the absence of a labour policy. . . . Qualified personnel . . . are drifting away because of red tape, lack of opportunities and standardisation of salaries in the public sector. Cost accounting in the public sector is still in its infancy and the system of financial control, including the demands of the Auditor-General, is cumbersome. . . . Absenteeism at Rourkela has sometimes gone up to 25%.[85]

> It must, however, be admitted that we in Rourkela, as well as in Bhilai and Durgapur, have to manage with a very large percentage of beginners. I do not call them inexperienced, for though they may be experienced, they are still beginners in so far as a steel industry is concerned, and especially for a plant with a million ton capacity which has started from scratch. Only 2% of our staff have really got the experience in steelmaking which is necessary for running a plant of this magnitude.[86]

> Americans are beginning to learn this [from Rourkela] and therefore they are stipulating conditions before consenting to undertake work on the project Bokaro. They want control and supervision during erection. The Germans were not strict about it in Rourkela and they suffered as a result and will continue to suffer in reputation. . . .

> If erection is not controlled completely by those that have constructed the machinery then the working of such machinery might offer recurring difficulties and then the temptation to lay the whole blame at the doors of the foreign designers would be irresistible. At a later date it would be difficult to apportion the blame accurately between the designers and between those that have executed the designs. The benefit is always

given to the local men and fault is always found with the outsiders. . . .

. . . At present the Germans are in Rourkela only in an advisory capacity and are therefore helpless if their advice is not listened to. The public however blames them for every defect in the working. . . .

. . . Responsibility without authority is certainly demoralising. If the Indian tactics of doing things in a slovenly way and then attributing responsibility for everything that has gone wrong to foreigners continues then respectable manufacturers in non communist countries would refuse to cooperate in the development of our country.[87]

Our object here is not to apportion blame; the sole purpose of quoting these few brief remarks on the problems within the steel plant is to give an idea of the atmosphere in which Indians and Germans alike were required to work.

The Germans' initial position

Many of the difficulties the Germans encountered when they came to tackle the actual project had their roots in the preparatory negotiations, which were far from successful, and in the terms of the ensuing agreement. Individual contracts, no syndicated management, no right to be consulted on final decisions, having to hand over the plant on a piecemeal basis as each unit came into operation and not as a complete works, virtually no possibility of getting completion or commission schedules altered, no means of opposing the Indians' insistence (for political reasons) on overambitious construction or production schedules (to the detriment of the installation): these and many other conditions equally prejudicial to fruitful collaboration were established at the very outset. Without any doubt the Germans made their first mistakes *before* the work had even begun. The endless to-ing and fro-ing over the financial arrangements had already excited Indian public opinion: "there is a general awareness of the period of off-and-on relationships with the Germans in connection with the financing of the mill of Rourkela." [88] The Soviets undoubtedly played their hand far better by offering credit at low rates of interest from the start and demanding and obtaining a statisfactory working agreement in return. The Germans, on the other hand, waited before offering acceptable credit arrangements until it was too late, from a tactical point of view, to insist on the kind of conditions which would have facilitated the construction work.

It is true . . . that the Russians impose tough conditions on the developing countries with which they collaborate and only hand over the establishments to the people concerned when they, the Russians, are persuaded that the time is ripe. The Russians are tougher collaborators and yet—or perhaps for that very reason—they are more accepted than the representatives of the Western countries.[89]

Wilfred Malenbaum, an American observer, made much the same point when he said that it was not because of their friendly attitude that the Russians won friends but because of the kind of aid programs they offered.[90]

The second great disadvantage arose out of the piecemeal way in which the plant was transferred to the Indians; each German firm handed over the particular section which it had erected and was then immediately absolved from all further responsibility.

The fact that the German technicians, who had erected the plant and brought it into commission, were sent home too soon was certainly a mistake. It was only natural that their firms, who were in urgent need of their services, should have been agreeable and as the Indians were pressing [for their repatriation] there seemed little reason for not bringing them home, especially since this had been provided for in their contracts. But as a result a whole crop of difficulties arose, which could have been avoided. And to crown it all the Indians then tried to blame the Germans for these difficulties. It is to be hoped that both sides will have learned their lesson. Especially the Germans! [91]

It is significant that for some considerable time many Indians, especially those of the lower and middle classes, were not even aware that when the Germans left Rourkela upon completion of the construction work, they did so at the express wish of the Indian authorities. When this was pointed out to them they replied that in that case, the Germans, with all their experience to guide them, should have "forced their attentions" on the Indians.[92]

The Americans were particularly interested in the outcome of Indo-German collaboration in Rourkela since they had offered—under certain conditions—to finance and erect India's fourth state-owned steel plant in Bokaro. Consequently, they were well informed about events in Rourkela:

Ironically, part of the Germans' trouble, at least, stemmed from the rush to be the first. They were successful in their drive to get on-site work started before the others—but in doing so they made certain mistakes. By the time the Russians and the British got underway they were able to avoid these mistakes. . . . And from the beginning, the German technicians accepted the role of advisers to Hindustan Steel. The result: The Germans soon found that scant attention was being paid to their advice; that decisions were being made and work being performed with little regard for sound engineering principles.[93]

Although this description is generally correct, it overlooks the fact that the German firms themselves had no ambitions whatsoever to keep to their completion dates at all costs and against all reason, much less to improve on them; the truth of the matter was that they had no means of opposing Indian ambitions, especially since they were unable to form a united front. This meant that they were frequently played off one against the other with great dexterity in the course of the many bilateral negotiations instigated by the Indian authorities.

These, then, were the conditions under which the plant was erected and under which the construction personnel were required to work. If we compare these conditions with those of the German operation and maintenance personnel, who went out to Rourkela in 1961 to boost production and are still working there today (1968), we find that the situation has scarcely changed. True, production has again reached a satisfactory level and numerous mistakes have meanwhile been rectified, but today, in accordance with the terms of their new contracts, the Rourkela Germans are still employed in a purely advisory capacity. Moreover, since there are no longer any German managements in Rourkela, and the German personnel are all official employees of HSL, support from Bonn is not so readily available. Joseph Hunck, an expert on Indian affairs, has rightly observed in this connection that "it would be . . .

desirable, if there were something like a 'German Commissar' in Rourkela . . . who could deal with complaints, wrong decisions, etc. as soon as they occur and who could above all maintain the human contacts, which are so important." [94]

A number of Rourkela Germans were already aware of this need in 1958! The German Secretary of State, Gabriele Wülker, has said: "We are doubtless right in assuming that, despite all efforts, the mistakes made by the 'ugly American' have been repeated by the 'ugly German.'" [95]

German power of authority

All Rourkela Germans, whether construction or operation personnel, should have the power to give binding orders to those placed under their supervision. Not only the German supervisors and the Indian trainees but all impartial observers are agreed on this point; and yet the authorities on both sides would appear to hold a contrary view, with the result that the German personnel are left to cope as best they may with the ensuing difficulties. Specialists in the field of tropical medicine have also insisted that for psychological reasons all contractual rights should be clearly defined. Drascher, who has had considerable experience in a wide variety of developing countries and is well aware of the great diversity of the problems involved, nonetheless insists that development workers should be provided with all requisite powers for the simple reason that the Western technician is only able to help if his suggestions and instructions are complied with.[96] An American observer has drawn the following conclusions from his experiences in Rourkela: "For the recipient nations, the lesson is equally clear: When you invite an expert to do a job, let him do it. Take his word for it on technical matters; after all, that's why you asked him to do the job in the first place. And do your best to keep from strangling him in bureaucratic red tape." [97]

Behavior patterns of the Indians

From conversations held with Rourkela Germans during the construction period it is clear that the question of authority did not pose such a problem for the German fitters as it did for the operation personnel. This was owing to the fact that most fitters were dealing with Indian workers who had been employed—directly or indirectly—by the German firms themselves and were therefore prepared to take orders from Germans. Those Indian workers over whom the Germans had no authority were the members of HSL, which was still being organized during those early years and only came to assume a dominant role toward the end of the construction period. Consequently, it was only at the top management level that questions of authority presented any real problems during this time, although it should be added that since the problems were at such a high level, their material repercussions tended to be all the greater.

But even during the construction period, especially in the maintenance sector, the combination of inadequate powers of authority with a high degree of responsibility was a subject which often came up for discussion among the construction personnel. For the operation personnel, who followed them, this question became all-important, for the German backing that the fitters had received from their superintendents was not available to them, since there was no German management structure within HSL or its departments to which they might have turned. In a survey that was carried out among more than fifty members of the operation personnel, this was one subject which had only to be alluded to, to receive an almost instantaneous response. When asked how things were going at work three-quarters of those interviewed immediately replied that it was impossible to achieve any results if they were not allowed to tell their "men" anything. "We can't make them do anything, because we weren't given any backing in the first place. So all we can do is try and 'kid them along' in the hope that they'll learn something. You can imagine the result." This was the view advanced by one of the men. Another, when asked if he had ever experienced any difficulties, replied: "No, come what may, I avoid them. If a man falls asleep on the night shift, I let him sleep. Otherwise there'd only be a row. I have learned that you can't just go and rouse them. They expect to be asked why they were asleep. That would get me worked up, and so I don't do it." Another answered along much the same lines, adding quite ingenuously, "anyway, I find it quite impossible to be angry with them; they're far too puny."

Another man was asked how he got on with his Indian superiors and whether there were ever any problems in that sphere; he replied: "No; they don't have much to say to me. Their technical knowledge is none too good and they aren't all that interested. It looks as if the Germans are helping them here against their will." A similar response was: "One thing I'll never understand is why the Indians are so determined not to be helped by us. You get the feeling they're trying to sabotage their own machines. Why? For political reasons? Intrigue? Or is it that they prefer to be idle and hate the machines because they're being driven by them?" And yet another view: "This is the crux of the problem: what *we* make is examined under a magnifying glass; what *they* make doesn't matter and is scarcely even checked."

A number of the operation personnel expressed the opinion that the German fitters had been responsible for the Indians' subsequent outlook; these workers were asked how they got on with the Indians in general: "All right in private; things are more difficult in the plant. But in the light of past events I find this understandable. It was we Germans who made the Indians mistrustful in the first place." Another man merely complained: "My Indian colleagues don't do a hand's turn. My counterpart is so arrogant that the gulf between us is quite insuperable. He lets me know that he has 'studied' and that I am only a worker. He asks my advice only on very rare occasions." In this connection it should be pointed out that the men interviewed were nearly all chargehands or foremen, members of an industrial stratum that does not exist as such in India, where the equivalent posts have to be filled by graduate engineers. But let us close our brief account of this survey with a more positive comment on the question of private contacts with Indian colleagues: "Yes, we often meet. We often have a drink together. I must say, I shall leave here with a good impression of the Indians. They're cheerful people without any morbid ambitions, they're more peaceful than we are."

The chief point to emerge from these statements, which constitute a representative selection, is that many of the Rourkela Germans were not happy in their collaboration with the Indians. These men found no satisfaction in their work, they regarded themselves as timeservers and were chiefly concerned with getting through the various rounds of their engagement. By comparison with earlier surveys it was quite clear that the majority of the later Rourkela Germans were far more interested in the Indians and far more willing to enter into contact with them than were the fitters. This is borne out by their observations and thoughts on the Indians' social life and on their patterns of behavior, such as their attitude to machines. A further fact to emerge from these interviews is that the off-duty relations between Indians and Germans are also no longer quite as unfavorable as they once were. The opinion was expressed on repeated occasions that the behavior of the Rourkela Germans during the early years of the project had been so prejudicial to the general reputation of the German colony that it was no longer possible for a German to come to terms with the Indians. Some went even further than this, maintaining that the construction personnel had also indulged in technical "bodgery," which they, the operation and maintenance men, had had to sort out.

Occasional mishaps, of course, were bound to occur, since the construction personnel were engaged in what was in every sense a pioneering venture. It is also probable that the technical difficulties and the problems of collaboration with the Indians were greater than those posed years later for the members of the operation personnel. One might in fact go so far as to say that it was owing to the achievements of the construction personnel—both as workers and as supervisors—that the operation personnel now enjoy far easier conditions, which enable them to devote more of their time to improving human relations. There is some truth in the assertion, frequently made by the construction workers, that because they were so pressed to keep to their schedules, they simply did not have the time to ensure that an Indian colleague had at last mastered a particular technique that they had already demonstrated to him five times.

There is absolutely no doubt that the attitude adopted toward their work by the Indian workers and even the Indian engineers was something quite alien to the Rourkela Germans, and an attitude they found difficult to accept. Punctuality and work discipline have yet to be established, seniority has yet to be superseded by achievement as a general criterion, the idea that greater authority presupposes greater responsibility and greater obligations has yet to be recognized, and the realization that a machine needs oil and regular maintenance if it is to function properly has yet to sink in. These things will come, but they will come in their own time. "Work is worship" is written on the walls of the various plant units in Rourkela for all to see; but it will take a little while yet before those who do see them every day of their working lives have grasped their meaning and accepted its implications.

Behavior patterns of the Germans

Until this happens a great deal of patience will be needed, often more than the average Rourkela German has to offer. What is particularly trying is the feeling that he is "talking to a brick wall" or that the help which he is offering is not wanted by the Indians. An expert on local conditions in Rourkela came to the conclusion that "the aversion felt by the Indian engineers towards Germany and more especially towards the German engineers and workers who were or still are in Rourkela is considerable." [98] But he went on to modify this opinion, which was formed on the basis of numerous discussions and conversations with younger Indians of various social levels, by adding that the Indians were full of praise for "the good workmanship, the industriousness, and the technical knowledge" of the German fitters, although they subjected them to harsh but extremely well-founded criticism as human beings; the German operation personnel received a better report for their human qualities, but certain doubts were expressed as to their technical capabilities.

Other observers were regaled with even more forthright assessments, which still made the same basic distinction but in which the critical assessment of the technical abilities and knowledge of the operation personnel were based on well-founded statements.[99]

It is almost as though the Indians had sensed that the construction workers had identified more with their work, while the members of the operation and maintenance staff had apparently remained more objective. To the latter Rourkela was just an assignment like any other and they developed a kind of job philosophy which would normally be regarded as not typically German. Both groups' frustration and disappointment in their Indian colleagues was probably much the same, but the more constructive nature of the earlier work was doubtless more satisfying and consequently better calculated to enable the fitters to work off any tensions which arose. On the other hand the philosophy adopted by the operation personnel made it possible for them to show patience in situations which were more than trying.

There were the odd occasions during the construction period, when a fitter would "let fly" with his hand or even his foot. In a number of cases this led to serious trouble, and sometimes the press would get hold of the story. When this happened the whole of the German colony was naturally made to suffer. There were some fitters who refused to take any "risks" and so insisted on doing everying themselves, using the Indians simply to hand them their tools. Others—but not very many—explained to the Indians what had to be done, gave them practical demonstrations, and then let them do it themselves.

The construction personnel were undoubtedly a tougher lot and were also tougher in their dealings with their Indian colleagues, who certainly did not enjoy the experience. But by and large, collaboration between Germans and Indians functioned far better during the construction period than during the subsequent operation and maintenance period.

Social Structure: The Group

At no time can it be said that the Rourkela Germans constituted a firmly structured community under a central authority. During the period of construction they came under the various construction managements, who were able to bring a greater or lesser degree of influence to bear on their members within the framework of the employer-employee relationship and in accordance with the terms of their contracts. At the end of this period, when a number of groups were transferred to the operation staff and were joined by new personnel from Germany, the whole of the operation and maintenance staff became employees of HSL and were subject to its rules and regulations. From that moment onward—despite the fact that the post of technical director (general superintendent) within HSL was held by a German until 1966—the amount of influence which any German body (GSC, for example) was able to exercise was strictly limited. In the overseas contracts signed by the German personnel there was a clause to the effect that they must at all times behave in such a way as to protect the good name of their firm and of the German Federal Republic. But that was all; and it was not enough to enable the German authorities in Rourkela to influence the personal conduct of the German workers in any decisive way. The Indians were always surprised at this "extreme liberalism," which was censured by some and misunderstood by others. The younger Indian engineers were said to feel that

the German Federal Republic failed to take any interest in the events in Rourkela until a very late stage; it neglected to appoint an official to represent the German firms, with whom the Indian authorities could have negotiated. The Indian engineers gained the impression that the success or failure of the Rourkela project was a matter of indifference to the German Federal Republic.[100]

Looking back on the behavior patterns of the Rourkela Germans we must concede that the lack of a central authority was certainly a disadvantage. Hellpach's thesis is more or less applicable to the Rourkela Germans: when subjected to a certain degree of pressure from external forces the German is a reliable subordinate, but when entirely freed from such external forces he is quite incalculable.[101] Restated in more positive terms this would mean that the admirable technical achievements and the immense output of the construction personnel would probably not have been accompanied by such harmful side effects in the sphere of human relations if, instead of being left to their own devices and their own inadequate powers of self-discipline, the Germans had been subject to the firm control of experienced leaders who could have encouraged their better human qualities, such as their staunchness, their willingness to give of themselves, and their willingness to make sacrifices.

Having established that the Rourkela Germans were not "organized" we must now ask: What sort of social structure did they have? Were they a group in the sociological sense?

A group is an interpersonal structure, which is so constituted in respect of duration and conformity that its members may be said to belong together in a general sense.[102] Certainly the Rourkela Germans belonged together in this way, even in the formal sense of the word—for example, in their capacity as members of the German Club. But even if we define a group simply in terms of its relationship to another group or other groups, then quite apart from their common membership of their club, the Rourkela Germans must be regarded as a group in this sense also, which naturally leads to the comparison between "the Germans" and "the Indians."

The feeling that binds one human group together also distinguishes it from others. It constitutes the fundamental structural characteristic of all such associations and so gives rise to the categories of "in-groups" and "out-groups." [103] These twin concepts are also referred to as "we groups" and "they groups," and consequently we may speak of "we-behavior patterns" and "they-behavior patterns."

The "we-behavior pattern" is one of sympathy and indulgence vis-à-vis the individual concerned, and it interprets every single thing unhesitatingly and unequivocally to the greater glory of "our" group. The "they-behavior pattern" is one of suspicion and condemnation vis-à-vis the individual concerned, and it interprets every single thing unhesitatingly and unequivocally to the disadvantage of "his" group. . . . If the [suspect] individual is a member of the "we group," then "his action appears incredible" or "there must be a mistake," for "that sort of thing can't happen to us"; if the worst comes to the worst, he is considered to be untypical of "our" group, thank God. But if the [suspect] individual is a member of the "they group," then the report of his action is taken at its face value and the worst possible construction placed upon it.[104]

In-group and we-feelings

A variety of factors combined to promote "we-feelings" among the Rourkela Germans in a particularly intense form. A we-group is conceivable only within the context of a contrasting environment. The more strange, different, uncanny, hostile, and problematical the other group (or groups) and the environment which they have fashioned happen to be, the stronger the we-feelings will become. Even if it should have little else in common, the in-group will grow more cohesive the more it is subjected to outside pressures; in such conditions the automatic reaction of the group is to close its ranks. The Rourkela Germans behaved in much the same way as the German tourist groups described by one observer: they felt

> welded together by the strange environment and were thus able to compensate for their inferiority feelings by demonstrations of [corporate] courage. The fear released by the environmental pressures, which were mostly imaginary, was reflected in an "overbearing" emotional condition . . . with all its accompanying symptoms: all personal characteristics were weakened, individual behavior became primitive and uninhibited; the members of the group appeared as conquering heroes in a foreign land, yelling their heads off, "consciously" provocative and bereft of any sense of self-criticism.[105]

As far as Rourkela was concerned it should be pointed out—although this was no doubt intended by the author of the above passage—that any inferiority feelings, like those induced by the alien environment, were of course unconscious. It would seem, incidentally, that it is by no means uncommon for the development of exaggerated we-feelings within a German group to produce objectionable patterns of behavior; the Rourkela Germans were not an isolated case, as is quite evident from the numerous examples reported both in sociological literature and in the daily press. One German author, however, who has dealt at great length with "the" German, would appear not to have recognized this fact; in considering the opinion expressed by Goethe, in a conversation with the young Professor Luden, that whereas the individual German commands respect, Germans en masse are an abomination, this author stated: "one is tempted to reply that it is scarcely possible to ruin an omelette if it is made with good eggs." [106]

The German superintendents in Rourkela were astonished to find that the very fitters who had demonstrated their excellence over a period of years on primitive construction sites in the jungle of southern India—where they had been the only Germans among an all-Indian labor force whose members had thought highly of them—very soon drew attention to themselves in Rourkela on account of their bad behavior. Although the greater personal responsibility devolving on a man working on his own will doubtless have had some significance in these cases, the principal factor underlying such changes in behavior is more likely to be the individual's identification with the we-feelings of the in-group. This thesis has in fact been borne out by a considerable body of evidence from other quarters. It has frequently been said, and with some justification, that Germans abroad are always welcomed as individuals but often create a distinctly unpleasant impression en masse. We are told by Leonhardt that foreign visitors to Germany often remark on the amiability of the individual German and the frightfulness of the aggregate.[107] This is corroborated by reports of the "massed attacks" mounted by Germans on foreign countries on big sporting occasions, when they literally "take over" the stadium with flags flying, rattles sounding and banners hoisted aloft: "We take our oath, Germany will gain a place." This sort of scene was well described by Horst Peets in an article he wrote for *Die Welt*: The "Schnaps bottles stick out of their pockets and they believe in all sincerity that everybody must be nice to them." [108] The *Times* also once causticly observed: "Like Americans, Germans abroad like to be loved, but are perhaps slower to understand when they are not." [109] This comment might well have been made with the Rourkela Germans in mind, many of whom failed to realize, even after a lengthy stay, that Asians are extremely sensitive and are not to be won over by the cheap expedient of back-slapping joviality.

What we have defined as we-feelings were referred to by men in responsible positions in Rourkela, who were frequently confronted with this phenomenon, as a "sense of cohesion leading to a form of camaraderie so extreme as to be incomprehensible," in the face of which any attempt to present rational arguments, to bring influence or guidance to bear, or to exercise a calming effect appeared to have little success and little point: everything broke down in the face of such weird conformity. Once, when a Hungarian violinist was about to appear at the German Club, one group of Germans decided that they "didn't want a concert and [they] were going to show everyone whose club it was," even though some forty other Germans and thirty Indian guests were waiting for the concert to begin. In such a case arguments will accomplish nothing. The tomatoes are at hand, ready for throwing, and even before the soloist appears on stage the noise reaches disturbing proportions. The only thing that does any good in such a situation is for somebody to treat the group to a round of drinks and then get them so engrossed in something else that they forget all about the concert. Discussion, persuasion, arguments are a waste of time. Not one of the malcontents would be prepared to lay himself open to ridicule by being the first to respond to an argument or enter into a discussion. To do so would be to disengage from conformity. As Fromm has rightly said, a man feels most secure

> when he is most like his fellows. His principal object is to gain the approbation of others, his principal fear that he might fail to do so. To differ from those around him, to find himself in a minority, these are the dangers which threaten his sense of security; hence his ardent striving for boundless conformity. It is clear that this very striving will produce a constant and no doubt secret sense of insecurity. Every departure from the established scheme of things, every criticism, arouses fear in him and threatens his security. He depends on the approval of others as an addict depends on his drugs.[110]

This passage also points to the "deindividualizing" proclivity of group life, which may begin with the members of the group all wearing the same insignia, articles of clothing, uniforms, and the like and usually ends up with rather more extreme manifestations of loyalty, as in the case of a group of Rourkela fitters who all decided—much to the amusement of the colony—to sport beards and subsequently—even more amusing!—to have their heads shaven. But over and above such deindividualization the groups also revealed a tendency to regress into primitive modes of conduct.[111] Virtue lay in allegiance to the group and to the customary practices of the group. All were at pains to follow the group ideal or group pattern. Consequently, only those who have understood the group pattern—which is the sole criterion of behavior—are able to form a correct assessment of the group. As we have already noted, this criterion appears to have been fixed in Rourkela by a specific clique, whose loud-mouthed, swaggering ways attracted many adherents. The younger fitters especially seemed greatly impressed and were only too eager to follow their leaders. The American concept of the "peer group"—the group of contemporaries who establish the rules of conduct for a given neighborhood or professional community—should also be mentioned in this connection.[112] From his observations and reflections on this subject, Riesman has arrived at his categories of "inner-directed" types, who are bound by traditional precepts, and "other-directed" types, who are guided by conformity to the group. He regards the "other-directed" type as the typical product of the mass civilization of our modern technical world.[113]

But from a practical point of view the important question is how to bring influence to bear on the group or its individual members. Events in Rourkela—such as the incident of the concert wreckers—have shown that the only way to set about this successfully is by trying to influence the group as a whole: at first sight conversations with individual members of a group always appear fruitful and often enough one is astonished at the insight and good sense of the *individual*. But the object of such conversations is that they should be passed on to the other members of the group with a view to influencing them, and in this respect they are almost, if not entirely, ineffective. Walter Dirks is quite right when he says that "there are large numbers of workers with whom it is possible to speak a sensible word—good, candid people. . . . Unfortunately they are not the majority group—in which class are such men in the majority?—but neither are they hopelessly isolated." [114] And yet experience in Rourkela tells us that if such individuals form part of an undesirable group, it is usually easier to try to change the behavior of the whole group than to tackle each such individual on his own account, unless of course he should decide to remove himself from the group entirely. "As long as the group values are unchanged the individual will resist changes more strongly the farther he is to depart from group standards. If the group standard itself is changed, the resistance which is due to the relation between individual and group standard is eliminated." [115]

Leopold von Wiese has said much the same thing: "It would be quite wrong to try to free the ordinary members of a group from their dependence on the 'pattern.' It would in fact prove quite impracticable; however, the patterns themselves should be made more positive." [116]

A German pastor who gave a talk to a group of technicians attending a preparatory course prior to their departure for India tried to impress on the men that they must do better than their predecessors: "We cannot afford to set out [for India] as if we were going there merely on our own account!" He then posed the question: "Would it not be conceivable for a number of people who work together in the same place to cheer one another up and to keep one another in check?" [117] Clearly, the pastor was of the opinion that any influence, any guidance towards better patterns of behavior, could only come from within the group, and so he placed his hopes in the new recruits. But all observations made in Rourkela would suggest that such hopes must be discarded as Utopian. No matter how good their intentions may have been, the influence of the new arrivals was always speedily submerged by the tried and trusted views of the "old hands." In the words of one observant foreman, "the old hands corrupt the newcomers." The newcomers have a hard time of it anyway among their workmates; they are not treated as equals, nobody meets them halfway or gives them very much consideration at all, and there is certainly no question of their being introduced.[118] They have to prove themselves. "In old groups newcomers are accepted only after a long period of mistrust." [119] Consequently, it is quite impossible for individual newcomers to exercise a formative influence. On the contrary: "If they are to be accepted they must be prepared to discard the orientation they have brought with them and accept the one prevailing in the group; and even then the 'new settler' is treated with a certain amount of contempt." [120] For the most part this contempt takes the form of occasional reminders—delivered at appropriate moments—to the effect that the newcomer has only been there for a few weeks or months. The insinuation might also be framed as a question: "How long have you been here?" Asked in the right tone of voice and accompanied by a stern look, this is quite enough to put the new man in his place.

In addition to the in-group of the Germans and the out-group of the Indians, which were the really basic categories in Rourkela, there were also a number of other clearly defined groupings, such as the firm communities, the housing communities, and the various communities based on common interests or activities. At one time there were over thirty bowling clubs, a number of soccer teams (many representing particular firms), a water polo group (although this was less prominent), and even a group of Carnival enthusiasts. Many Rourkela Germans belonged to more than one group.

The strongest we-feelings were to be found within the firm groups; these feelings were quite strong enough to give rise to a system of in-groups and out-groups between the members of the different German firms. In January, 1959, there was an incident in the German Club that illustrates this point: M. was on his way to the toilet and was "just passing" a table near the door when, as he claimed, one of the two fitters sitting at the table, who both belonged to a different firm, called him a "drunken swine" for no reason; at this K., a colleague of M.'s and a member of his firm, fell upon one of the two fitters and beat him up. This was the signal for still more of M.'s colleagues to attack the two men with the result that the fight developed into a general scrimmage with men threshing about on the floor. Quite apart from the unseemly sight presented by bloodstained shirts and suits and swollen and battered faces, five chairs, one circular card table with a glass top, and a number of glasses were broken.

We have already mentioned on various occasions that the life of the German Club was controlled by a permanent clique of dissidents. The leading lights in this clique were nearly always men who also played a prominent part in other forms of group activity, above all the members of the various soccer teams. Their we-feelings were so well developed and they appeared to be so conscious of their reserves of corporate strength that they were only too prone to disregard the feelings of other Rourkela Germans. This exaggerated sense of power resulted from the we-feelings engendered by the consciousness of belonging to the large in-group of Rourkela Germans and in many cases to other smaller in-groups as well and caused many Rourkela Germans to lose all control of themselves. This is also illustrated by an incident which occurred in 1959: After the bar had been closed for the evening and the German manageress in the club restaurant had impressed on R. that no more beer could be sold to him because it was past licensing hours, he forced his way into the stock room and removed five bottles of beer from the cold storage installation, which had not yet been locked since stocktaking was still in progress. The (Indian) barkeeper, who was in the stockroom at the time, was unable to stop the man. Immediately after this R. was interviewed by the club manager. Because he made no attempt to argue and also because it was his birthday the matter was pursued no further. Fifteen minutes later R. left the clubhouse with his friends. But, before leaving, he wantonly destroyed three wooden chairs in the presence of the manageress.

There were any number of such incidents, many of them far worse than this. Alcohol was not always a factor, but usually it was. One would feel inclined to regard such incidents as examples of the famous "tropical frenzy" which has haunted the pages of sociological and medical literature for many a long year, were it not for the fact that there is no such thing. This has been rightly pointed out by Hellpach, who has found a whole series of plausible explanations for such excesses, the most important being the consumption of alcohol,

which in the sultry atmosphere is particularly liable to induce excitation and rowdyism and also combines with sociopsychic factors that, in cases where the character make-up is unfavorable, quite understandably exercise a similar influence. . . . The absence of many customary taboos, the entry into a sphere of what appear to be more primitive modes of conduct, the genuine need for self-preservation, the fact of having "savages" as workmates, the need to control their natural instincts and to keep them to their work schedule . . .—all these factors combine to explain the [European's] inclination to let himself go.[121]

In another work the same author touches on another important point, one which has scarcely been mentioned by the majority of sociological writers but which, to judge by events in Rourkela, can scarcely be emphasized enough, namely, the European's "unaccustomed position of authority over more primitive people [savages]."[122] The fact that many of the people concerned are not really primitives or savages but are wrongly assessed as such is, of course, quite immaterial. It was their position as masters which "went to their heads" and which—coupled with other motivations —made the Rourkela Germans so prone to all manner of excesses. Many of these additional motivations have already been established; Han Suyin also mentions isolation in this connection. With her sensitive understanding for the European milieu in Asia she describes how on "mess evenings" in Malaya the pent-up feelings of isolation would explode into bad behavior while the native servants looked on, some with a sense of shame, others with amusement.[123] In Rourkela the reactions of the bearers, who served the Germans on their alcoholic sprees in the club and so witnessed their excesses, also differed greatly. Some were visibly—and not unjustifiably—afraid when their masters began to get rowdy, and they did their utmost to keep in the background lest they should be seized upon and subjected to rough horseplay. Others were less fearful; they remained in close attendance and seemed to find amusement, which was mixed with contempt, in the conduct of their sahibs. But when things really warmed up, they also kept their distance. Ultimately the point was reached where the Indian employees in the club refused to carry out their duties; even the bus driver, whose last journey was scheduled to depart from the clubhouse when the bar was closed and who therefore drove most of the guests home, eventually refused to make this trip because he had been beaten up on a number of occasions.

In the summer of 1958 a Rourkela German wrote to his family at home: "I am sorry to say that unpleasant situations arise quite regularly due to the lack of discipline of a number of the fitters. As I have already told you, it is always a small minority that tries to terrorize the majority in the clubhouse." In certain cases there was no choice but to punish the worst offenders by repatriating them.

In Germany, too, repatriation would appear to be a trusted method of dealing with such problems, whether Italian "guest" workers attack German policemen in Wolfsburg or English soldiers create a row in the pubs of Minden. After the incidents in Wolfsburg it was said that "only in a very few cases had it proved necessary to repatriate blackguards. But in any camp of that size there are bound to be a few bad characters. Such things have nothing to do with nationality." [124] In the Minden affair the German press remained remarkably objective and consequently the episode was not blown up out of all proportion.[125] In the case of Rourkela, where they were dealing with their own countrymen, the German reporters showed less restraint.

As a result of the change effected in the Rourkela colony by the withdrawal of the construction personnel and their replacement by growing numbers of operation and maintenance personnel, there was a noticeable decrease in the intensity of the we-feelings within the community. This has also been reported by pastor Peusch.[126] The self-sufficiency previously demonstrated by the in-group—at least in its dealings with the Indian out-group—was greatly diminished. This also produced a corresponding reduction in the intensity of the they-feelings, as we have already intimated.

Out-group and they-feelings

The out-group of the Indians forms the counterpart to the in-group (or we-group), which, by promoting we-feelings, enabled the Rourkela Germans to develop their excessive strength and consequently their excessive behavior. The feelings entertained toward the members of an out-group, that is, toward "the others," are "they-feelings." The resulting state of affairs is not far removed from the condition of ethnocentrism, in which all members of the in-group are regarded as equals and all members of the out-group —here, a different ethnic group—are regarded as inferiors. At the deepest level all group conflicts are promoted by the sense of superiority felt by one group vis-à-vis another, irrespective of whether their differences are occasioned by pride of race, by nationality, culture, religion, or politics.

In this connection Arnold Zweig has spoken of the differentiating affect and the centralizing affect as typical of group feelings.[127] The differentiating affect refers to they-feelings. The "consciousness of being different [i.e., Zweig's differentiating affect], which can become a veritable passion,"[128] finds its necessary complement in the centralizing affect, which is to say, in the feeling of standing at the hub of the world. This leads to the conception of the in-group as something important and faultless. Zweig comments on the "exaltation" felt by the members of an in-group:

> The members of any group are under the sway of an inner experience, which impresses itself upon them in two ways: as members of this group they may stand—to overstate the case—at the hub of the universe. Such importance does not accrue to them in the form of thoughts —only in the case of particularly naïve groups and group members does this attitude attain the status of consciousness, of a program—but rather in the form of feelings, in fact as an attitude. But when they are excited they behave as if possessed by this instinctual conviction. Their group is *the* most important thing and the whole world of values and reality is grouped around it in zonal patterns; this group is the very tip of the pyramid of creation; other terrestrial groups, especially those of a similar nature, and also all people who are not members of groups, are inferior by comparison with them.[129]

Although Zweig's ideas were formulated with the object of explaining anti-Semitism, they are also applicable to many of the attitudes adopted by the Rourkela Germans towards the Indians as representatives of an out-group.

In Rourkela countless discussions were held in specific situations in an attempt to clarify and objectify the relationship to individual Indians or to "the" Indians; and at the end of these talks it was usually felt that the problem had been successfully reduced to rational and objective terms. It was all the more disappointing, therefore, for those who had gone to the trouble of mounting such discussions to discover that they had been mistaken: the emotional attitude had proved stronger. Zweig also comments on this point: "In the light of reason it is perfectly clear that a cobbler is just as important as a tailor. . . . But you can hardly hope to persuade either one of them that this is unreservedly true. In the end he will laughingly agree; but a certain reservation, the bit of group-ego within him, will always remain sceptical." [130]

Ethnocentrism

When Rourkela Germans give expression to their they-feelings by referring to the Indians as "Kanakas" or "blacks," then—whether they do so from conviction or simply from a desire to conform—their behavior falls within the sphere of what is known as ethnocentrism.

The "whites" and the "coloreds"—these divisions are based on characteristics which are too obvious to be ignored. Although it is conceded that color is by no means the only or even the principal guide to racial characteristics, yet for most of us, both here and over there, no sooner do we see a person whose pigmentation is other than our own than we immediately and involuntarily think of him as essentially different, essentially alien. Although these notions may well be extremely vague, initially they are our most significant notions and are dominant at each new meeting. They assert themselves as a negative force in the face of all other criteria and continue to do so at all subsequent meetings; even in a relationship of long standing they will yield only very slowly and sometimes not at all. If they are to be overcome, or at least ignored, which is of course a prerequisite for a better understanding of the other person, much good will and intellectual self-discipline are called for. For racial differences are omnipresent, and we are reminded of them with every day that passes; they impress on us that our neighbor is not the same as we are and must therefore be assessed by quite different criteria. If we are to overcome these difficulties, the first essential is to realise that the color of a man's skin provides no indication whatever as to his character, his outlook, and his inner qualification.[131]

In view of the many biased assessments which have been advanced in the past it is particularly necessary when dealing with India to remind ourselves that pride of race, arrogance, and the desire to keep at a distance from people who are different and are perhaps thought to be inferior are not the prerogative of Europeans and Americans alone. "In India even the better-class prostitutes avoided contact with the English lest they should be soiled by intimate association with them and so lose caste." [132] As late as 1925 Glasenapp, the late German Indologist, wrote: "thus, for example, on a modern caste list the English soldiers are placed just above the man-eaters and are said to be the descendants of a marriage between a *Turushka* [Turk] and a *Shudra*-woman [lowest Indian caste]." [133] In 1964 a group of African students in Madras found themselves in the news when they accused the Indians of practicing racialism; they complained bitterly that they were debarred from social contact with Indian students and Indian families because they were black. Several of these students who were unable to cope with their homesickness and their loneliness returned home shortly afterwards without having completed their studies. Finally, it should be remembered that the concept of caste designates an institution that was first introduced as a means of preserving racial purity and which has remained virtually unchanged to this day, especially in the higher castes. "Pride of race and nobility of birth have still a fascination for Indians." [134]

Considered in this light it is scarcely surprising that the Indians should be particularly sensitive to the insults, the disparagements, and even the ineptitude of the Rourkela Germans. But while the Germans often show a lack of consideration in this respect, the Indians often show a lack of objectivity when anticolonialists appeal to the dark instincts of racial hatred and disseminate the view that the attitude of the whites today is still exclusively determined by racial arrogance and that their apparent willingness to come to terms is simply a cover for the devious measures by which they intend to re-establish the old order of discrimination.[135]

Isolation in the ghetto

The following passage provides a comment on various conversations which were held with Indians both in the plant and in the trainees' hostels:

It has also been noted with bitterness that the majority of the fitters used the German Social Center in order to build for themselves a Little Germany to which no Indian would have access. Many Indians still believe to this day that it is not possible for them to become members [of the German Club]. The "German Club" is still reputed by not a few of the Indian engineers to serve as a locale for "drinking orgies." Above all else it is the excessive consumption of alcohol and the drunkenness [of the German fitters] which induces feelings of bitter scorn in the majority of Indians.[136]

These few sentences are in complete accord with remarks constantly being made by Indians in the course of general conversation in Rourkela; they not only fairly relate the difficulties facing the German Social Center (which had what was often the thankless double role of providing welfare for the German community and mediation for the Indian authorities), but they also reveal the essential problems underlying Indo-German relations.

The Germans' urge to build a "Little Germany" for themselves in Rourkela and then retire within its walls is easily explained and was certainly not motivated by a typically German desire "to seek isolation from the world" and "to build protective walls," which were the reasons given by an Italian for the self-imposed isolation of the Italian workers in the Federal Republic.[137] The examples already quoted, in which individual German fitters showed an outstanding capacity for adaptation when working on their own elsewhere in India but were conformist to a degree once they entered the mass community in Rourkela, prove that "the" German is not naturally given to seclusion. In fact, it is the numbers which make all the difference. The individual who is thrown back on his own resources has no other choice, if he wishes to satisfy his need for social intercourse, than to establish contact with the members of his temporary environment, whether they be Indians or Africans and regardless of the difficulties he may encounter due to the language barrier, personal dislikes, or the strange customs of an alien people. His need for social contact will be strong enough to overcome all such obstacles.

But once the individual German meets up with another German or group of Germans he is no longer obliged to go to such bother or to contend with such difficulties. Contact with his fellow Germans is so much easier, for there are no language problems, no strange customs, and no really major points of divergence. It is understandable, therefore, that he should neglect the more onerous contact with the foreign people in his environment in favor of his own countrymen, until eventually he finds himself living, together with them, in isolation from the environment. And of course the larger this minority becomes, the easier it is for its individual members to satisfy all their needs for social intercourse within its confines. Consequently, the growth of the minority is also a factor in persuading the individual German to refrain from cultivating more onerous contacts outside the minority group. Ultimately this development leads to a state of affairs that might well be described as a kind of "ghetto existence," and by analogy the "Little Germany" in Rourkela may be regarded as a form of ghetto.

We must repeat, however, that this is by no means a typically German phenomenon. But for Rourkela one might almost have assumed that it was primarily an American practice, for wherever large groups of Americans have appeared in the world they have tended to erect their "Little America" and to isolate themselves within it. This is a point which Lederer and Burdick have demonstrated and pilloried time and again in their book *The Ugly American*.[138] As a result of the negative experiences in a wide variety of developing countries, a number of authors have subjected the striking isolation of the American communities in those countries to detailed investigations.[139] In his novel *Fandango Rock*, John Masters has shown that this phenomenon is by no means restricted to the developing countries of Asia, Africa, and Latin America. On the contrary, a "Yankee Ghetto" has also been created on the continent of Europe, namely in Spain.[140] Experiences within the Federal Republic have been of a similar order—there is an American enclave in Kaiserslautern—and from this it follows that the racial question was by no means the only motivation underlying the attempt to build a "Little Germany" in Rourkela.

Indian sensitivity to the Germans' desire to isolate themselves stems largely from their colonial past. This was clearly implied by a comment in an Indian newspaper: "in fact they live rather like the British used to live before them." [141] Nothing can have a more harmful or lasting effect on the Indians than behavior that is reminiscent of the practices of the "hated oppressors" of colonial days. Countess Dönhoff has written: "The political struggle to win over the neutral powers is not like a game of soccer; it's not your achievements that count—not the number of goals you score—but the mistakes that you make." [142] Mehnert advanced a similar view when he said, "if it is true that the Asians' antiwhite feelings are not inherited but conditioned by the intensity and recentness of the colonial oppression to which they were subjected, then we might reasonably conjecture that antiwhite feelings will yield to the extent to which memories of colonial rule recede." [143] This seems all the more plausible if we consider just how much the English lived a life of their own and how clearly they gave the Indians to understand that in this life there could be no place for them save as "servants and merchants."

India became an unknown country to the English inhabitants of Calcutta and Madras, and what is unknown a natural conservatism will always condemn. So in 1827 "it was the extremity of bad taste to appear in anything of Indian manufacture—neither muslin, silk, flowers nor even ornaments however beautiful." The sentiment became general, which is still sometimes expressed, "How nice India would be if it wasn't for the Indians." [144]

From the descriptions given by Reinhard Raffalt in a recent radio program it is clear that conditions have not changed much since 1827: "Life is pleasant in Calcutta. In Calcutta? No, above Calcutta, half a meter above the ground, comfortable and completely isolated from the Indian soil, gently cushioned on the air so as not to put out roots, unrelated, civilized, sterile." [145] What seems quite incredible is the tolerance with which the Indians still allow those Englishmen who have stayed on to maintain their isolation in the form of an institutionalized exclusivism. It is only in recent years that Indians have begun to object—for example, in letters to the press—about the English swimming clubs in Bombay and Calcutta, where membership and entry is restricted to "whites." Up to now Indians have not even been admitted as guests.

Racial differences are undoubtedly one of the chief reasons why it is so difficult to overcome feelings of mutual strangeness. The well-meaning attempts being made today to ignore the very existence of the problem merely serve to obscure this very real issue. Nobody who has lived overseas for any length of time and had dealings with colored peoples can play down, let alone deny, the significance of racial differences.[146]

These daring words may well meet with a very mixed reception, but for large numbers of people of different races there is undoubtedly an element of truth in them. And at this point we must turn to consider the exclusivism of the German Club in Rourkela.

At the beginning of this chapter we spoke of the censure leveled at the Rourkela Germans by the Indians and referred to the difficult position of the German Social Center in this respect. In 1959, when the Indian newspapers asserted that the Germans in Rourkela had their own club, hospital, and swimming pool to which Indians were normally denied access, it must be admitted that they were printing the truth. The installations erected by the German Social Center were intended for the use of the German construction personnel; it had never occurred to the people back home in Germany who had first thought of providing these amenities or to those who had planned them that the Indians might feel offended. To have realized this in advance, they would have needed specialized knowledge of India and her peoples, and particularly of the links that still bind modern India to her colonial past. When the German hospital was completed and commissioned, a few Indians—usually senior employees who were friends or acquaintances of the German medical officers or of other leading German officials—would come from time to time for a medical consultation or for treatment. All such cases were treated privately and there was never any great trouble as a result. Nonetheless, the fact that the German doctors had no legal right to practice medicine within the Indian economy and, despite repeated applications, were never allowed to set up as "registered practitioners" meant that these consultations with Indian patients were a delicate matter. But thanks to a tacit "gentlemen's agreement" between all the parties concerned, including the Indian doctors in Rourkela, they always passed off smoothly. On one occasion, in February, 1959, when the German doctors diagnosed in the child of one of the senior Indian police officers a serious condition that could only be cured by a special operation that was available in the Federal Republic but not in India, both parents and child were flown to Hamburg, and the operation was successfully performed. In order to make this possible the German fitters organized a collection, the airline reduced its flight charges to a minimum, and the German surgeon in Hamburg refused to take a fee.

The German hospital in Rourkela practiced what might be called an "elastic exclusivism" and owed its success primarily to the fact that it was operated by a small number of discerning men. Just how important this factor was becomes quite clear if we consider that the treatment of Indian patients by the German medical officers became a bone of contention *only* on those occasions when the waiting rooms were full of German fitters who then saw an Indian either leaving or entering one of the consulting rooms. This certainly gave rise to a wave of resentment, which led to disapproving comments in the course of conversation and occasionally to an official complaint.

In addition to these private consultations the Indians employed by the GSC, about 200 in all, were also treated in the German hospital. Cooperation between German and Indian doctors was excellent and they freely consulted with one another to the benefit of both Indian and German patients. Even if we disregard the fact that the German hospital was completed before the Indian HSL hospital (250 beds) and was not joined with this in a single building, the elastic exclusivism practiced by the German hospital can scarcely be censured.

In the German Club matters were far less satisfactory. When the clubhouse was opened in 1958 and the first German swimming enthusiasts—who had long waited for this day—appeared at the swimming pool, they found two Indians in their midst. A number of the Germans asked what the Indians were doing there and whether this was not *their* club, which had been promised to them in their contracts as part of the welfare provided by their firms. After the questioners had first been appeased and assured that "of course" it was their club and that the matter would be cleared up as soon as possible, it was discovered that one of the German construction managements was employing two Indians, who had been sent to them by their parent firm in Germany with precisely the same contracts as those given to German fitters. From this it clearly followed that these two Indians were entitled to enjoy the social welfare provided by their firm and consequently to use the club amenities. And so it was. The Germans got used to the idea, although many of them made no secret of their resentment. The two Indians did not feel particularly at ease, but they nonetheless put in an occasional appearance. The situation was much the same for the Indian wives of German fitters. Officially they were club members from the very beginning, but they seldom, if ever, availed themselves of the club amenities: at most they would attend the evening cinema shows.

Any member wishing to invite an Indian guest had to obtain permission from the club management; this was a necessary measure, for it would have been undesirable if the Germans had brought their ayahs with them, a thing which actually happened on a number of occasions in the early days. But above all the club management could not and would not run the risk of having Indians in the club when the waves of alcoholic good cheer began to rise. Some Germans thought of inviting Indian acquaintances and some actually did invite them, but they soon lost all desire to do so because they could never be sure—especially in the evenings when the men were drinking—that their guests would not be insulted by one of the Rourkela Germans. Because of the large number of Germans working in Rourkela between 1958 and 1962 the club premises were often overcrowded and so it was seldom possible during that time to find a quiet corner where it would be possible to sit with Indian guests in relative seclusion.

In December, 1959, by which time the number of Germans had decreased to some extent, the German Social Center and some of the German superintendents began to take the first steps towards extending the club to include Indian members. But when the question was discussed with the men's representatives it met with an unfavorable reception and in the ensuing ballot it was firmly rejected. The personnel of a number of German firms threatened to walk out of the club in a body if Indians were admitted as members. They had four arguments: The club is not big enough for us anyway (an argument which had in fact been invalidated by those who advanced it, for it was they who had driven a large number of their fellow Germans from the club as a result of their bad behavior); we have to put up with these foreigners, whom we don't understand, all day long and so we want to spend our free time among ourselves; we want to be at liberty to behave in our club in the way that we enjoy and we don't want any foreigners watching us; the club has been built for us by our firms and back home in Germany strangers aren't allowed into a works' club, so why should they be here?

This attitude gradually softened, although it was not until 1960 that the first Indians, who had been hand-picked for their understanding and their Western attitudes, were made provisional members. By 1961 their numbers had swelled and by 1962 were so large that it was finally possible to transform the German Club into the "Indo-German Club Rourkela."

One important factor in this development was the changeover from construction to operation and maintenance personnel, which completely transformed the make-up of the German colony. In the first place the operation personnel were much less of a homogeneous group, and because the "inner contact" among the group members was considerably weaker, their we-feelings and, consequently, their tendency to reject the out-group were also weaker. Also, the majority of the operation personnel were presented with the Indo-German Club as a *fait accompli,* which meant that, since they had never known it in its original all-German form, they had less reason for opposing the change. If this had been realized in 1957 and 1958, it is probable that the development of the club would have proceeded along entirely different lines. When the club was opened in 1958, it is most unlikely that it would even have occurred to the Rourkela Germans to protest against Indian membership if, during the preceeding twelve months in which the club was being planned, designed, and built, it had been clearly stated that it was envisaged for the use of both nationalities.

Even during the period when a "tough line" was being pursued by the German fitters concerning the use of the club, attempts were made both in and through the club to cultivate relations with the Indians in Rourkela by arranging special events for both Indian and Indo-German groups; these soon came to be accepted even by the anti-Indian elements among the Rourkela Germans and were gladly patronized by large numbers of the Indians themselves. Sometimes it even proved possible to persuade the German "troublemakers" to join in the preparations for these festive occasions. For weeks on end men would be hard at work, sawing, constructing, painting, and getting things ready for the annual *Oktoberfest.* When these troublemakers saw that several hundred Indian guests and colleagues took pleasure in the festival, then they too appeared to be well pleased. The various collections which were organized in Rourkela show that the German construction personnel had every sympathy for Indians in need: they contributed over $3,000 for the young Indian child who was flown to Germany for an operation, and they provided similar amounts on a number of occasions for flood victims in Orissa.

Despite the difficult situation obtaining in those early years, then, it still proved possible to use the club as a means of improving Indo-German relations in Rourkela; from this it is quite evident that the problem cannot be reduced to the simple formula: the Rourkela Germans are so anti-Indian that, apart from the absolutely essential contacts in the plant, they simply do not want to have anything to do with the Indians.

Frustration and Aggression

After a short visit to Rourkela the Swiss publicist Peter Schmid wrote:

"If you show a thing to the Indians five times, then leave them to it, they'll still do it wrong the sixth time." This pious ejaculation has become something of a *Leitmotiv* in Rourkela. "And when they have finally got the hang of it and you try to teach them something new, then in no time at all they will have forgotten the old skill." In a word: "It will take generations before they are able to operate a steel plant." This contemptuous assessment is so unabashed, so outspoken, that it could not possibly remain concealed from the Indians for long. And the Indians are a proud and sensitive people. If they feel offended, they do not easily show it; but they are offended nonetheless. This state of affairs has led to a curious hardening of attitudes in Rourkela: the Indians meet the Germans' bitterness and irritation with provocative defiance. They do not like one another and they make no attempt to conceal the fact. In his impotence the Indian reacts to insults with a smile. But in his heart he is intent on sabotage. When I saw the [Indian] workers in Rourkela talking to the German foremen, there was something in their look which I did not like. The German, who senses this hostility, studiously disregards the Indian and, if he becomes insistent, treats him as if he were a nonentity—or some troublesome insect. What this comes down to in practical work-a-day terms is: Go to the devil, I can do it better myself.[147]

Just how much of this report is true and how much was invented by its author is not a matter which we wish to enter into; whether it is possible to speak of German contempt or whether the Indians respond with defiance is not our immediate concern. But if we disregard its inaccuracies and false interpretations, the underlying mood presented in this report corresponds more or less to the atmosphere in Rourkela during the construction period. But how was this atmosphere created? We have already considered a number of motivations. We now propose to approach the question from a different point of view. In various of the preceding sections we have dealt with the fact that the German abroad tends to develop a number of qualities that prejudice his ability to live and work with indigenous peoples. We have dealt in some detail with the difficulties arising out of the close communal life led by the Rourkela Germans, which also had a harmful effect on their corporate attitude to the Indians. In what follows we shall be trying to find an explanation for these attitudes and reactions, which were to be observed in the behavior patterns of *individual* Germans to the Indians (and vice versa) and which exceeded what might be regarded as a normal measure of indifference or even rejection, since the explanation already provided within the context of German and Indian attitudes, both individual and group, does not cover all cases.

Workers, Leonhard considers, are not slow to criticize. "When the German worker is dissatisfied he blames the management, then he curses bureaucratic red tape and finally the government." [148] Hermann Eich says the same thing but goes one step further: "The need to compensate for having to lick one man's boots by insulting some other man is one of the gravest of German characteristics." [149] An American observer has presented a similar view: "There is plenty of evidence that the meek, submissive German can, when frustrated, become insufferably arrogant. The patient, phlegmatic subject can, when thwarted, suddenly become emotionally violent." [150]

Various attempts have been made to explain the Indians' patterns of behavior, most of which derive from their sudden confrontation with industrialization and its accompanying effects, of which the most important has been the change brought about in their whole system of values. The following quotation from Mitscherlich provides a synopsis of these views:

The severance from traditional patterns of life and the assumption of new techniques with no knowledge of the historical background against which they have developed must activate primary fear. The less the old patterns of behavior are able to afford security, the stronger the regressive tendencies and the eruption of the primitive instinctual manifestations contained within them, especially those of an aggressive type.[151]

Fromm formulates the same conception of the disintegration of old patterns of behavior but in stronger terms: It is only

for as long as the external conditions of a society remain stable that the social character continues to exercise a primarily unifying function. When external conditions change in such a way that they no longer correspond to the traditional social character, then a "rupture" takes place, as a result of which the social character is often transformed from an element promoting preservation to an element promoting disintegration, from "social mortar" into dynamite.[152]

These quotations represent an arbitrary selection from a whole series of views that have been presented in sociological literature on the question which interests us here, namely, how is it that the individual Germans and Indians came to adopt their "hostile" patterns of behavior. The authors in question are all agreed on one point: certain needs have failed to find gratification and this has given rise to affective reactions.

Although in actual fact people seek gratification of a large number of needs, these have been reduced by certain authors to a few basic needs or desires. Fromm speaks of happiness, harmony, love, and freedom in this connection and claims that they are immanent in man.[153] From extensive experience with the workers in his factories the Hamburg industrialist Kurt Körber stipulates five basic needs whose gratification is essential to the working man—security, recognition, justice, freedom, and information.[154] Wiese maintains that "people strive for the fulfillment of four principal desires: security, response, recognition, and new experiences." [155]

But however we may choose to categorize existent or conceivable human needs, what is quite certain is that in Rourkela, in the case of Indians and Germans alike, a number of quite specific needs were either not satisfied at all or only to an inadequate extent. For example, the need for internal and external security was certainly not satisfied: with the growth of industrialization and its requirements the Indians lost the security previously afforded by their traditional social systems (castes, multitiered families), while the Germans in Rourkela felt themselves threatened by tropical illnesses, by the strangeness of an exotic land, by the political significance attributed to their work (which they found quite incomprehensible), and last but not least by the bloody riots of militant religious or regional groups.

The same was true of the need for recognition. It was not long before the Rourkela Germans discovered that, contrary to their expectations, the Indians did not receive them with open arms and with a genuine desire for collaboration and that they were in fact obliged to "help the Indians against their will"; for their part the Indians not only saw themselves subjected to constant criticism but also interpreted the Germans' attempts at guidance and instruction in the light of criticism because of the unfortunate way in which these were handled. Indian engineers who often had a better theoretical knowledge of engineering than the Germans with whom they worked were given no credit for this and were required to carry out dirty manual tasks; the Germans paid no tribute to the cultural values and skills which India was able to offer in such abundance.

The need for justice also received scant satisfaction, for when disputes between Indians and Germans had to be settled the German authorities were always at pains to exonerate the Indian, while the Indian authorities were also frequently courteous and accommodating enough to decide in favor of the German, irrespective of the evidence. The fact that Germans were charged by the Indian police only in the most extreme cases and even then were let off with minimal fines (drunken driving resulting in severe physical injury had a fine of approximately 40 dollars) must also have appeared unjust to the Indians. And then the German community felt that it was unjustly treated by the press, and the Indians complained because the Germans received far higher wages.

Not even the need for freedom was fully satisfied; the anti-ayah measures, the consistent supervision of their behavior even in off-duty hours, the fact that Rourkela was so isolated because of poor communications and the lack of transport in Rourkela itself—all these things were regarded by the Rourkela Germans as restrictions of their personal liberty. The Indians' freedom was also restricted to an every increasing extent as a result of the technology introduced by the Germans: discipline and punctuality were suddenly demanded of them, they were allowed to leave the construction site only for stipulated leave periods, and they had to come to work regardless of the weather, the harvest, or other "important" matters.

For the Germans the need for information was certainly not satisfied. Air mail rates for newspapers were too expensive, surface deliveries took several weeks, most Germans did not understand the Indian newspapers or the Indian radio programs, the German short wave could only be heard by the few who had powerful receivers, there was no television; consequently the Rourkela Germans were largely reduced to gossip and rumor. And finally the need for response, in so far as this was meant to be mutual, also failed to achieve gratification either on the Indian or on the German side: the Germans did not receive the sympathy which they had expected from the Indians, while the Indians were disappointed to find that the Germans were not all ardent admirers of Indian culture.

The condition induced by the nonsatisfaction of basic needs is called frustration. An American dictionary of sociology defines frustration as "emotional tension produced by failure to attain a desired goal or to terminate an act successfully." [156] Mitscherlich states: "Frustration is unwilling renunciation; this not only rouses fear but also frees aggression with which to counter this condition." He also says that "enforced renunciation breeds contempt." [157] König speaks of the "pattern of frustration and aggression" in this connection.[158] Frustration does not have to produce aggression; there are a number of feasible reactions to frustrating experiences, but one of these reactions is aggression. A further important point to be noted here is that when a Rourkela German feels frustrated because one of his needs has not been gratified, and when he is subsequently aggressive to an Indian, it does not follow that his aggressive feelings were prompted by an Indian (or group of Indians). A German may experience frustration-engendering conflicts that have nothing whatsoever to do with any Indians, and he may then try to abreact these conflicts in the form of aggression towards an Indian (or group of Indians). "Since the inner conflict was not mastered . . . the aggressiveness, which was induced by frustration, does not take the form of self-chastisement but of extrapunitivity. Extrapunitivity denotes an attempt [on the part of the individual] to punish others for his own moral inadequacy." [159] Or to put it in another way: "Minority groups really are used as 'lightning conductors' for the frustrations felt by the majority for quite different reasons. . . . Their own failure, their inability to overcome misfortune, their hurt pride produce aggression towards the scapegoat." [160] Thus aggression may take the form of "diffuse aggressiveness" [161] such as that displayed by the Rourkela Germans in their hostility toward a delegate from the German Federal Parliament in the German Club.

The hostile behavior demonstrated in Rourkela, then, by Germans toward Indians, by Indians toward Germans, and by Germans toward one another did not necessarily derive from actual conflicts of interests or group conflicts alone, but may also have been due to a combination of individual conflicts with the "pattern of frustration and aggression."

4/ IMPLICATIONS OF ROURKELA

What have we learned from this long hard look at the Rourkela Germans? What conclusions may we draw from it for the future, for similar undertakings in other places? What lessons are to be gleaned from the behavior patterns of the German personnel for other projects on the part of German industry or within the framework of the German Federal Republic's aid program or even of the technical assistance projects of the Western world in general? Must we assume from the evidence of Rourkela that Germans are less suitable for assignments in developing countries than the members of other industrial nations? Or was it merely the size of the Rourkela project, combined with the general shortage of labor in the Federal Republic, which gave rise to the problems within the sphere of human relations that have been described in this book? Was it due to lack of foresight and planning on the part of the industrial firms or to their lack of any real sense of responsibility that the human side of the Rourkela project was less successful than it might have been? Was the German government at fault in failing to recognize at an early stage that the construction of the Rourkela steel plant would burst the bounds of a private enterprise project and assume political significance? Or is it simply that, despite the great technical achievements and the tremendous work output of the German personnel in Rourkela, which deserve the highest praise, it is asking too much to expect them and their families to behave in any other way or to develop a more positive attitude to a foreign land and its people?

These are difficult questions, but they are also important questions. To some extent they have already been answered in the course of the preceding chapters, but we shall now be enlarging on these answers in an attempt to show how such large-scale projects can be handled better in the future.

Preliminary Discussions in Germany

We have already indicated in earlier chapters that many decisions that come to have important repercussions on the behavior patterns of the German technicians and their families in the construction town are made during the preliminary discussions, when the contracts are being negotiated. Usually these discussions are concerned primarily with technical, legal, and business matters, but it would be extremely desirable for other factors to be considered at this initial stage as well. Easier working conditions, better living conditions, and better working relations between German and indigenous personnel are all crucial matters, as has been amply demonstrated in the course of this book.

Whether or to what extent it is justifiable or even feasible for such questions to be dealt with in the preliminary discussions is an issue which cannot be analyzed in detail within the framework of this present study. At the same time, however, we would recommend to those concerned that it might well be worth while to consider whether proposals which appear to be uneconomical from a strictly financial point of view might not in fact pay a handsome dividend in the long run if they helped create a better working atmosphere, thus contributing to more harmonious relations between the men actually engaged on the construction site and consequently to a more favorable assessment of the whole project by the international community.

Any recommendations which make for easier and unambiguous working conditions on the site are important and must, if possible, be dealt with in the preliminary discussions. Should the visiting technicians have authority over their indigenous counterparts and subordinates, and if so, what kind of authority? How could such powers be implemented or enforced? These are the kinds of questions which, as we have seen, could and should be clarified beyond all possible doubt *before* the technicians actually arrive on the construction site.

If collaboration between foreign and native workers is to be mutually satisfactory and if the indigenous peoples are to profit from it, then the terms of contract for the technicians must allow them an adequate amount of time in which to train the indigenous personnel. In Rourkela this was not the case; the Germans were under constant pressure to meet tight construction schedules, and when one phase of the work was completed they had to rush straight on with the next.

A rational approach to the preparation of a construction site would not be restricted to technical and administrative matters alone but would also consider questions impinging on the life of the workers. The whole complex issue of accommodations for the technicians and their families would need to be worked out in adequate terms. This is not simply a matter of providing suitable and properly appointed houses which would be pleasant to live in. What is needed here is for a really effective housing policy to be evolved in detail. One point that should certainly be dealt with in the preliminary discussions is how to prevent a situation in which large numbers of construction workers are concentrated in a single complex and thus isolated from the local population. Meaningful coexistence between foreign and indigenous peoples should be the aim. Whether this can be achieved, and if so, how it can be achieved, are matters that should really be considered at the planning stage.

The question of supplies for the visitors should not only be discussed with the representatives of the host country but should also be thoroughly investigated and checked by their own officials on the spot. Experience has shown that where large numbers of Western development workers are concentrated on an overseas site, the demand for certain articles such as modern water closets, air conditioners, hygienic installations, special kinds of food, tends to assume massive proportions; no matter how good their intentions may be, this is a matter which the representatives of the host country simply are not able to assess because their whole outlook is geared to different criteria.

The idea of isolation raises the further important problem as to the availability or procurability of personal transport. In this respect it is certainly preferable to advise Western people who intend to live in a construction town to take with them, or to acquire upon arrival, either bicycles or scooters, rather than to let them labor under the delusion of grandeur—presumably a relic of the colonial era—which prescribes motor cars as the only means of transport "in keeping with their rank" in a developing country.

It goes without saying that the personal safety of the construction personnel must be adequately ensured and this problem should be worked out in detail in the course of the preliminary discussions.

Another matter of paramount importance at this early stage is that raised by the individual contracts issued to the technicians prior to departure. In the close-knit communal life of a construction site settlement, as described in the earlier chapters of this book, it is quite impossible for the individual workers to keep their contract conditions secret. In Rourkela, certainly, a number of these conditions frequently became the main topic of conversation. Discrepancies between the conditions of employment stipulated by different firms were felt—especially by the fitters—to constitute an injustice and so gave rise to discontent and discord, which had a harmful effect on both living and working conditions within the community. It would therefore be highly desirable for the responsible departments (or firms) to get together on this question and standardize their terms of contract. The most important thing of all in this connection is for the daily allowances paid out on the construction site to be leveled to a fixed norm. This is imperative and could be quite easily done; any readjustment that might seem desirable could be effected by raising or lowering the wages or salaries paid out in the home country. Understandably enough, it is these daily allowances that are most frequently discussed on the site, whereas the salaries paid out at home are rarely mentioned. But insurance and maintenance and such matters are also popular themes and should also be adjusted to a fixed norm. The departments responsible for sending personnel overseas could also help them to acquire a greater personal interest in the indigenous peoples and their country by inserting a clause in their contracts to the effect that part of their leave—or, alternatively, an additional local leave—should be spent in the host country.

A further clause that seems to be extremely important is that requiring all personnel to respect the local proprieties and customs and to behave in such a way as to enhance the reputation of their country abroad. But this is not enough in itself. This "disciplinary clause" should also give full powers to the representatives of the construction firms on the site to threaten with, or actually to impose, sanctions on any employee who behaves in an objectionable manner and, if necessary, to send him home under instant dismissal and at his own expense. In view of the high wages normally paid on overseas sites this harsh measure appears fully justified.

Suitability and Selection

We have already shown in some detail how difficult it is to make universally valid pronouncements on the question of the suitability and selection of technicians for overseas construction sites. But there is one overriding consideration, which certainly bears repetition: even for a technician *temperamental* suitability may well be more important as a precondition of successful collaboration in a developing country than the possession of outstanding technical abilities. However, it is quite evident from the case of Rourkela that, given the conditions obtaining in the labor market within the German Federal Republic today, the feasibility of applying stringent criteria to determine suitability and selection must depend to some extent on the size of the particular overseas project.

To recapitulate on a number of the points learned from the Rourkela undertaking: it is absolutely essential that every worker and every member of a family going overseas produce a certificate of fitness for tropical duties. Construction personnel should also be allowed to take their families with them wherever possible, even if this should create temporary problems of accommodation or finance.

Knowledge of languages must also be regarded as an important factor when it comes to selecting personnel. Authors of recent sociological works dealing with the subject of development aid seem to be entirely agreed as to the linguistic shortcomings of the great majority of development workers and have considered various possible ways of improving this situation. At a session of the German Foundation for the Developing Countries in 1962 it was said to be quite evident from conversations with the representatives of the younger African states that foreign technicians are able to exert a very considerable politico-psychological influence on the indigenous peoples with whom they work, if they are able to intersperse just a few polite phrases from the local language in the course of conversation.[1] Drascher has confirmed this finding from his own experiences in the developing countries, where, he says, the tone of the conversation becomes very much warmer when the visitor has even a moderate command of the local language: from being a stranger he becomes "a welcome guest, for his knowledge of the other language is [taken as] a token of respect, which establishes a relaxed mood from the outset."[2] Alsdorf, a Hamburg Indologist, also insists on the urgent need for language training. He points out, however, that in view of the great urgency of this problem it would be impracticable to think in terms of a full language course in the academic sense and suggests that all desire for perfection must yield to the great need for partial knowledge. "The chief emphasis must be laid on high-speed courses, which would impart a basic knowledge of a given language. Within a short period of time (between two and six weeks) quite considerable progress can be made."[3] And with this the language problem enters a sphere which follows quite logically from that of suitability and selection: the preparation of technicians for their assignment in a developing country.

Preparation

The representative of a Swiss firm underlined the importance for foreign technicians of a knowledge of local languages, when he said: "I know from personal experience that the Russian and to some extent the Czech and the Chinese representatives have an advantage over us in this respect, but we can't force our people, we can't order them to learn Chinese [or any other language] within the year. In Moscow that can be done, but in Berne, I am happy to say, it cannot." [4]

Nonetheless, some means should be found of giving the technicians the sort of language training envisaged by Alsdorf before they set off on their assignment. This seems all the more desirable and all the more feasible since preparation, if it is to be successful, cannot possibly be encompassed by a seven- or ten-day course prior to departure but—as we shall come to see—must be continued and sustained by subsequent instruction during the assignment. Whether such language training should be designed to furnish a sound working knowledge of one of the major foreign languages (French, English, Spanish) or whether it should be restricted to the provision of a basic vocabulary of some 50 to 200 phrases either in one of these languages or in some other language spoken in the host country would have to be decided on a purely individual basis. The experience gained in Rourkela indicates that it may be desirable for any regular language course to be framed with a view to the specific requirements of the construction site. When the student notices from one lesson to the next that he is better able to converse both on the site and off—for example, when he goes shopping—when he sees that he is making tangible progress, this will urge him on to greater efforts.

All departments intending to send personnel overseas should think very carefully about their preparation and should lay their plans well in advance, unless—and this is undoubtedly the better course—they decide to entrust the whole operation to one of the various institutions that already have considerable experience and a great deal of specialized knowledge in this field (such as, in Germany, the German Foundation for the Developing Countries in Bonn, Haus Rissen in Hamburg, the Institute for Foreign Relations in Stuttgart, church foundations in all parts of the Federal Republic, universities, and so forth). The planning of preparatory courses calls for precise knowledge of the conditions to be expected at the site, for part of the purpose of such preparation is to reduce the severity of the shock that the newcomer may quite conceivably feel upon being confronted with so many strange and new experiences. This will only be achieved if the person concerned is adequately prepared and supplied with precise, relevant, and detailed information.

By now the firms responsible for sending personnel overseas should at last be realizing just how important such preparatory courses are. Moreover, the two groups that have been virtually excluded from such courses in the past should certainly be admitted to them now: the wives and the senior officials. We have already dealt with the special significance attributed to the behavior of the German wives. As for the superintendents and other senior officials, it goes without saying that they should be better informed about the conditions and problems of the developing country than anybody else, since they must be in a position to advise and enlighten their men if the need should arise. But, however obvious such facts may appear to be, a number of the German firms sending personnel overseas have so far failed to recognize them or to act upon them. Only a small portion of the Germans who have gone out to Rourkela were advised to attend a preparatory course. The numbers attending the courses run by the German Federation especially for Rourkela Germans have been very low indeed and constitute no more than a small fraction of those working in Rourkela during the relevant periods:

Year	No. attending courses
1961	24
1962	27
1963	93
1964 (first 6 months)	12

IMPLICATIONS OF ROURKELA

In December, 1963, a few months after they had arrived in Rourkela, thirty-five members of the operation personnel were asked if they considered that their preparatory courses had been of value. The results were encouraging. All of those interviewed spoke well of the courses and said that they had been greatly helped in a number of situations by the knowledge they had gained. A point which came in for special mention was the "shock" set up by their initial impression of the misery and poverty in Calcutta. Although this had not been entirely eliminated by the objective description of Calcutta provided during the course, the men felt that it had been greatly ameliorated. All were agreed that the German wives should also be invited to attend the courses and that the curriculum should, if possible, be adjusted to meet the practical needs of life in Rourkela, including the problems of coexistence with Indians, of work relationships, of personal conduct, and so forth.

But the preparatory courses should not be restricted to such questions alone. In addition to acquiring a knowledge of local languages and conditions, the technicians should also be given some idea of the problems of development aid and of the special part played within this sphere by the process of "decolonialization" and any other political issues of current concern. The information supplied to men preparing for an assignment in a developing country cannot be too realistic. As part of their education they should certainly be advised of the unfortunate and widespread tendency within the Federal Republic—and doubtless elsewhere—to link development aid and international good will with overseas business considerations and the insistence on a common political outlook; they should also be disabused of the spurious conception of development aid as an "act of love" which is extended only to "friends." It is unfair to German or any other technicians to allow them to set off for a developing country with the idea that they will be welcomed with open arms and that their help will be gladly accepted. It would be far more to the point if they were told quite openly of the kind of assessments that have been formed by foreigners, such as, for example, the statement made by the Indian

Ambassador Tyjabi upon his departure from Bonn in 1961, in which "the" Germans were described as "inert, egocentric, irresponsible, and unwilling to really help against want in the world." [5] In a real preparatory course the worker should also be asked about his own personal attitude to the problems of the developing countries and what he is prepared to contribute over and above the work for which he is being paid so handsomely. Germans in general are accused—not without some justification—of failing to show any real involvement with the misery and the problems of these countries. The comment made by Carl Weiss with regard to Indonesia is applicable to both individual and corporate German attitudes: "The Federal Republic appears as a trading nation, as a warehouse, richly furnished with consumer goods, keeping to delivery dates, giving value for money, dealing fairly with her customers, but above all in search of profits. There are many who think that in the long run this will not be to our advantage." [6] The same could probably be said of many highly industrialized nations.

It is also advisable to deal realistically with the people in the developing countries. For example, we should be thinking about how to inform the technicians in the host country of any idiosyncrasies in the attitude to work or the habitual way of life of their Western counterparts. If we were able to do this, a considerable number of misunderstandings would be greatly alleviated and unpleasant surprises might well be avoided. The kind of stereotype thinking that was described earlier is to be found on both sides. The question as to whether it is possible to influence or eliminate such "character images" of ethnic groups, once they have taken root, by supplying fresh information, by attempting to correct false impressions, and by providing general enlightenment has been assessed very differently by sociological writers, although the majority have tended to adopt a negative rather than a positive attitude. According to E. and R. Hartley:

Man tends simply to disregard everything that does not fit in with his emotional pattern; contrariwise he lays stress on everything which conforms to this pattern and supports it. If one tries to draw people's attention to facts that demonstrate the falsity of their emotionally-based views, one runs the risk of being soundly rebuffed and perhaps even abused or, alternatively, one's arguments are rejected as meaningless. In our society this frequently happens when, for example, one counters strong ethnic prejudices with factual arguments. This merely serves to strengthen the original emotional bias.

Gehlen also refers to these problems.[7]

On the other hand, however, there are many powerful advocates of the view that these irrational stereotypes can in fact be influenced to some extent by means of rational enlightenment. But, owing to their rigidity, their universality, and their relative intangibility, preventive measures are likely to prove more successful than any attempts to tackle existent stereotypes as such. In this connection an interesting and most welcome experiment has been reported from England, where a number of Nigerians, who were selected for their intelligence and general suitability, have been employed as teachers both in all-white and multiracial schools in an attempt to counteract racial prejudices or misguided opinions either by preventing them from arising in the first place or by nipping them in the bud when they do.[8]

In general we may say that information, enlightenment, and anything which helps to promote understanding and knowledge of the foreign (ethnic) group works against the stereotypes and that the earlier the anitdote is applied the more effective it will be. All relevant information is of value in this respect: school lessons, further education classes, and above all the special courses designed to furnish technicians bound for overseas with background knowledge of the developing countries in which they will be working.

In our analysis of the behavior patterns of the Rourkela Germans we isolated three particularly painful factors which influenced adaptation. First there was the initial encounter with the misery of Indian living conditions immediately upon arrival in Calcutta, then the difficulty of fitting in with the daily routine in Rourkela, and finally the meeting between the newcomer with his new ideas and his good resolutions and the "old hands." If these three obstacles to successful adaptation are to be overcome more readily, and subsequent patterns of behavior improved, then the preparation given to the personnel for their assignment in Rourkela prior to their departure must be regarded as no more than an introductory phase, which would then be followed up by the provision of welfare and advice upon their arrival both in Calcutta and in Rourkela and of active guidance in their encounter with the experienced workers on the site. In other words, the preparation of personnel for a site the size of Rourkela can only really succeed if it is subsequently backed up by the resources of welfare and advisory services on the site, which must therefore be set up for the technicians and their families with all possible speed.

Welfare

Although the German Social Center, which was responsible for the cultural, social, and medical welfare of the whole of the German community in Rourkela, admirably illustrates both the importance and the great complexity of this kind of institution, it also reveals its weaknesses and dangers.

The first point that must be clarified in respect of the welfare services provided for foreign workers in a developing country is whether and to what extent their amenities can be extended to the indigenous population. Sooner or later the welfare workers are bound to run up against considerable difficulties. Although some of these will be of a purely practical nature, such as the provision of services and goods for the Western workers, the majority will be brought about as a direct result of the workers' isolation from the indigenous population and from the local environment. The central core of all such welfare work should be carried out by highly qualified and experienced social workers. They should have ultimate control of all departments. At the same time, however, the members of the community—especially if it is a big one—must also be encouraged to do things for themselves. The need for this was made very clear in Rourkela. We have already seen that it is useless to expect the members of a German group to "keep one another in check" and that the influence brought to bear on the entrenched mores of the community by well-intentioned newcomers is for the most part ineffectual.

However, Hans Paul Bahrdt has indicated one way in which a large group might be influenced from within, that is, by the actions of individual members of the group. Although this idea was developed with a view to improving the general welfare and the sense of civic pride and responsibility of city dwellers, it is also applicable to overseas construction sites, since the problems involved are analogous. Bahrdt insisted that the upper strata of society must concern themselves more with civic affairs, that is, "the doctors, the teachers, the political economists, the engineers and the socially critical intellectuals, who could all gain access [to the community] from their own specialized spheres, if they took the trouble." [9] In Rourkela the plain fact of the matter was that the "upper strata" —the superintendents, the engineers, the priests, teachers, doctors, and administrative officers—seldom spent an evening in the one place where they could have "gained access" to the large group of the German fitters, namely in the German Club. Their dealings— and often enough, no doubt, their annoyance—with the men in the course of their day's work had been quite enough for them; and of course they also knew that the atmosphere in the club was vulgar and disagreeable. Why expose themselves to it? But what they may well have overlooked is that by their absence they were in fact deepening the gulf which already separated them from the men and were making it all the more difficult for themselves to bring any effective influence to bear. This is likely to prove a particularly important factor on future projects.

In his community study König describes this vicious circle, which has been aptly called the "self-fulfilling prophecy": "Under the pressure of the inferior assessment placed on them from 'above' the members of the lower class react with coarseness and aggression, which is taken by those 'above' as proof of the validity of their original assessment." [10] And yet the influence and guidance of the "upper strata," their participation in the life of the community, would seem to offer the only viable solution. On future projects the superintendents, engineers, teachers, priests, and doctors must all be urged, or, better still, required, to afford consistent support to the full-time social workers in order to ensure the well-being of the entire community, which means of course that under their terms of contract they would have to be given both the time and the facilities for doing so. But the community will only accept such guidance if it is pursued consistently. The occasional attempts made in Rourkela by individual superintendents (acting in their capacity as head of their department and relying on the sense of discipline of the members of their own firm) to control the behavior of a whole group (composed of men from a number of different firms) by asking one of their own men to use his influence with his colleagues frequently proved abortive. Even if the superintendent approached his "best man" and even if the man was extremely popular with his workmates, the degree of influence that he was able to exert in such situations was very slight. Mitscherlich has explained the mechanism underlying such cases:

The threat of losing contact with the group is a terrifying experience; it releases feelings of panic and forces the individual to exert himself in every conceivable way to re-establish conformity; simply to acquire rational control over the situation would not suffice, for this kind of rational outlook would only strengthen the conflict within the individual whose patterns of behavior are not approved by the others. Voluntary isolation from the group, . . . or at least abstention from its affective stimulations, would appear to be one of the most difficult of all aspects of ego control. If we recall the medieval practice of banishment, it is clear that what threatens the individual who loses his membership of the group is death.[11]

But if the forces available within the community for the structuring of communal life are to be utilized to the full, then enlisting the services of the senior personnel is clearly no more than the first step. Over and above this the full-time welfare workers and their assistants must somehow contrive to open up new sources of help by mobilizing positive, democratic forces from within the group. There is surely no reason why effective supervisory and organizational committees should not be recruited from the ranks of the community to deal with a number of the tasks arising within the general sphere of welfare, internal administration, discipline, leisure structuring, and so forth. The interests and requirements of such committees would have to be coordinated with the interests and requirements of the site managements and of the welfare departments; and this in turn would call for a reappraisal of the over-all situation whenever conditions on the site changed. Events in Rourkela have shown that unless there is effective coordination, such committees do not always function satisfactorily and do not last very long. The principal reasons for this are the lack of continuity resulting from the constant changes of personnel, the heavy demands made both by the nature of the work and by the variations of climate, inadequate knowledge of the land and its peoples, and other factors. Nor should we overlook the fact that the workers on an overseas construction site are certainly not a representative cross section of the population of their native land.

A further important aspect of welfare work within a Western community on a construction site in a developing country is the direct or indirect effect which it has on the indigenous population. For example, anybody who arranges for European or American films to be shown on such a site must bear in mind that these films are bound to create an impression—either positive or negative—on those local people who see them. Similar considerations are called for when the construction of a national school is mooted. Even if the project is regarded simply as an educational expedient to cater to the temporary needs of the children of the construction workers, the question of whether it would not be preferable to build a multiracial school, which would provide a meeting place for Western and indigenous children, should certainly be explored, since this would not only counteract any tendency towards isolation on the part of the Western families, but would also bring an important cultural influence to bear on the indigenous population. In certain cases it might well prove even more advantageous to integrate Western children into an already existing local school.

Public Relations

We do not intend to enter into a full-scale discussion of the extremely complex issue of public relations, which is of such vital importance for the work now going on in the developing countries. It is of course perfectly true that the provision of information about the developing countries in the industrialized nations and about the industrialized nations in the developing countries forms an integral part of public relations work and as such has an indirect bearing on the questions and proposals advanced in the course of this book. But the specific issues raised by the actual development project is of more immediate interest to us. The public relations work undertaken by the German authorities in connection with the Rourkela project began far too late and was initially on far too small a scale. We have already pointed out, with reference to Bhilai and Durgapur, that the public relations work for such projects must begin before the construction work has even started —in other words, *before* the first foreign technicians have arrived on the site.

Happily enough it is no longer necessary to regard the Soviet Russians and the English as pre-eminent in this sphere. During the later stages of the construction period in Rourkela, by which time a number of the German firms engaged on the project had become concerned about the bad reputation of the Indo-German enterprise, the public relations work, both in India and in the Federal Republic, was tackled far more energetically and professionally and has been quite exemplary ever since. Both in terms of organization and method it sets an example that may be safely followed for future projects of this order. The most important single issue for the planner, then, is to give early consideration to all aspects of the undertaking, including public relations, and so ensure a rational system of work and the correct deployment of all available resources.

Will this prove possible on future projects in developing countries?

APPENDIX

Songs Composed and Sung by the German Fitters in Rourkela

1. One of these days it will all be forgotten

One of these days it will all be forgotten:
One of these days the turbines will roar
And we won't be needed any more;
One of these days they will never know
That this was all jungle years ago.

One of these days it will all be forgotten:
The beat of the drums in the jungle night
And the jackal's cry in the bright moonlight;
Rourkela town will be so smart,
With a barber's shop and a mini-mart.

One of these days it will all be forgotten:
Missing buttons, trouble with *dhobis*,*
Genuine miniature Christmas trees;
Power cut off and taps run dry,
The cost of living shooting sky-high.

One of these days we will all go home:
We'll take our fill of television,
Enjoy our German civilization,
Look at the pictures in our apartment,
And think of India, "land of enchantment."

* Members of a low Indian caste employed as washermen.—TRANSLATOR.

2. Oh sahib, please *bakshish*

As a simple German fitter
With a picture in my mind
Of a land of milk and honey
I left Germany behind.
But when my Skymaster touched down
In old Calcutta Town
I knew at once that this fair land
Would damn soon get me down.
Oh sahib, please *bakshish*,*
Oh sahib, no mama, no papa.

We piled into a taxi
To get to our hotel,
The driver drove at a rare old pace
But he didn't drive too well.
When something thumped against the car
And we sat there all agog
That Indian just turned round and said:
"No matter, only a dog!"
Oh sahib. . . .

The following day we wandered out
And had a look around;
The men, the women, the holy cows
Were stretched out on the ground,
A smell of car and animal
Was clinging in the air;
Calcutta dear, a town like you
I've not seen anywhere.
Oh sahib. . . .

From Calcutta up to Rourkela
It's twelve hours on the grid.
I never thought we'd make it
But in the end we did.
And when we left the train at last
We'd not got very far

---

* Gift of money for favor or reward; tip; alms.—Translator.

APPENDIX

When they started up their bakshish wail
"No mama," "no papa."
Oh sahib. . . .

So then we saw old Rourkela
And it wasn't hard to tell
The people in that shanty town
Weren't doing all that well.
The pick-up came, we all climbed in
And drove about a mile
To be welcomed by the management
In truly regal style.
Oh sahib. . . .

The welfare people talked to us,
The superindendents too,
They told us all the things we could
And all we couldn't do.
The big boss came along as well
To sing his little song:
"Those men who keep an ayah here
Do not stay healthy long."
Oh sahib. . . .

It took some time, but in the end
We got our bungalow
And a half-share in a *mali* *
Just to make the flowers grow.
We had a bearer, had a cook,
A bed and furniture,
It seemed that we were all fixed up
For the next twelve months and more.
Oh sahib. . . .

But first we had the dysentry
And then we had the rain;
It flooded through the bungalow,
Then flooded through again.
You couldn't go to bed at all
Without an umberella,

* Gardener.

Imagine paying such high rents
For living under water.
Oh sahib. . . .

All the firms have autos
They're thick upon the ground
Bus, pick-up, Jeep, Ambassador,
And the station run-around.
But if you ever need a car
You're out of luck, my lad.
You'll find, no matter where you look,
There's not one to be had.
Oh sahib. . . .

We also have a hospital,
Tip-top and white as snow,
But not the sort of place, my friend,
We fitters like to go.
It's twenty-eight rupees a day
For any man that's sick,
And when you're paying rent at home
That's a bit too bloody thick.
Oh sahib. . . .

There'd be lots more to sing about
But it's time to call a halt,
For Carnival is not the time
To keep on finding fault.
Our song has scored a point or two,
That must be clear by now,
And so we'll say *"Aufwiedersehen,
Helau, Alaaf, Helau!"*
Oh sahib. . . .

3. Rourkela, Rourkela, Rourkela

I sat beneath the moon with Erika
When suddenly my thoughts returned to India;
I knew, yet scarcely had the heart to say,
My airplane would be taking off next day.
And when I told my Erika at last
Her tears began to fall so thick and fast,

She sobbed and sighed and turned upon me then:
So now the wedding gets put off again.
Rourkela, Rourkela, Rourkela,
On the distant plains of India,
You will never want for construction crew,
For my heart delights at the thought of you.
Dear little girl in Germany, in our little town in Germany,
Just wait a little longer, for soon we shall be home.

The following day she still felt pretty blue
And said to me: "I don't think much of you,
Going off again to be a fitter
And leaving me the way I'll be too old."
But when the engine note begins to swell
A man thinks to himself, ah what the hell!
Why, there'll be girls galore in India
And probably more beautiful than here.
Rourkela. . . .

And in my airplane up among the clouds
I dreamed of pretty Indian girls and crowds
Of little monkeys climbing forest trees,
I dreamed of beer and whisky and rupees.
But just one day of heat in old Bengal
And things weren't all that super after all.
In Rourkela they made me very welcome
And took me off to see my brand new home.
Rourkela. . . .

'Twas then I had my first almighty shock,
A narrow bed, a mattress stuffed with flock,
"Your bungalow," the bearer proudly said.
My bungalow was like a cattle shed!
But at least I soon had company:
A thousand insects came to live with me,
Big and small and black and white and red;
So friendly too, they even came to bed.
Rourkela. . . .

I've been to see the German Club, you know;
The *Spiegel* wrote it up some months ago.
It's nice there, you can eat and drink your fill,

But heaven help you when you get the bill.
They cleaned me out down to my last rupee,
There's no more beer and whisky now for me
Until they pay us out ten days from now.
So I'll just sit at home and milk the cow.
Rourkela. . . .

The stink of cooking fills the bungalow,
The ayah's fixing *khana* * laced with mango,
The *mali*'s† catching snakes out in the garden,
While I sit here and write a letter home.
Oh Erika, I can't believe its' true,
In six short months I'll be back home with you;
We'll sit together underneath the moon
Upon the bench in our dear little park.
Rourkela. . . .

* Food or meal.
† Gardener.

NOTES

1/ Germans for Rourkela

1. Dieter Oberndörfer, *Von der Einsamkeit des Menschen in der modernen amerikanischen Gesellschaft* (Freiburg in Breisgau, 1961), p. 11.

2. Walter Ballerstedt, "Das Angebot von Fachkräften für die Entwicklungsländer" (lecture given at the Evangelische Akademie Loccum at a conference, "Personnel Selection as a Problem in Development Aid," July 2–5, 1963). See also "Deutsche arbeiten im Ausland: Ausländer bilden sich in Deutschland" (article in "The Bulletin" of the Presse- und Informationsamt der Bundesregierung, No. 82 [June 10, 1963]), p. 722.

3. Friedrich A. Wagner, "Der Urlauber, das unbekannte Wesen," Frankfort *Allgemeine Zeitung*, April 18, 1964.

4. For a very typical example see Klaus Röh, *Rourkela als Testfall für die Errichtung von Industrieprojekten in Entwicklungsländern* (Hamburg, 1967), p. 385.

5. Charles E. Hendry, *The Role of Groups in World Reconstruction* (New York, 1952), p. 180.

6. Ludwig Homburger, "Es ist alles ganz anders," Frankfort *Allgemeine Zeitung*, January 6, 1962.

7. Kurt Hesse, *Entwicklungsländer und Entwicklungshilfen* (Berlin, 1962), p. 392.

8. René König, "Kulturelle Determination des Arbeitsstils," in *Fragen der Entwicklungshilfe aus soziologischer Sicht* (report of a session of the German UNESCO Commission and the Friedrich-Ebert Foundation in May, 1960), p. 42.

9. Peter R. Hofstätter, *Sozialpsychologie* (Berlin, 1956), pp. 79 f.

10. "Bericht über Begleiterscheinungen der Industrialisierung im sozialen Bereich im Raume Rourkela, Indien" (unpublished report pre-

pared on behalf of the Federal Ministry for Economic Collaboration, Bonn, 1964), p. 133.

11. "The German Worker," *Hindu Weekly Review* (Madras), July 13, 1963.

12. "The Most Up-to-Date Steel Plant in India," *International Management*, XVII (August, 1962), p. 25.

13. Heinz Küpper, *Wörterbuch der deutschen Umgangssprache*, vol. 111: Hochdeutsch—Umgangsdeutsch, Gesamtstichwortverzeichnis (Hamburg, 1964), p. 19.

14. Wahrhold Drascher, *Auslandsdeutsche Charakterbilder* (Stuttgart, 1929), p. 40.

15. Willy Hellpach, *Der deutsche Charakter* (Bonn, 1954), p. 210.

16. Wahrhold Drascher, *Schuld der Weissen?* (Tübingen, 1960), p. 310.

17. Horst Symanowski and Fritz Vilmar, *Die Welt des Arbeiters* (Frankfort, 1963), p. 31.

18. Hellpach, *Der deutsche Charakter*, p. 217.

19. Leander Feiler, "Die Deutschen aus der Sicht der indischen Ingenieure und Arbeiter Rourkelas" (MS at the German Consulate in Calcutta, Rourkela, 1962), pp. 5 ff.

20. Rudolf Walter Leonhardt, *X-mal Deutschland* (Munich, 1961), p. 486.

21. John Lewis Gillin and others, *Social Problems* (New York, 1952), pp. 50 f.

22. Quoted in Erich Sturtevant, *Vom guten Ton im Wandel der Jahrhunderte* (Berlin, 1917), p. 148.

23. Hermann Glaser, *Spiesser-Ideologie* (Freiburg, 1964), p. 201.

24. Max Bauer, *Der deutsche Durst* (Leipzig, 1903), p. 86.

25. Richard Müller-Freienfels, *Die Psychologie des deutschen Menschen und seiner Kultur* (Munich, 1922), p. 116.

26. Drascher, *Schuld der Weissen?* p. 244.

27. Dietrich Rüschemeyer, "Ergebnisse der soziologischen Vorurteilsforschung," in Friedrich-Ebert Foundation, *Überwindung von Vorurteilen* (Hanover, 1960), p. 31.

28. Hofstätter, *Sozialpsychologie*, p. 78.

29. Eugene L. and Ruth E. Hartley, *Die Grundfragen der Sozialpsychologie* (Berlin, 1955), p. 461.

30. Arnold Gehlen, *Die Seele im technischen Zeitalter* (Hamburg, 1957), p. 47.

31. Hortense Powdermaker, *Coppertown: Changing Africa* (New York, 1962), p. 78.

32. Hans-Joachim Knebel, *Soziologische Strukturwandlungen im modernen Tourismus* (Stuttgart, 1960), p. 135.

33. See Gehlen, *Die Seele*, pp. 48–49; also Hartley, *Die Grundlagen*, pp. 463 ff.

34. Percival Spear, *The Nabobs: A Study of the Social Life of the English in 18th Century India* (London, 1963), p. 145.

35. Carl Weiss, "Im indischen 'Ruhrgebiet' rauchen deutsche Schlote," *Neue Zeitung* (Vienna), November 14, 1959.

36. König, "Kulturelle Determination," p. 40.

37. Joseph Maria Hunck, *India Tomorrow* (Düsseldorf, 1963), p. 97.

38. Wahrhold Drascher, "Wissenschaftliche Aspekte der Entwicklungshilfe," *Merkur*, XVI (1962), p. 739.

39. Drascher, *Schuld der Weissen?* p. 311.

40. Alexander Mitscherlich, *Auf dem Weg zur vaterlosen Gesellschaft* (Munich, 1963), pp. 18, 369.

41. Ernst Rodenwaldt, *Tropenhygiene* (Stuttgart, 1957), pp. 19 ff.

42. Michael Rehs, "Zur Vorbereitung ausreisender deutscher Fachleute," *Mitteilungen des Instituts für Auslandsbeziehungen*, April–June, 1960, pp. 109 ff.

43. Alfons Otto Schorb, *Pädagogische Voraussetzungen und Aspekte eines deutschen Beitrags zur Entwicklungshilfe* (Mannheim, 1962), p. 72.

44. Oskar Splett, "Entwicklungshilfe in ihren menschlichen Zielen," in Robert Siegert (ed.) *Entwicklungshilfe einmal anders* (Baden-Baden, 1963), p. 133.

45. Drascher, *Schuld der Weissen?* pp. 258 ff.

2 / The Indians in Rourkela

1. J. Bodo Sperling, *Rourkela: Sozioökonomische Probleme eines Entwicklungsprojektes* (Bonn, 1963), p. 16.

2. Government of India, *India: A Reference Annual, 1962* (New Delhi, 1963), p. 15.

3. "No Central Police: Disturbances at Rourkela," *The Statesman* (Calcutta), August 26, 1959. See also "Mahatab Condemns Rourkela

Riots," *Amrita Bazar Patrika* (Calcutta), August 26, 1959; "Streik in Rourkela," *Handelsblatt* (Düsseldorf), December 12, 1960; "Gefahren für Indiens Einheit," *Süddeutsche Zeitung* (Munich), February 28, 1961; "Der Inder im Lendenschurz hat von Nehru noch nie gehört: Kampf um die Einheit des Landes," *Die Welt* (Hamburg), October 5, 1961.

4. A. K. Majumdar, "Deutschland im Licht der indischen Philosophie," in Hans-Joachim Netzer, (ed.), *Deutschland von aussen gesehen* (Berne, 1963), p. 155.

5. Quoted in Howard M. Teaf, Jr., "Origins of a Private Village Improvement Project," in Teaf and Peter G. Franck (eds.), *Hands Across Frontiers* (Ithaca, N. Y., 1955), p. 106.

6. Richard F. Behrendt, *Dynamische Gesellschaft* (Berne, 1963), p. 141.

7. The Most Up-to-Date Steel Plant. *International Management*, XVII (August, 1962), 25.

8. K. M. Pannikar, *Asien und die Herrschaft des Westens* (Zürich, 1955), p. 407.

9. Gardner Murphy, *In the Minds of Men* (New York, 1955), pp. 276 f.

10. Prodosch Aich, *Farbige unter Weissen* (Cologne, 1962), p. 251.

11. Klaus Mehnert, *Asien, Moskau und wir* (Stuttgart, 1961), p. 39.

12. Gerhard Ritter, *Das deutsche Problem* (Munich, 1962), pp. 55 f.

13. Charles H. Heimsath, *Indian Nationalism and Hindu Social Reform* (Princeton, N. J., 1964), p. 133.

14. Wilhelm E. Mühlmann, *Chiliasmus und Nativismus* (Berlin, 1961), pp. 329 f.

15. Kai Uwe von Hassel, "Gestraffte Entwicklungshilfe," *Christ und Welt* (Stuttgart), November 10, 1960.

16. Eugen Lemberg, *Nationalismus I* (Munich, 1964), p. 302.

17. Mühlmann, *Chiliasmus*, p. 233.

18. Max Weber, *Gesammelte Aufsätze zur Religionssoziologie* (Tübingen, 1963), pp. 11 ff.

19. Mühlmann, *Chiliasmus*, p. 236.

20. Prodosch Aich, *Farbige unter Weissen*, p. 250.

21. Commentary on an unpublished study, "Die Entwicklungshilfe aus Indischer Sicht," carried out by the EMNID Institute for International Market and Social Research, Bielefeld, on behalf of the Studienstelle für Entwicklungsländer, Bonn, 1961.

22. "Das Deutschlandbild in zehn Ländern Asiens, Tabellenteil" (unpublished inquiry carried out by the EMNID Institute for International Market and Social Research, Bielefeld, 1962), pp. 92 ff.

3/ The Germans in Rourkela

1. Willy Hellpach, *Geopsyche* (Leipzig, 1939), p. 159.
2. J. Grober, *Die Akklimatisation* (Jena, 1936), p. 104.
3. *Ibid.*, p. 63.
4. *Ibid.*, p. 92
5. Hellpach, *Geopsyche*, pp. 117 f.
6. R. J. Harrison Church, *Modern Colonization* (New York, 1951), p. 28.
7. Kurt Bergter, "Fünf Jahre deutsches Krankenhaus Rourkela," Special edition of Hamburg *Ärzteblatt*, October, 1963, p. 2.
8. Ernst Rodenwaldt, *Tropenhygiene* (Stuttgart, 1957), p. 168.
9. See, for example, Arthur Fürer, "Probleme der industriellen Entwicklung," in S. Fürer (ed.), *Die wirtschaftlich und gesellschaftlich unterentwickelten Länder und wir* (Berne, 1961), p. 283; Grober, *Die Akklimatisation*, p. 83; Rodenwaldt, *Tropenhygiene*, p. 168.
10. See, for example Hellpach, *Geopsyche*, pp. 118, 152; also Grober, *Die Akklimatisation*, p. 59.
11. Rodenwaldt, *Tropenhygiene*, p. 168.
12. See Werner Röllinghoff, "Erhaltung und Pflege der Gesundheit in den warmen Ländern," in Bundesverwaltungsamt (eds.), *Merkblatt No. 23 für Auslandstätige und Auswanderer* (Cologne, n.d.), p. 13.
13. Bergter, "Fünf Jahre," p. 2.
14. *Techno-Economic Survey of Orissa* (New Delhi, 1962), p. 138.
15. Taken from Bergter, "Fünf Jahre," p. 2.
16. *Ibid.*
17. See also B. de Rudder, *Grundriss einer Meteorobiologie des Menschen* (Berlin, 1952), pp. 165 ff.
18. Grober, *Die Akklimatisation*, p. 80.
19. Hellpach, *Geopsyche*, p. 117.
20. Rudolf Lütkens, *Die geographischen Grundlagen und Probleme des Wirtschaftslebens* (Stuttgart, 1950), p. 63.
21. Rodenwaldt, *Tropenhygiene*, p. 23; for a similar view see also Friedrich Plehn, *Die Kamerun-Küste* (Berlin, 1889), p. 255.

22. Hilton Brown (ed.), *The Sahibs* (London, 1948), p. 46; for similar views see also Plehn, *Die Kamerun-Küste*, p. 260.
23. "Fleisch auf dem Speisezettel," Frankfort *Allgemeine Zeitung*, April 25, 1964.
24. Grober, *Die Akklimatisation*, p. 130.
25. Hellpach, *Geopsyche*, p. 37.
26. Warhold Drascher, *Schuld der Weissen?* (Tübingen, 1960), p. 248.
27. Hellpach, *Geopsyche*, p. 116.
28. Rodenwaldt, *Tropenhygiene*, p. 24.
29. Plehn, *Die Kamerun-Küste*, p. 256.
30. Fred Majdalany, *State of Emergency* (Norwich [U.K.], 1962), p. 13.
31. Brown, *The Sahibs*, pp. 148 f.
32. M. Ganapati, "Planning and Construction: Rourkela Steel Project," *Indian Construction News* (Calcutta), December, 1958.
33. Rodenwaldt, *Tropenhygiene*, pp. 31 f.
34. Plehn, *Die Kamerun-Küste*, p. 313.
35. Alphons Silbermann, *Vom Wohnen der Deutschen* (Cologne, 1963), pp. 14 f.
36. Eugen Diesel, *Die deutsche Wandlung* (Stuttgart, 1929), pp. 74 f.
37. Hans Paul Bahrdt, *Die moderne Grossstadt* (Hamburg, 1961), p. 84.
38. Silbermann, *Vom Wohnen*, p. 38.
39. Leander Feiler, "Die Deutschen aus der Sicht der indischen Ingenieure und Arbeiter Rourkelas" (MS at the German Consulate in Calcutta, Rourkela, 1962), p. 5.
40. See Elspeth Huxley, *Die Grashütte* (Stuttgart, 1961), p. 19.
41. T. Axenfeld, Letter in *Der Kontinent: Mitteilungen für die Mitglieder der Deutschen Afrika Gesellschaft*, No. 9, 1962.
42. Hortense Powdermaker, *Coppertown: Changing Africa* (New York, 1962), pp. 79 ff.
43. "Bericht über Begleiterscheinungen der Indistrialisierung im sozialen Bereich im Raume Rourkela, Indien" (unpublished report prepared on behalf of the Federal Ministry for Economic Collaboration, Bonn, 1964), pp. 140 ff.
44. For a further report on this topic see also the Oriya daily newspaper *Matrabhumi* (Cuttack), September 3, 1958.
45. Thilo Bode, "Zarte Gemüter sprechen von 'Tanzmädchen,'" *Die Welt* (Hamburg), May 1–2, 1961.

46. Rodenwaldt, *Tropenhygiene*, p. 149.
47. From the minutes recorded by one of the Germans present at the discussions.
48. "Plant for producing Bastards?" *Film India*, June, 1958.
49. Eberhard Peusch, "Die geistige Situation der deutschen 'Kolonie' in Rourkela, Indien," *Kulturarbeit*, XIV, No. 10 (1962), p. 193.
50. See, for example, Rodenwaldt, *Tropenhygiene*, p. 149; also Grober, *Die Akklimatisation*, p. 135, and Röllinghoff, "Erhaltung und Pflege," p. 6.
51. Feiler, "Die Deutschen," p. 6.
52. See also Pater Josef Duschl, *Der Ring: Mitteilungen für die deutschsprachigen Katholiken in Indien* (Rourkela), V, 9.
53. Han Suyin, *Der Wind ist mein Kleid* (Frankfort, 1957), p. 124.
54. Hans Floerke, *Deutsches Wesen im Spiegel der Zeiten* (Berlin, 1916), p. 281.
55. Silbermann, *Vom Wohnen*, p. 217.
56. René König, "Kulturelle Determination des Arbeitsstils" *Fragen der Entwicklungshilfe aus soziologischer Sicht* (report of a session of the German UNESCO Commission and the Friedrich-Ebert Foundation in May, 1960), p. 44.
57. Alexander Mitscherlich, *Auf dem Weg zur vaterlosen Gesellschaft* (Munich, 1963), p. 423.
58. Adolf Weber, *Die Grosstadt und ihre sozialen Probleme* (Leipzig, 1908), pp. 121 f.
59. *Umfragen, Ereignisse und Probleme der Zeit im Urteil der Bevölkerung* (Frankfort on the Main, 1962), p. 147.
60. Peusch, "Die geistige Situation," p. 193.
61. David Riesman, *The Lonely Crowd* (Oxford, 1950).
62. Powdermaker, *Coppertown*, p. 72.
63. Alfred Vierkandt, *Kleine Gesellschaftslehre* (Stuttgart, 1961), p. 67.
64. For example, Hugo Grothe, *Grundfragen und Tatsachen zur Kunde des Grenz- und Auslandsdeutschtums* (Dresden, 1926), pp. 43 ff.; also Leopold von Wiese and Leopold Max Walter von Kaiserwaldau, *Die Weltwirtschaft als soziologisches Gebilde* (Jena, 1923), p. 43.
65. Fürer, "Probleme der industriellen Entwicklung," p. 283.
66. Diesel, *Die deutsche Wandlung*, p. 71.
67. Rodenwaldt, *Tropenhygiene*, p. 142.
68. Willy Hellpach, *Der deutsche Charakter* (Bonn, 1954), p. 221.
69. Mitscherlich, *Auf dem Weg*, p. 44.

NOTES

70. Friedrich A. Wagner, "Das bescheidene Deutschland," Frankfort *Allgemeine Zeitung*, August 12, 1964.
71. Adolph Freiherr von Knigge, *Über den Umgang mit Menschen* (Munich, 1954), pp. 12 f.
72. Lily Abegg, "Knigge für Asien," Frankfort *Allgemeine Zeitung*, July 22, 1961.
73. Mitscherlich, *Auf dem Weg*, p. 32.
74. Harlan Cleveland, "The Pretty Americans," *Harper's Magazine*, March, 1959, p. 31.
75. Percival Spear, *The Nabobs: A Study of the Social Life of the English in 18th Century India* (London, 1963), p. 140.
76. Leslie H. Palmier, *Indonesia and the Dutch* (London, 1962), pp. 33 f.
77. Suyin, *Der Wind*, p. 64.
78. Plehn, *Die Kamerun-Küste*, p. 341.
79. Dieter Danckwortt, "Probleme der Anpassung an eine fremde Kultur," in *Materialien zur Entwicklungshilfe* (Cologne, n.d.), p. 172.
80. *Ibid.*, pp. 173 f.
81. Gustav Adolf Henning, "Indien baut ein 'Ruhrgebiet,'" *Hamburg Abendblatt*, September 20–21, 1958.
82. Thilo Bode, "Keine 'Herrenmenschen' in Rourkela," *Die Welt*, April 28, 1960.
83. Klaus Mehnert and Giselherr Wirsing, "Der grosse deutsche Probefall Rourkela," *Christ und Welt* (Stuttgart), February 25, 1960.
84. Thilo Bode, "New Delhi: Kritik an Rourkela unberechtigt," *Die Welt*, April 6, 1960.
85. *Times of India* (New Delhi), May 24, 1962.
86. "Rourkela Run by Beginners" (report of a speech by Mr. Ganapati, the Resident Director of the Rourkela Steel Plant, in August, 1959), *The Statesman* (Calcutta), August 17, 1959.
87. Poona *Daily News*, January 17, 1962.
88. Wilfred Malenbaum, *East and West in India's Development* (Washington, D.C., 1959), p. 53.
89. Gabriele Wülker, *In Asien und Afrika* (Stuttgart, 1962), p. 15.
90. Malenbaum, *East and West*, p. 54.
91. "Was Rourkela lehrt," *Handelsblatt* (Düsseldorf), October 3, 1961.
92. Feiler, "Die Deutschen," p. 5.
93. "The Most Up-to-Date Steel Plant in India," *International Management*, XVII (August, 1962), p. 23.
94. "Noch ein 'Solveen-Bericht,'" *Handelsblatt*, January 16, 1964.

95. Wülker, *In Asien*, p. 16.
96. Drascher, *Schuld der Weissen?*, pp. 262, 228.
97. "The Most Up-to-Date Steel Plant," p. 25.
98. Feiler, "Die Deutschen," p. 3.
99. René König, "Kulturelle Determinationen des Arbeitsstils," p. 133.
100. Feiler, "Die Deutschen," p. 3.
101. Hellpach, *Der deutsche Charakter*, p. 143.
102. Leopold von Wiese, *Allgemeine Soziologie* (Munich, 1929), p. 128.
103. René König, *Soziologie* (Frankfort on the Main, 1960), pp. 105 f.
104. Karl N. Llewellyn, "Gruppenvorurteil und Erziehung zur Gemeinschaft," in R. M. MacIver, (ed.), *Zivilisation und Gruppenbeziehungen* (Berlin, 1951), p. 42.
105. Hans-Joachim Knebel, *Soziologische Strukturwandlungen im modernen Tourismus* (Stuttgart, 1960), pp. 105 f.
106. Hermann Eich, *Die unheimlichen Deutschen* (Düsseldorf, 1963), pp. 12 f.
107. Rudolf Walter Leonhardt, *X-mal Deutschland* (Munich, 1961), p. 521.
108. Horst Peets, "Die unheimliche Kanaille," *Die Welt*, June 14, 1958.
109. "German Yearning for the South," *Times* (London), August 23, 1958.
110. Erich Fromm, *Der moderne Mensch und seine Zukunft* (Frankfort, 1955), p. 177.
111. Wiese, *Allgemeine Soziologie*, p. 171.
112. Mitscherlich, *Auf dem Weg*, p. 231.
113. See Riesman, *The Lonely Crowd*.
114. Walter Dirks, "'Arbeiterbildung' und der heutige Arbeiter," *Frankfurter Hefte*, October, 1960, pp. 685 f.
115. Kurt Lewin, "Frontiers of Group Dynamics," *Human Relations*, June, 1947, p. 35.
116. Wiese, *Allgemeine Soziologie*, p. 184.
117. J. Hermelink, "Niederschrift Indien II," (course designed for the Evangelische Zentrale für Auswandererhilfe, Stuttgart, 1957), p. 215.
118. Horst Symanowski and Fritz Vilmar, *Die Welt des Arbeiters* (Frankfort, 1963), pp. 18 ff.
119. Mitscherlich, *Auf dem Weg*, p. 335.

120. *Ibid.*
121. Hellpach, *Geopsyche*, p. 116.
122. Willy Hellpach, *Sozialpsychologie* (Stuttgart, 1951), p. 201.
123. Suyin, *Der Wind*, p. 124 f.
124. Klaus Wiborg, "Eine Stadt für 4,300 Gastarbeiter in Wolfsburg," Frankfort *Allgemeine Zeitung,* September 26, 1962.
125. "Die Zwischenfälle um britische Soldaten," *Neue Züricher Zeitung,* July 6, 1962.
126. Peusch, "Die geistige Situation," p. 193.
127. Arnold Zweig, *Caliban oder Politik und Leidenschaft* (Potsdam, 1927), p. 55.
128. Wiese, *Allgemeine Soziologie,* p. 170.
129. Zweig, *Caliban,* p. 54.
130. *Ibid.*, p. 55.
131. Drascher, *Schuld der Weissen?* p. 238.
132. *Ibid.*, p. 240.
133. Helmuth von Glasenapp, *Indien* (Munich, 1925), p. 19.
134. P. Thomas, *Hindu Religion, Customs and Manners* (Bombay, 1956).
135. Drascher, *Schuld der Weissen?* p. 76.
136. Feiler, "Die Deutschen," p. 6.
137. Giacomo Maturi, "Aus einer anderen Welt," *Die Welt,* August 8, 1964.
138. William J. Lederer and Eugene Burdick, *The Ugly American* (London, 1959).
139. D. H. Radler, "Our National Talent for Offending People," *Harper's Magazine,* August, 1961, John C. Caldwell, *Let's Visit Americans Overseas* (New York, 1958). Harlan Cleveland and Others, *The Overseas Americans* (New York, 1960).
140. John Masters, *Fandango Rock* (London, 1961), p. 39.
141. "Rourkela and Bhilai," *Hindustan Standard* (Calcutta), September 27, 1959.
142. Gräfin Marion Dönhoff, "Neutral gegen wen?" *Die Zeit* (Hamburg), September 15, 1961.
143. Klaus Mehnert, *Asien, Moskau und wir* (Stuttgart, 1961), p. 15.
144. Spear, *The Nabobs,* p. 142.
145. Reinhard Raffalt, program on Bavarian Radio, Munich, May 9, 1957.
146. Drascher, *Schuld der Weissen?* p. 237.

147. Peter Schmid, *Indien mit und ohne Wunder* (Stuttgart, 1960), pp. 125 f.
148. Leonhardt, *X-mal Deutschland*, p. 185.
149. Eich, *Die unheimlichen Deutschen*, p. 55.
150. Charles W. Thayer, *The Unquiet Germans* (London, 1958), p. 227.
151. Mitscherlich, *Auf dem Weg*, p. 313.
152. Fromm, *Der moderne Mensch*, p. 76.
153. *Ibid.*
154. Kurt Körber, "Pflege und Förderung zwischenmenschlicher Beziehungen" (special publication based on a lecture given to an audience of local government experts in Hamburg, March 6, 1963).
155. Wiese, *Allgemeine Soziologie*, p. 178.
156. Henry Pratt Fairchild, (ed.), *Dictionary of Sociology and Related Sciences* (Patterson, N.J., 1961), p. 125.
157. Mitscherlich, *Auf dem Weg*, p. 263.
158. René König, *Grundformen der Gesellschaft: Die Gemeinde* (Hamburg, 1958), p. 100.
159. Peter Heintz, "Vorurteile und Minoritäten," in René König (ed), *Soziologie* (Frankfort, 1958), p. 305.
160. Dietrich Goldschmidt, "Das Vorurteil gegen Minderheiten in soziologischer Sicht," in Friedrich-Ebert Foundation, *Überwindung von Vorurteilen* (Hanover, 1960), p. 15.
161. Eugene L. and Ruth E. Hartley, *Die Grundfragen der Sozialpsychologie* (Berlin, 1955), p. 211.

4/ *Implications of Rourkela*

1. Hellmuth Wagner, "Förderung sprachlicher Vorbereitung für Fachkräfte, die in Entwicklungsländer gehen" (report of a discussion of May 7–8, 1962, held at the German Foundation for Developing Countries), *Deutschland-Union Dienst* (CDU), VIII, No. 95 (A).
2. Wahrold Drascher, *Schuld der Weissen?* (Tübingen, 1960), p. 312.
3. L. Alsdorf, "Förderung sprachlicher Vorbereitung für Fachkräfte, die in Entwicklungsländer gehen," *Deutschland-Union Dienst* (CDU), VIII, No. 95, p. 9.
4. Hans Keller, "Technische Hilfe durch Schweizer Sachverständige

in Entwicklungsländern," in *Die wirtschaftlich und gesellschaftlich unter-entwickelten Länder und wir* (Berne, 1961), p. 341.

5. Annual Report of the Indian Embassy, "India 1961," Bonn, 1961.

6. Carl Weiss, "Die deutsch-indonesische Rechnung geht nicht auf,' in Hans Joachim Netzer (ed.), *Deutschland von aussen gesehen* (Berne, 1963), p. 149.

7. Eugene L. and Ruth E. Hartley, *Die Grundfragen der Sozialpsychologie* (Berlin, 1955), p. 224. Arnold Gehlen, *Die Seele im technischen Zeitalter* (Hamburg, 1957), p. 5.

8. H. E. O. James and Cora Tenen, *The Teacher Was Black* (London, 1953).

9. Hans Paul Bahrdt, *Die moderne Grossstadt* (Hamburg, 1961), pp. 87 f.

10. René König, *Grundformen der Gesellschaft: Die Gemeinde* (Hamburg, 1958), p. 103.

11. Alexander Mitscherlich, *Auf dem Weg zur vaterlosen Gesellschaft* (Munich, 1963), p. 195.

BIBLIOGRAPHY

Apart from a number of articles in newspapers and periodicals and a few isolated passages in various books, there is no literature dealing with the behavior of the Germans in Rourkela. Although the bibliography provided here is fairly extensive and lists more than 200 books and nearly 100 essays and documents, it consists for the most part of reference works that were used primarily to check and collate the empirical material obtained in Rourkela.

For Parts One and Two of this book reference was made to works which helped to establish the basic characteristics of both Germans and Indians, since these tended to set the pattern of their behavior in both their working and their social relations. The works consulted for Parts Three and Four fall into three main categories: (a) writings from the field of tropical medicine, (b) social science literature, and (c) books and reports dealing with situations which in one way or another were comparable to that in Rourkela.

Books

Achinger, Hans. *Sozialpolitik als Gesellschaftspolitik.* Hamburg, 1958.
Allemann, Fritz René. *Bonn ist nicht Weimar.* Cologne and Berlin, 1956.
Alsdorf, Ludwig. *Vorderindien.* Brunswick, Germany, 1955.
Atteslander, Peter M. *Probleme der sozialen Anpassung.* Cologne and Opladen, 1962.
Ausländische Arbeitskräfte in Deutschland. Ed. Hessisches Institut für Betriebswirtschaft. Düsseldorf, 1961.
Bahrdt, Hans Paul. *Die Gemeinde in der Industriegesellschaft.* Cologne, 1962.
Barley, Delbert. *Jugend im Blickpunkt: Grundzüge und Probleme der Soziologie.* Berlin-Spandau, 1962.

Barnett, H. G. "Wer nimmt Neuerungen an und wer lehnt sie ab?" in *Soziologie der Entwicklungsländer,* ed. Peter Heintz, pp. 73–109. Cologne and Berlin, 1962.

Barth, Hans. *Masse und Mythos.* Hamburg, 1959.

Bauer, P. T. *United States Aid and Indian Economic Development.* Washington, D.C., 1959.

Behrendt, Richard F. *Der Mensch im Licht der Soziologie.* Stuttgart, 1962.

Benedict, Ruth. *Patterns of Culture.* London, 1947.

Bentley, Arthur F. "Die Tätigkeit von Gruppen," in *Die Politische Wissenschaft,* ed. Carl Joachim Friedrich, pp. 374–409. Munich, 1961.

Billerbeck, Klaus. *Deutscher Beitrag für Entwicklungsländer.* Hamburg, 1958.

Björnson, Björn. *Vom Deutschen Wesen.* Berlin, 1917.

Bodamer, Joachim. *Der Mann von heute.* Stuttgart, 1956.

———. *Gesundheit und technische Welt.* Stuttgart, 1955.

Bogardus, Emorg S. *Sociology.* New York, 1954.

Bon, Gustave le. *Psychologie der Massen.* Stuttgart, 1961.

Bowles, Chester. *Ambassador's Report.* London, 1954.

Brecher, Michael. *The New States of Asia: A Political Analysis.* London, New York, and Toronto, 1963.

Brepohl, Wilhelm. *Der Aufbau des Ruhrvolkes im Zuge der Ost-West-Wanderung: Beiträge zur deutschen Sozialgeschichte des 19. und 20. Jahrhunderts.* Recklinghausen, 1948.

Brown, J. A. C. *The Social Psychology of Industry: Human Relations in the Factory.* London, 1963.

Bühler, Charlotte. *Psychologie im Leben unserer Zeit.* Munich and Zurich, 1962.

Caplow, Theodore. *The Sociology of Work.* London, Bombay, and Carachi, 1954.

Carrington, C. E. *The British Overseas.* Cambridge, 1950.

Clark, Colin. *Growthmanship.* London, 1962.

Cohen, Albert K. *Kriminelle Jugend: Zur Soziologie jugendlichen Bandenwesens.* Hamburg, 1961.

Comas, Juan. *Racial Myth.* Paris, 1958.

Constantine, Learie. *Colour Bar.* London, Melbourne, Sydney, Auckland, Bombay, Cape Town, New York, and Toronto, 1954.

Coser, Lewis A., and Bernard Rosenberg. *Sociological Theory.* New York, 1959.

Coulmas, Peter. *Der Fluch der Freiheit: Wohin marschiert die farbige Welt.* Oldenburg and Hamburg, 1963.
Dahrendorf, Ralf. *Gesellschaft und Freiheit.* Munich, 1962.
Danckwortt, Dieter. *Zur Psychologie der deutschen Entwicklungshilfe.* Baden-Baden and Bonn, 1962.
Dreitzel, Hans P. *Elitebegriff und Sozialstruktur: Eine soziologische Begriffsanalyse.* Stuttgart, 1962.
Drucker, Peter F. *Die nächsten zwanzig Jahre.* Düsseldorf, 1957.
Duisburg, Adolf von. *Wer will in die Kolonien?* Berlin, 1938.
Dunckmann, Karl. *Soziologie der Arbeit.* Halle on the Saale, 1933.
Eickstedt, Egon von. *Rassendynamik von Ostasien.* Berlin, 1944.
Eltridge, Seba, and Others. *Fundamentals of Sociology.* New York, 1950.
Eysenck, Hans Jürgen. *Uses and Abuses of Psychology.* London, 1953.
Fausel, Erich. *Das Zipser Deutschtum.* Jena, 1927.
Freyer, Hans. *Das soziale Ganze und die Freiheit der Einzelnen unter den Bedingungen des industriellen Zeitalters.* Göttingen, Berlin, and Frankfort, 1957.
Fröhlich, Walter (ed). *Land Tenure, Industrialization and Social Stability: Experience and Prospects in Asia.* Milwaukee, Wis., 1961.
Die Front der Farbigen. (Author not named.) Munich, 1957.
Gaitanides, Johannes. "Von der Ohnmacht unserer Literatur," in *Ich lebe in der Bundesrepublik,* ed. Wolfgang Weyrauch. Munich, n.d.
Gebser, Jean. *Asienfibel: Zum Verständnis östlicher Wesensart.* Frankfort and Berlin, 1962.
Gehlen, Arnold. *Der Mensch.* 7th edition. Frankfort on the Main and Bonn, 1962.
———. *Anthropologische Forschung.* Hamburg, 1961.
———, and Helmut Schelsky. *Soziologie.* Düsseldorf and Cologne, 1964.
Gerling, Walter. *Kulturgeographische Untersuchungen,* Vol. I. Würzburg, 1963.
Gerwig, Ernst. *Die soziologische Struktur des Industriebetriebes.* Stuttgart, 1960.
Glass, Ruth. *The Social Background of a Plan: A Study of Middlesborough.* London, 1948.
Haller, Albert von. *Die Letzten wollen die Ersten sein.* Düsseldorf and Vienna, 1963.
Harrison, Selig S. *India: The Most Dangerous Decades.* Princeton, N. J., 1960.

Hayek, F. *Individualismus und wirtschaftliche Ordung.* Erlenbach-Zürich, 1952.
Heer, Friedrich. "Europa vor der Aufgabe der einen Welt," in *Die wirtschaftlich und gesellschaftlich unterentwickelten Länder und wir,* ed. S. Fürer. Berne and Stuttgart, 1961.
Heimsath, Charles H. *Indian Nationalism and Hindu Social Reform.* Princeton, N.J., 1964.
Hellpach, Willy. *Mensch und Volk der Grossstadt.* Stuttgart, 1939.
——. *Der Sozialorganismus: Menschengemeinschaften als Lebewesen.* Cologne and Opladen, 1953.
——. *Sinne und Seele.* Stuttgart, 1946.
——. *Einführung in die Völkerpsychologie.* 3rd edition. Stuttgart, 1954.
——. *Kulturpsychologie.* Stuttgart, 1953.
Hofstätter, Peter R. *Einführung in die Sozialpsychologie.* 2nd edition. Stuttgart, 1959.
——. *Einführung in die quantitativen Methoden der Psychologie.* Munich, 1953.
——. *Gruppendynamik: Die Kritik der Massenpsychologie.* Hamburg, 1951.
Homans, George Caspar. *Theorie der sozialen Gruppe.* Cologne and Opladen, 1960.
Hussmann, Horst. *Studien zur Entstehungsgeschichte der deutschen Betriebssoziologie.* Cologne 1958.
Huszar, Georg B. D. *Anatomy of Racial Intolerance.* New York, 1946.
Huxley, Aldous. *Brave New World.* New York, 1932.
India, Government of. *India: A Reference Annual, 1959.* New Delhi, 1960.
Jahoda Gustav. *White Man.* London, New York, and Accra, 1961.
Janaki, Ammal E. K. "Report on the Humid Regions of South Asia," in *Problems of Humid Tropical Regions.* Paris, 1958.
Jenny, Hans. *Afrika ist nicht nur schwarz.* Düsseldorf, 1961.
Kapeller, Ludwig. *Das Schimpfbuch.* 3rd edition. Herrenalb, 1964.
Kapferer, Clodwig. *Unabhängige technische Beratung.* Hamburg, 1954.
Karst, Heinz, Friedrich Beermann, and Franz Grosse (eds.). *Menschenführung, Personalauslese, Technik in Wirtschaft und Armee.* Darmstadt, 1954.
Katz, Elihu, and Paul F. Lazarsfeld. *Persönlicher Einfluss und Meinungsbildung.* Munich, 1962.
Kauffmann, Richard. *Gebrannte Kinder.* Düsseldorf, 1961.
Kellner, Wolfgang. *Der moderne soziale Konflikt.* Stuttgart, 1961.

Kesting, H., H. Popitz, H. P. Bahrdt, and E. A. Jüres. *Das Gesellschaftsbild des Arbeiters.* Tübingen, 1957.
Kläge, Walther. *Von deutscher Biederkeit.* Hamburg, n.d.
Klages, Helmut. *Der Nachbarschaftsgedanke und die nachbarliche Wirklichkeit in der Grossstadt.* Cologne and Opladen, 1958.
Klineberg, Otto. *Race and Psychology.* Paris, 1951.
———. *Social Psychology.* New York, 1955.
Krüger, Karl. *Technik für alle Länder.* Berlin, 1959.
Kübler, Fritz. *Deutsche in Bolivien.* Stuttgart, 1936.
Lauterbach, Albert. *Psychologie des Wirtschaftslebens.* Hamburg, 1962.
Little, Kenneth L. *Race and Society.* Paris, 1958.
Mackensen, Rainer and Others. *Daseinsformen der Grossstadt.* Tübingen, 1959.
MacIver, R. M. (ed.). *Zivilisation und Gruppenbeziehungen.* Berlin and Bad Nauheim, 1951.
Mannheim, Karl. *Mensch und Gesellschaft im Zeitalter des Umbaus.* Darmstadt, 1958.
Marfeld, A. F. *Der Griff nach der Seele.* Berlin, 1962.
Maurer, Emil H. *Der Spätbürger.* Berne, 1963.
Mayntz, Renate. *Soziologie der Organisation.* Hamburg, 1963.
Mead, Margaret. *Sex and Temperament in Three Primitive Societies.* London, 1935.
Messner, Johannes. *Das Gemeinwohl.* Osnabrück, 1962.
Middendorf, Wolf. *Soziologie des Verbrechens.* Düsseldorf and Cologne, 1959.
Miller, Delbert C. *Unternehmung, Betrieb und Umwelt.* Cologne and Opladen, 1957.
Mohanty, H. B. *Location of Steel Plant in Orissa: Rourkela.* Bhubaneswar, 1954.
Morant, G. M. *The Significance of Race Difference.* Paris, 1952.
Muchow, Hans Heinrich. *Jugend und Zeitgeist.* Hamburg, 1962.
———. *Sexualreife und Sozialstruktur der Jugend.* Hamburg, 1962.
Muller, Phillippe. *Berufswahl in der rationalisierten Arbeitswelt.* Hamburg, 1961.
Nair, Kusum. *Blossoms in the Dust.* London, 1961.
Neidhardt, Friedhelm. *Studenten im internationalen Wohnheim.* Tübingen, 1963.
Noetzel, Gerte M. *Persönlichkeit und Gemeinschaft.* Munich and Basel, 1957.
Ogburn, William F., and Meyer F. Nimkoff. *Sociology.* 2nd edition.

Boston, New York, Chicago, Dallas, Atlanta, and San Francisco, 1950.
Opler, Morris E. *Social Aspects of Technical Assistance in Operation* ("Tensions and Technology Series"). Paris, 1954.
Oppen, Dietrich V. *Familien in ihrer Umwelt.* Cologne and Opladen, 1958.
Ortega y Gasset, José. *Der Aufstand der Massen.* Munich, 1962.
Packard, Vance. *The Hidden Persuaders.* London, 1960.
Redfield, Robert. *The Little Community.* Uppsala, 1955.
Richter, Hans Werner (ed.). *Bestandsaufnahme: Eine Deutsche Bilanz, 1962.* Munich, 1962.
Röh, Klaus. *Rourkela als Testfall für die Errichtung von Industrieprojekten in Entwicklungsländern.* Hamburg, 1967.
Röpke, Wilhelm. "Die unterentwickelten Länder als wirtschaftliches, soziales und gesellschaftliches Problem," in Albert Hunold, *Entwicklungsländer Wahn und Wirklichkeit,* pp. 11–82. Zürich, 1961.
Rose, Arnold. *The Roots of Prejudice.* Paris, 1951.
Rumney, Jay, and Joseph Maier. *Soziologie.* Frankfort, 1956.
Salisbury, Harrison E. *Die zerrüttete Generation.* Munich, 1962.
Schelsky, Helmut. *Die skeptische Generation: Eine Soziologie der deutschen Jugend.* Düsseldorf and Cologne, 1960.
——. *Die sozialen Folgen der Automatisierung.* Düsseldorf and Cologne, 1957.
——. *Soziologie der Sexualität.* Hamburg, 1962.
Schilling, Kurt. *Geschichte der sozialen Ideen.* Stuttgart, 1957.
Schmitt, Matthias. *Partnerschaft mit Entwicklungsländern.* Stuttgart, 1960.
Schulenberg, Wolfgang. *Ansatz und Wirksamkeit der Erwachsenenbildung,* vol. I. Stuttgart, 1957.
Schulze-Maizier, Friedrich. *Deutsche Selbstkritik.* Berlin, 1932.
Sherif, Muzafer. *Intergroup Relations and Leadership.* New York and London, 1962.
Shonfield, Andrew. *The Attack on World Poverty.* London, 1960.
Sperling, J. Bodo. *Rourkela.* Bonn, 1963.
Taylor, Carl C., and B. F. Brown. *Human Relations.* New York and London, 1926.
Vallentin, W. *Das Deutschtum in Südamerika.* Berlin, 1908.
Vermeer, Hans Josef, Heinz Walz, and Heinrich Klebes. *Sprache und Entwicklungshilfe.* Heidelberg, 1963.
Wolf, Charles, Jr. *Foreign Aid: Theory and Practice in Southern Asia.* Princeton, N. J., 1960.

Wright, Richard. *Schwarze Macht*. Hamburg, 1956.
Wülker, Gabriele. *Die Entwicklungshilfe aus indischer Sicht*. Bonn, 1961.

Documents and Reports

Behrendt, Richard F. "Zellen und Träger des gesellschaftlichen Entwicklungsprozesses," in *Fragen der Entwicklungshilfe aus soziologischer Sicht* (report of a session of the German UNESCO Commission and the Friedrich-Ebert Foundation), May, 1960, pp. 15–26.
"Förderung sprachlicher Vorbereitung für Fachräfte die in Entwicklungsländer gehen" (report of a discussion of May 7–8, 1962, held at the German Foundation for Developing Countries), in *Deutschland-Union Dienst* (CDU), VIII, No. 95 (A).
Heus, Theodor. Speech delivered in the German Social Center in Rourkela on November 11, 1960.
Osner, Karl. "Ausbildung von deutschen Experten für die Arbeit in Entwicklungsländern," *Fragen der Entwicklungshilfe aus soziologischer Sicht* (report of a session of the German UNESCO Commission and the Friedrich-Ebert Foundation), May, 1960, pp. 56–62.
Sperling J. Bodo. "Hindustan Steel Limited—Rourkela Steel Plant" (unpublished study carried out for the Federal Ministry of Economics, February, 1962).
Thierbach, Hans. "Grundsätzliche Gestaltung und Anforderung an länderkundliches Material—aus der Sicht der Auslandsberatung und Vorbereitung" (report of a discussion of March 20–21, 1962, Deutsche Stiftung für Entwicklungsländer, Bonn, 1962, pp. 7–8.
United States Foreign Service Institute. "When Americans Live Abroad." Washington, D.C., 1955.

Magazines and Newspaper Articles

Amrita Bazar Patrika (Calcutta), November 19, 1959.
Benkiser, Nikolas. "Die Missionare der Entwicklung," Frankfort *Allgemeine Zeitung*, March 20, 1961.
Blomfield, Richard B. "Overseas Employment: Are You Ready for It?" *Pipe Line Industry*, September, 1962, pp. 73–75.
Bodamer, Joachim. "Zwischen Beruf und Familie," *Die Politische Meinung*, February, 1964, p. 54.
Bode, Thilo. "Der Inder im Lendenschurz hat von Nehru noch nie gehört," *Die Welt* (Hamburg), October 5, 1961.

——. "Klubmitglieder in Calcutta—nach der Hautfarbe sortiert: Kampf um die Einheit des Landes," *Die Welt*, July 8, 1961.
Böhm, Anton, "Falsches Leben," *Die Politische Meinung*, 1962, pp. 54–64.
Corsten, Rüdiger. "Menschen nach der Arbeit," *Die Politische Meinung*, May, 1963, pp. 48–61.
"Deutsche arbeiten im Ausland: Ausländer bilden sich in Deutschland," "The Bulletin" of the Presse- und Informationsamt der Bundesregierung, June 10, 1963, p. 722.
Funkenberg, Alexander. "Für die Wohlfahrt aller Völker: Deutsche Sachverständige im Dienste der Vereinten Nationen," *Vereinte Nationen*, March, 1962, pp. 55–58.
——. "Deutsche Mitarbeit an den Entwicklungsprojekten der United Nations Organisation," *Vereinte Nationen*, June, 1963, pp. 98–100.
"Gefahren für Indiens Einheit," *Süddeutsche Zeitung* (Munich), February 28, 1961.
Hausmann, Gottfried. "Der pädagogische Aspekt der Entwicklungshilfe," *Offene Welt*, December, 1962, pp. 484–493.
Hellpach, Willy. "Kosmische Einflüsse im Seelenleben," *Die Naturwissenschaften*, 1924, pp. 1079–1086.
Hildebrandt, Walter. "Die epochale Aufgabe der Entwicklungshilfe," *Wirtschaftsdienst*, III (1962), pp. 105–111.
Hindustan Standard (Calcutta), November 14, 1959.
Hindu Weekly Review (Madras), October 8, 1962.
"Italiener haben Heimweh," Frankfort *Allgemeine Zeitung*, October 5, 1962.
"Key Posts Should Go to Oriyas," *Hindustan Standard*, July 26, 1959.
Koch, Herbert R. "Deutsche Schulen in Lateinamerika," *Offene Welt* (special issue: "Lateinamerika"), June, 1963, p. 258.
Manndorf, Hans. "Soziale Umwandlungsprozesse als Folgeerscheinung der Industrialisierung in Südasien," *Sociologus* II (1957), pp. 181–183.
Muddathir, Ahmed. "Der Intellektuelle in den Entwicklungsländern angesichts der sozialen und wirtschaftlichen Dynamik," *Offene Welt*, June, 1962, p. 218.
Nauck, E. G. "Die Akklimatisation und ihre Bedeutung für die Siedlung in den Tropen," *Zeitschrift der Gesellschaft für Erdkunde zu Berlin*, III–IV (1938), p. 81.
Oberhumer, Eugen. "Medizinische Geographie," *Petermanns Mitteilungen*, 1935.

Pfeffer, Karl Heinz. "Die Ausbildung qualifizierter Führungsschichten in spät industrialisierten Ländern," *Wirtschaftsdienst,* XXXVI, No. 7.

Schwenke, Dietrich H. "Entwicklungshilfe und der Ingenieur," *Intertechnik,* April, 1961, pp. 104–106.

Sonnenhol, Gustav Adolf. "Der Ingenieur in der Entwicklungshilfe," *BDI-Nachrichten* [Bundesverband der Deutshen Industrie], VI–VIII, 1963.

Sperling, J. Bodo. "Soziale Probleme in Rourkela," *Indo Asia,* July, 1961, pp. 260–274.

———. "Auslands-ABC für 'Rourkela-Deutsche': Vorbereitung vor der Ausreise nach Indien," *Handelsblatt* (Düsseldorf), August 7, 1963.

Sterner, Siegfried. "Knigge für amerikanische Manager," Frankfort *Allgemeine Zeitung,* May 19, 1964.

"Streik in Rourkela," *Handelsblatt,* December 12, 1960.

"Wandlungen der Arbeitermentalität," *Neue Züricher Zeitung* (Zurich), August 14, 1962.

"Weisse Polizeistreifenwagen," Frankfort *Allgemeine Zeitung,* June 1, 1964.

"'White' Swimming Pool," readers' letters in *Times of India* (Bombay), October 27, 1961.

Witzel, Dietrich. "Sicherheit für Rourkela," Frankfort *Allgemeine Zeitung,* April 18, 1964.

Wülker, Gabriele. "Fragebogen in Asien: Meinungsforschung in Entwicklungsländern," "The Bulletin" of the Presse- und Informationsamt der Bundesregierung, January 12, 1962, pp. 69–70.

INDEX

Abegg, Lily, 129, 132
Accidents: industrial, 62; road, 62
Acclimatization, 55 ff.
Accommodations for Germans in Rourkela, 71 ff.; *see also* Bungalows *and* Fitters' hostels
Adaptation: problems of, 117 ff., 189; and homesickness, 122, 127 ff., 131 ff.
Adivasis, 21, 33-34, 35-36, 37, 53, 87 ff., 91
Aggression, 173 ff.
Alcohol, 16 ff., 67 ff., 95, 109 ff., 159; Indian prohibition of, 67
Alcoholism in various European races, 70
American Friends Service Committee in India, 37
American workers in Rourkela, 4
Amoebiasis: of the intestines, 62; of the liver, 62
Amoebic cyst carriers, 62
Amoebic dysentery, 64
Ancylostomiasis, 60, 62
Arsenical poisoning, 62
Asthenia, acute or tropical, 63
Austrian workers in Rourkela, 3, 74
Ayahs, 83, 86 ff., 121

Bahrdt, Hans Paul, 191
Balasore, 109
Barpali, 37-38
Bearers, 82 ff.
Bengal, 36; Bay of, 34, 58
Bengalis, 123
Bergter, Kurt, 59, 63
Bhattacharya, Bhabani, 45n

Bhilai, 20, 81, 137, 141, 194
Bhubaneswar, 104
Bites, animal, 62
Bokaro, 141, 144
Bombay, 35
Boveri, Margaret, 128
Brahmani Club, 112, 113
Brauer, Max, 17
Buddhists, 34
Bungalows, 73 ff.; equipment of, 75, 80; rents of, 76

Calcutta, 35, 89, 92, 104, 133, 134, 189, 190
"Calcutta shock," 133
Carmelite nuns, Indian, 115
Characteristics of European workers in India, 12, 52
Cholera in Calcutta, effects of on German morale, 64
Chota Nagpur, 33
Christ und Welt, 137
Christians, Indian, 34
Churches, 117-118; Indian attitude toward, 118
Cleveland, Harlan, 130
Climate, effects of, 55 ff.
Club life in Rourkela, 108 ff.; *see also* German Club
Coarseness, German, 13
"Coletti Team," 82
Confinements of German women in Rourkela, 60
Construction personnel, 1 ff.
Consultations, medical, 63-64
Contracts, 139 ff., 180 ff.

INDEX

Cultural detail, knowledge of, 26-27
Cuttack, 109

Danckwortt, Dieter, 132
Deaths of Germans in Rourkela, 61 ff., 64, 65-66
Deussen, Paul, 37
Deutsche Stiftung für Entwicklungsländer (German Foundation for the Developing Countries), 126, 184, 186
Deutscher Akademischer Austauschdienst (German Academic Exchange Service), 16
Diet, problems of, 25-26, 66-67
Dirks, Walter, 156
Disciplinary powers, need for, 183
Dönhoff, Countess, 167
Drascher, Wahrhold, 68, 145
Drinking, see Alcohol
Durgapur, 137, 141, 194
Dutch workers in Rourkela, 3
Dysentery, 60, 62

Eckermann, Johann Peter, 119
Eich, Hermann, 174
EMNID Institute for International Market and Social Research, Bielefeld, 49
Encephalitis, 62
Epidemics among Rourkela Indians, effects of on German morale, 64
Erasmus of Rotterdam, 16-17
Ethnocentrism, 163 ff.
Exclusivism, 168 ff.
Exotic environment: as cause of insecurity, 122 ff.; German interest in, 124 ff.

Family status of workers, 3
Fear of illness, 64, 65
Financial incentive as motivation for work overseas, 7 ff.
First impressions of India, 133 ff.
Fitters' hostels, 71 ff., 84-85, 90 ff.
Foreign wives, 3
Fromm, Erich, 155, 175
Frustration, 173 ff.

Gandhi, 44-45
Ganjam, 109
Gehlen, Arnold, 189

German Club, 20, 78, 99, 100, 101, 104, 108 ff., 152, 165, 168, 170 ff., 191; cinema, 101, 110; library, 110; swimming pool, 110
German Foundation for the Developing Countries, see Deutsche Stiftung für Entwicklungsländer
German hospital, 61-62, 168 ff.
German Industrial Press Office, New Delhi, 135
German school, 114 ff., 193
German Social Center (GSC), 73, 93, 105 ff., 113, 116, 125, 138, 151, 169 ff., 190; see also German Club
Germans: authority of, 145 ff.; behavior patterns of, 149-150, 189-190; children of, 60-61; characteristics of, see *individual characteristics*; wives of, 3, 130 ff., 186-187
Glasenapp, Helmuth von, 127, 164
Glaser, Hermann, 17
Goethe, 119, 154
Gossip: German, 99-100; Indian, 99-100
Grober, J., 56, 59
Grobian (roughneck), 15
"Guest peoples," 45

Hamirpur Mission School, 87, 114 ff.
Haus Rissen, Hamburg, 186
Heatstroke, 62
Hellpach, Willy, 15, 63, 151, 160
Hesse, Kurt, 11
Heuss, Theodor, 5
Hindi, 19-20
Hindu, The, 12-13
Hindustan Steel Limited (HSL), 71, 75, 76n, 77, 79, 80, 90 ff., 96, 97, 106 ff., 118, 134, 135, 140, 144, 146, 151; hospital, 170
Hirakud Dam, 37-38
Hofstätter, Peter R., 11
Homesickness, 120 ff.
Housing policy, need for, 181
Housing sectors, 73, 76
Hunck, Joseph, 144
Huxley, Aldous, 103
Hygiene, problems of, 25-26
Hymenolepis nana, 62

Immigrant workers, Indian, 35-36
Indian attitudes: toward foreign

224

Indian attitudes (*cont.*)
  workers, 49 ff.; toward Germans in Rourkela, 36 ff., 53-54; toward Western economic aid, 37 ff., 48 ff.; toward Western technology, 41-42
Indian hospital, 170
Indian Institute of Public Opinion Research, New Delhi, 49
Indians: behavior patterns of, 145 ff.; nationalism of, 43-44; nativism of, 44-45; political reactions to Germans, 138-139; riots, 123; in Rourkela, 33 ff.; traditional thought of, 45; trainees in Germany, 46 ff.
Indo-German Club Rourkela, 171-172
Indo-German collaboration in the plant, 139 ff.
In-groups, 152 ff.
Institute for Foreign Relations, Stuttgart, 30, 186
Intestinal diseases, 61
Intolerance, German, 13, 16
Isolation, feelings of, 160, 165 ff.
Itinerant workers, 2

Jains, 34
Jamshedpur, 89
Jharkand, 33

Kaffirs, 22
Kanaka, 22-23, 24, 163
Knigge, Freiherr August von, 129
König, René, 25, 100, 191
Koraput, 109
Körber, Kurt, 175
Küpper, Heinz, 13-14

Lack of consideration, German, 13
Lambliasis, 62
Languages, knowledge of, 18 ff., 184-185
Lederer, William J., and Eugene Burdick, 166
Leisure, 86; structuring of, 101 ff., 192-193
Leonhardt, Rudolf Walter, 154, 174
Lichen tropicus, 62
Lippmann, Walter, 21
Living quarters, *see* Bungalows *and* Fitters' hostels

Madras, 36
Maintenance and operation personnel, 1 ff.
Malaria, 60, 61, 62
Malenbaum, Wilfred, 143
Mali, 83, 121
Masters, John, 166
Medical welfare in Rourkela, 61-62
Mehnert, Klaus, 42, 167
Missions, Christian, 40
Mitscherlich, Alexander, 103, 129, 177, 192
Moksha, 45
Monsoon: effect of on health, 63; effect of on living conditions, 79
Motivations of overseas workers, 4 ff.; financial incentives, 7 ff.; personal experience, 9; personal problems, 5-6; promotion, 9; spirit of adventure, 5; status, 6-7; wanderlust, 5
Müller, Max, 37
Muslims, 34, 123
Mycosis, 62, 64

Nehru, 96
Neighborhoods, "strong" and "weak," 77
Neocolonial ambitions, 40
Neurosis, 65
New Delhi, 96
Nitu, 37

Oberndörfer, Dieter, 6
Oktoberfest in Rourkela, 110
Organization, German gift for, 10-11
Orissa, 34, 61, 104, 109; Government of, 37-38
Oriyas, 34-35, 36, 39, 123
Out-groups, 152, 158, 161, 162-163

"Pariah peoples," 45
Parties and entertainment, 96 ff.
Pedantry, German, 10-11
Peer groups, 156
Peets, Horst, 154
Perfectionism, German, 16
Permanent workers, 2
Personal characteristics of Germans in Rourkela, 9 ff.; *see also individual characteristics*
Personal contacts between Germans and Indians, 125-126

Peusch, Eberhard, 111, 161
Physical fitness of workers going overseas, 27-28, 59-60, 184
Plehn, Friedrich, 132
Precision, German, 11
Prejudices, German, 20 ff.
Preparation for work overseas, 185 ff.
Press reactions to Rourkela, 135 ff.
Promotion as motivation for work overseas, 9
Prostitution in Rourkela, 89-90
Psychoses, 64
Public relations, 108, 193-194
Punjab, the, 35
Punjabis, 21, 123
Puri, 109

Radio and television, lack of, 79-80
Raffalt, Reinhard, 167
Riesman, David, 114, 156
Ritter, Gerhard, 43
Rodenwaldt, Ernst, 29, 56, 60, 64, 69, 89, 121
Rourkela Club, 112
Rowdyism among the Germans in Rourkela, 111-112

Sacherl, Karl, 71n
Scheler, Max, 119
Schmid, Peter, 173
School children, German, 114 ff.
Selection of overseas workers, *see* Suitability and selection of overseas workers
Sense of order, German, 10-11, 15
Sepsis, 61
Servants, 81 ff.
Shiva, 126
Sita, 93
Smallpox, 61
Social differences in Rourkela, 97 ff.
Social facilities for the Germans in Rourkela, 108-109
Social life of the Germans in Rourkela, 95 ff.
Social structure of the Rourkela community, 151 ff.
Sombart, Werner, 119
Spear, Percival, 130
Spirit of adventure as motivation for work overseas, 5
Sporting facilities, provision of, 73

Standardized contracts, need for, 182
Status: as motivation for work overseas, 6-7; as mania in Rourkela, 97 ff.
Staunchness, German, 11
Stereotype thinking, 188-189
Stereotypes, German, 20 ff.
Studienstelle für Entwicklungsländer, Bonn (Study Center for the Developing Countries), 47-48
Suitability and selection of overseas workers, 27 ff., 183-184
Sundargarh, 110
Supervision of social activities, 113-114, 155
Suyin, Han, 95, 131, 160
Svadeshi, 44-45
Svaraj, 44
Sweepers, 83
Symanowski, Horst, 15

Temperamental suitability for work overseas, 28-29
They-feelings, 152, 161, 162-163
Thoroughness, German, 11
Thrombus, 62
Times, The (London), 154
Transportation, need for, 182
Tropical diseases and fevers, 61
Tyjabi, 188
Types, "inner-directed" and "other-directed," 156
Typhus abdominalis, 62

Verein Sozialbetreuung Rourkela, Essen (Association for Social Welfare in Rourkela), 46
Vierkandt, Alfred, 116
"V.I.P. feeling," 7
Von der Heydte, Freiherr Friedrich August, 71n
Von Hassel, Kai Uwe, 43-44

Wages: of Indian workers, 41; of German workers, 106-107
Wanderlust as motivation for work overseas, 5
Weber, Adolf, 104
Weber, Max, 45-46
We-feelings, 152 ff.
Weiss, Carl, 188
Welfare, 190 ff.

Die Welt, 137
Western goods, need for, 181
Wiborg, Klaus, 90n
Wide strip mill, 4, 96
Wiese, Leopold von, 119, 157

Woman problem, *see* Ayahs
Wülker, Gabriele, 145

Zweig, Arnold, 162-163